"This book is a joy to read. None, I believe, neither scholar nor common reader, can fail to respond to the originality of its subject, the lucidity of its prose, the intellectual richness of its concerns. I celebrate its publication."
—Vivian Gornick, author of *The Odd Woman and the City*

"Who knew? Who knew about the Japanese obsession with the most obsessive of all English novels? Look closely and you can find *Wuthering Heights* almost anywhere: anime, drag shows (Heathcliff with spit curls), serious fiction, manga that run for years and years . . . Who knew? Well, Judith Pascoe did—and thanks to this book of marvels now we do as well."
—Michael Gorra, Smith College

"A beautifully written, innovative book that brings together personal memoir and an ethnographic scholarly study of translation and transnational flows of culture focused around the reception of Emily Brontë's *Wuthering Heights*. The author's experience of Japan and the complex intersections of *Wuthering Heights* with Japanese culture are artfully layered and integrated."
—Adela Pinch, University of Michigan

On the Bullet Train
with Emily Brontë

Wuthering Heights in Japan

Judith Pascoe

UNIVERSITY OF MICHIGAN PRESS

Ann Arbor

First paperback edition 2019
Copyright © 2017 by Judith Pascoe

Published in the United States of America by the
University of Michigan Press
Manufactured in the United States of America
⊗ Printed on acid-free paper

2022   2021   2020   2019   4   3   2

A CIP catalog record for this book is available from the British Library.

Library of Congress Cataloging-in-Publication data has been applied for.

ISBN: 978-0-472-13060-3 (hardcover: alk. paper)
ISBN: 978-0-472-12335-3 (e-book)

Frontispiece: Emily Brontë on the Shinkansen platform. Courtesy of Iwashita Hiromi, © Iwashita Hiromi.

ISBN: 978-0-472-03740-7 (paper)

Illustrations (*clockwise from upper left*): (1) Detail of Emily Brontë from *The Brontë Sisters* by Patrick Branwell Brontë, © National Portrait Gallery, London; (2, 4, 6, 8) ocean wave, iStock.com/paul_june; (3) Catherine in *Arashi ga oka* [Wuthering Heights], © Iwashita Hiromi, Courtesy of Iwashita Hiromi; (5) Detail of book jacket, Mori Michiyo, *Arashi ga oka* [Wuthering Heights], © Kaisei-sha, 1954, Courtesy of Kaisei-sha Publishing Co., Ltd.; (7) Heathcliff, © Iwashita Hiromi, Courtesy of Iwashita Hiromi; (*Center*) Shinkansen [bullet train], iStock.com/ImageGap.

For my Japanese teachers and conversation partners

It is not true that it doesn't matter where you live, that you are in Hartford or Dallas merely yourself. Also it is not true that all are linked naturally to their regions. Many are flung down carelessly at birth and they experience the diminishment and sometimes the pleasant truculence of their random misplacement. Americans who are Germans, Germans who are Frenchmen, like Heine perhaps.
—Elizabeth Hardwick, *Sleepless Nights*

Someone remarked that you should give up any art of which you have not become a master by the age of fifty. At that age there is no prospect that you may acquire it by hard work. . . . If there is something you would like to know, study it if you like, but once you have learned the general principles and your curiosity is assuaged, you should stop. Best of all is to dispense with such desires from the start.
—Kenkō, *Essays in Idleness* (trans. Donald Keene)

Author's Note

Japanese names are written in the order of surname followed by given name, except in those instances when the person being referenced lives and works in a Western country and uses the Western name order.

Macrons are used throughout to indicate long vowel sounds (for example, ō) in Japanese, but they are omitted in the case of common place-names (such as Tokyo).

I have sought to apply these rules consistently throughout the book, but I apologize in advance for any unintended lapses from this practice, and for other language-related errors. The research for, and writing of, this book was carried out over eight years and four trips to Japan, and at varying stages of Japanese language acquisition.

Acknowledgments

This book was begun during the year I spent as a Fulbright Lecturer in Japan, and it advanced toward completion during my tenure as a Guggenheim Fellow. I am indebted to the Fulbright Scholar Program and the John Simon Guggenheim Memorial Foundation, whose combined support had a transformative effect on my research and teaching.

The line of Japanese scholars, artists, friends, colleagues, and strangers who contributed to this project, both directly and indirectly, extends from Iowa City to Tokyo. Muramatsu Chie, Takayama Hiromi, Nishi Yumiko, Naka Tomomi, Mizuno Kuriko, along with the rest of my Japanese instructors at the University of Iowa, supported my efforts in the classroom, as did my classmates in first- through fourth-year Japanese. During my Fulbright year in Japan, I benefited from the instruction and camaraderie provided by the Kodaira International Friendship Association, where my teacher Ike Asako cultivated her students' conversational skills, and where my Chinese and Brazilian classmates shared tips on how to make gyoza and where to purchase the best kanji pen.

Throughout most of the period during which I was working on this book, I was talking by means of Skype with Japanese conversation partners I met through The Mixxer web site: Serita Nahoko, Ono Kōji, Yoshida Isao, Tōne Emiko, and Hino Akira. Nakajima Miharu took me to rare book stores in the Jinbōchō area of Tokyo, and helped me track down Japanese editions of *Wuthering Heights*. Closer to home, Maiko John corrected my Japanese in a Coralville coffee shop, and Kawakami Kiyomi helped me discuss topics ranging from tango to slang in George's Buffet, which is a bar, not a buffet (English is baffling).

The generosity of the many Japanese artists and writers who have adapted or rewritten *Wuthering Heights*, and who shared their deep knowledge of Brontë's novel, made this book possible. They included the actress Koshiro Miyako, who explained how she prepared for playing the role of Heathcliff; the director Ōta Tetsunori, who cast light on his staging of *Wuthering Heights*; the manga artist Iwashita Hiromi, who discussed how he approached drawing Brontë's characters, and who drew the frontispiece illustration for this volume; and the manga artist Miuchi Suzue, who explained why she featured *Wuthering Heights* in her *Garasu no kamen* (Glass mask) series. The manga artists Hanabusa Yōko and Sanazaki Harumo were especially good at explaining Brontë's appeal for Japanese readers. The interpreter Kurosawa Ayako served as a skillful go-between in the conversations I shared with the people above. The manga artist Sakurai Mineko generously discussed by email the changes she worked on Brontë's novel. I shared a splendid lunch with the translator Tamura Taeko, her friend and illustrator Ichihara Junko, and Ichihara's students; their hospitality extended through an afternoon during which Tamura and Ichihara discussed fine points of Brontë translation, both verbal and visual. Aoyama Nanae helpfully responded to my query about Brontë's influence on her novel. By happy accident, I first met Mizumura Minae during Obon week in Oiwake, the time and place of Catherine's ghostly return in Mizumura's artful rewriting of Brontë's novel. In a subsequent meeting, she shared family photographs, three of which are reprinted in this book.

My gratitude extends to the many scholars, editors, and translators who allowed me to draw on their expertise. These included Nīmi Hatsuko, Noguchi Keiko, Iwakami Haruko, Okumura Maki, Juliet Winters Carpenter, Sasagawa Hiroshi, Kōnosu Yukiko, Tanizaki Yui, Hakui Ryoko, Kobashi Sumio, Iki Kazuko, Okada Akiko, Fujī Junya, Ogawa Kimiyo, Aoyama Seiko, Suzuki Masashi, Steve Clark, David Chandler, Thomas McLean, Michael Gorra, Kendall Heitzman, Nataša Ďurovičová, Toyota Horiguchi, John Picker, Alan Bewell, Andrew McConnell Stott, Nicholas Theisen, and the staff of the Ikeda Bunko Library. Japanese Studies Librarian Sakai Chiaki directed me to scholarly resources, contacted libraries on my behalf, hunted down obscure *Wuthering Heights* manga, and helped me write letters in Japanese.

I am grateful for the support of the University of Iowa College of Liberal Arts and Sciences, the Office of Research and Economic Development, and International Programs.

The faculty, staff, and students at Japan Women's University, Tsuda College, and Shōtoku Gakuen were kind and welcoming; I taught as a Fulbright Lecturer at the first two institutions, and my daughters attended school at the third. The warm friendships my family forged with the Tateyama family and with Hirayama Tomoko have enriched our lives. Shirai

Yoko, my colleague at Japan Women's University, helped me write conversation questions in Japanese, and Nagata Yoichi, the baseball historian and travel expert, helped me make train connections like a Tokyo denizen. I extend heartfelt thanks for their guidance, support, and companionship. Kōno Chiemi could be counted on to provide both practical and moral support for which I am greatly indebted.

I am grateful for the expert editorial work of LeAnn Fields, Marcia LaBrenz, and Elizabeth Frazier at the University of Michigan Press, for the efforts of the production and marketing staff, and for the astute comments of the two anonymous readers who read my book in manuscript. My gratitude extends to Amron Gravett, who created the index, and to Sara Sauers, who designed the cover.

Sara Levine, my companion on this book's journey, helped me figure out where we were headed, and fine-tuned five million sentences along the way. My husband and daughters, too, accompanied me on countless tangents and never complained about the price of the ticket.

Finally, I acknowledge my enormous debt to Kobayashi Akifumi and Kobayashi Yoko, who welcomed my family to Japan, and who opened doors there. Kobayashi-sensei's teaching, scholarship, and generosity kindled this exploration of *Wuthering Heights* in Japan.

Contents

Wuthering Heights and the Pursuit of Mastery

In 1987 a famous portrait of the Brontë sisters, painted by Branwell Brontë, was exhibited at a Japanese department store (fig. 1).[1] In the painting, one of only two surviving portraits of Emily Brontë, the sisters look a little wooden, and if Emily did not, in actuality, have the biggest head of the three, then Branwell faltered when it came to proportions. John Elliott Cairnes, who viewed the portrait at Haworth in 1858, called it "a shocking daub, not up to the rudest sign board style."[2] Others agreed; in 1914, the second wife of Charlotte Brontë's husband found the portrait folded like a washcloth and left on top of a cupboard. Still, for Japanese Brontë fans, it must have seemed like a piece of the true cross had come to call on its distant pilgrims. The Brontë Society of Japan, with the support of the Seibu Department Store corporation, transported the portrait from the London National Portrait Gallery to Tokyo, and displayed it as the centerpiece of an exhibit whose title, roughly translated, read "*Wuthering Heights* Exhibition: The Running Across the Heath Brontë Sisters' World."[3] By "roughly," I mean as it might be translated by someone who has not sufficiently mastered Japanese.

In the summer of 2009, I carried Emily Brontë's novel *Wuthering Heights* to Japan as I began a yearlong stint as a Fulbright lecturer.[4] When I arrived, I was unaware that the Brontë sisters were so popular in Japan that a department store had underwritten the transport of Branwell's awkward portrait for an exhibit of the Brontë sisters' world. I singled out *Wuthering Heights* to read in Japan partly because it is an oddity of the nineteenth-century literary canon, a screaming banshee of a book in the midst of well-mannered works.[5] But I also selected *Wuthering Heights* as the sole volume in my traveling library because my personal relationship with the novel was uneasy. I'd read it (halfheartedly) in high school and (hermeneutically) in graduate school, but I didn't *get* it in the way I get Charlotte Brontë's novels or even the more challenging works of Henry James.

Fig. 1. Patrick Branwell Brontë, *The Brontë Sisters* (Anne Brontë, Emily Brontë, Charlotte Brontë), © National Portrait Gallery, London.

When I brought *Wuthering Heights* to Japan, I imagined experiencing the kind of single-minded absorption that Louis Renza enacts in *A White Heron*, in which he presents multiple readings of a single Sarah Orne Jewett story; that T. J. Clark carries out in *The Sight of Death*, in which he visits and revisits the same two paintings; and that Geoff Dyer carries out in *Zona*, his obsessive meditation on Tarkovsky's *Stalker*.[6] My fantasy was further fueled by a Derrida documentary in which the philosopher was asked whether he had read all of the books in his library. "No," he responded, "only four of them. But I read those very, very carefully."[7]

My dream of mastering *Wuthering Heights* can also be traced to a lost rite of graduate school passage. Students in the class before mine had to pass a one-book exam and a fifty-book exam before commencing dissertation work. My class was tasked with passing only the fifty-book exam, that is, with demonstrating breadth, rather than breadth *and* depth of knowledge. It's easy to be nostalgic for an exam you never had to take. In my imagined version of the one-book exam's last invigilation, the final group of masters-in-training fill blue books with their vast accumulated knowledge of *Beowulf* or *Huckleberry Finn* or *The Tempest* while seated in the dome-shaped reading room of the old British Library, Karl Marx and Virginia Woolf scribbling nearby. When I resolved to concentrate on Emily Brontë's lone novel, I hoped to join the intellectual pantheon to which my upper classmates and their nineteenth-century progenitors belonged. "No one is more triumphant than the man who chooses a worthy subject and masters all its facts," wrote E. M. Forster with quaint confidence in 1927.[8] When I resolved to focus on Emily Brontë's novel, I imagined that I, belatedly, would become more like the dauntingly knowledgeable specialists who taught me back when professors carried broken-spined, much-glossed copies of Milton. At a moment in the early twenty-first century when search and browse were on the ascendant, I would attempt to meet the past century's definition of a well-educated person.

That I would be rereading Brontë's novel in a country in whose language I was illiterate would make it less likely that I would start wandering across a different moor. I could avoid becoming distracted by the Brontë family history, which hangs over the literary works like Spanish moss over a graveyard.[9] Because it is so implausible that geographically isolated siblings wrote some of the greatest works of nineteenth-century English literature, and because the family was beset by tragedy (Branwell and Emily were dead of tuberculosis within a year of *Wuthering Heights'* publication; their younger sister Anne succumbed to the same disease five months later), the Brontë family biography, as Henry James wrote, stands before us "as insistently as the vividest page of *Jane Eyre* or *Wuthering Heights*."[10] Emily occupies an especially prominent place in the family lore despite (or, perhaps, because of) her slender biographical remains. In Elizabeth Gaskell's *Life of Charlotte Brontë*, the forerunner of all subsequent Brontë biographies, Emily only occasionally snaps into focus, most notably when

Charlotte recalls her sister's love of the moors: "Flowers brighter than the rose bloomed in the blackest of the heath for her;—out of a sullen hollow in a livid hill-side, her mind could make an Eden."[11] Gaskell goes on to note that Emily studied German as she kneaded bread dough, and to describe her unhappy tenure as a teacher in the village of Halifax: "Emily—that free, wild, untameable spirit, never happy nor well but on the sweeping moors that gathered round her home—that hater of strangers, [was] doomed to live amongst them" (118). After her death, Emily became a specter haunting her sister's days. "The feeling of Emily's loss does not diminish as time wears on; it often makes itself most acutely recognized," Charlotte wrote. "It brings, too, an inexpressible sorrow with it; and then the future is dark" (307).

Contributing to Emily Brontë's mystique is the paltriness of her manuscript archive. "Her remains are so skeletal that the body seems to have gone missing altogether," Lucasta Miller writes.[12] The juvenilia of Branwell and Charlotte Brontë has been treasured and preserved by collectors and librarians, but the fantasy Gondal saga that Emily and Anne composed as children survives only in fragmentary and conjectural form. Charlotte Brontë's collected letters take up three impressive volumes published by Oxford University Press. By contrast, the letters Emily Brontë wrote to her siblings did not survive long enough to secure the scholarly edition treatment. Only ephemeral bits of her personal writings are still extant, such as the fifteen-year-old Emily's much-quoted diary paper in which she writes, "The Gondals are discovering the interior of Gaaldine Sally mosley is washing in the back Kitchin."[13]

The biggest absence of the many omissions that make up Emily Brontë's posthumous existence, however, is the loss of manuscript material from the last two years of her life, a period of time during which she is rumored to have been working on a second novel. Her biographer sternly asserts, "The absence of a manuscript of the novel (and of the Gondal prose) can be explained only by a deliberate act of destruction."[14] All eyes turn to Charlotte, who carried out damage control on Emily's reputation, expressing discomfort with her sister's first novel by writing, "Whether it is right or advisable to create things like Heathcliff, I do not know; I scarcely think it is."[15] Charlotte was justifiably embarrassed by press errors that proliferated in the first edition of *Wuthering Heights*. She complained, "The orthography and punctuation of the books are mortifying to a degree: almost all the errors that were corrected in the proof-sheets appear intact in what should have been the fair copies."[16] But along with correcting these errors for the second edition, Charlotte also changed paragraph breaks, altered punctuation, regularized style, and altered dialect. Neither the original manuscript nor any draft pages of *Wuthering Heights* survive. The Emily Brontë who wrote *Wuthering Heights* speaks to us only through the unreliable first edition of the novel, through two hundred or so poems, and through a few scattered diary pages and school exercises.

That, for me, was a large part of her appeal. Emily Brontë's papers had already been *edited* in the ruthless manner I wished I could apply to my e-mail mailbox; there, 9,368 messages hovered, waiting for me to determine their future, to toss them in a virtual trash can or to "file" them according to some archival logic. I did not even want to think about the boxes of paper letters that I had transported through three moves because I didn't have the nerve to throw them out without opening them, and because, if I opened them, I'd become thirteen again. Brontë seemed to have sheared through the world as cleanly as a knife, leaving only *Wuthering Heights* behind her.

Before I embarked on the Fulbright year, I made a start on learning Japanese, enrolling in my university's first-year Japanese class, which I attended daily, earning a reputation as the weakest student in the class. In a log I kept of my language-learning experience that first year, I penned an observation that proved prescient: "Nearly every day I have the humbling thought that I am not up to the task. I can't pull up the right word on command, and drop it into the correct spot in a sentence—I've got the beads but I can't string them into a necklace." After one discouraging class meeting, I noted: "Next week we have to read a paragraph of Japanese text for an oral quiz, reading at 'certain speed,' a phrase *sensei* said while looking pointedly at me."

The Japanese writing system is made up of two syllabaries (*hiragana* and *katakana*) used in tandem with Chinese characters (kanji), 2,136 of which are deployed in common usage (the total number of kanji is approximately 50,000). Over the course of first-year Japanese, I learned 90 of the common-use kanji. Knowing a little Japanese was better than knowing no Japanese at all. If nothing else, it allowed me to appreciate the difficulty of what I expected the Japanese students in my American literature classes at Japan Women's University and Tsuda College to be able to do. Achieving the ability to read a literary classic in another language often serves as a benchmark of foreign language acquisition.[17] My Japanese students could almost read English-language literature, whereas the ability to read Japanese literature was for me a distant aspiration. Even after I returned to Iowa and completed second-, third-, and fourth-year Japanese classes, I could only dream of being able to read with confidence and ease.[18]

Still, knowing a little Japanese allowed me to glean that the Japanese title of *Wuthering Heights* is 嵐が丘, which is read *Arashi ga oka*. One day, while running my eyes over the display racks in the Kinokuniya bookstore, its Japanese literary offerings dispiritingly beyond my ken, I recognized the *Arashi ga oka* characters on the book jacket of a manga volume. The image on the cover of Ōgi Yuzuha's manga depicts a grand turreted mansion in front of which a man sports a windswept coif of a style favored by Japanese pop idols.[19] On the book jacket the big-haired man puts his hand down the unzipped jeans of a blonde young man, who seems unfazed by this development. Emily Brontë's novel tells the story of Heathcliff, a Liverpool orphan who is raised as Catherine Earnshaw's childhood companion, and whom she abandons in order to marry Edgar Linton, the insipid son of an affluent neighbor. The rejected Heathcliff, resorting to furious revenge, marries Linton's sister Isabella, whom he loathes, and uses their child as a pawn to manipulate the daughter of Catherine and Edgar Linton. Brontë's novel presents a lantern slide show of riveting tableaux—a ghost child scratching at a window, a baby falling over a bannister, a dog hanging from a bridle hook—but it does not, so far as I recalled, depict an erotic encounter between two young men. Intrigued, I purchased Ōgi's manga and carried it home for closer analysis.

Electronic dictionary at my elbow, I applied myself to the manga with the assiduousness of a serious scholar. The blonde man, Reona, I discovered, arrives to take a job at the mansion and, while grooming a horse in the nude (Reona, that is, although the horse, too, wears no clothing), is spotted by Kaizaki, the big-haired man. Before long, Reona is buffing Kaizaki's shoes, and Kaizaki is whipping Reona's buttocks. Ōgi's manga belongs to a genre known as *yaoi*, featuring sexual relations among men, drawn by female manga artists, and targeted at female readers. Why had the Japanese title of *Wuthering Heights* been grafted onto a homoerotic manga, I asked my teenage daughters, who knew more about manga than I did, but who were reluctant to discuss the *yaoi* genre with their mother. By invoking the title of Brontë's novel, had Ōgi Yuzuha tried to give Kaizaki a Heathcliffean aura? Was *Wuthering Heights* so well known in Japan that *Arashi ga oka* had come to have a life of its own, evoking, in an untethered kind of way, tormented lovers or windswept moors or something else that was uniquely understood by Japanese people? These were questions that wanted answering as I wandered around with my English-language edition of *Wuthering Heights*, which now seemed tepid in comparison to Ōgi's version.

It seemed odd that *Wuthering Heights*, of all Western literary works, would be popular in Japan, a country that I, blithely stereotyping, associated with gentle arts like the tea ceremony and flower arrangement. I knew that *Anne of Green Gables* had a large fan base in Japan; so popular is *Akage no An* (Red-haired Anne) that its translator Muraoka Hanako inspired a 156-episode morning drama in which she rescues her manuscript translation from the flames of the 1945 bombing of Tokyo.[20] I could understand why Japanese readers liked the spirited Anne Shirley, or why, for that matter, they might like *Jane Eyre*—Jane's story arc, too, is triumphant, and although Rochester gets blinded, he and Jane are united at novel's end. In *Wuthering Heights*, a far more bleak and unsettling novel than *Jane Eyre*, Catherine Earnshaw perishes soon after Heathcliff tells the dying woman his tears will blight her. And then the novel drags on for another 160 pages, recounting the comparatively bland history of Catherine and Heathcliff's heirs.

Emily Brontë wrote *Wuthering Heights* in Haworth, England, approximately six thousand miles from Tokyo. Perhaps the closest she came to Japan was in her invention of Gondal, the imaginary Pacific island about which she and her sister wrote stories in microscopic script. As Brontë drafted her novel in the 1840s, the actual Pacific island country of Japan was undergoing rapid changes, as the country emerged from a period of isolation during which *rangakusha* (specialists in Dutch studies—Dutch traders in Nagasaki were the primary source of information) introduced innovations in Western technology: hot-air balloons and microscopes and electricity.[21] Twenty years after Emily Brontë's death in 1848, the Tokugawa shogunate fell from power, and the new Meiji government set out to modernize the nation.

Brontë's homeland, too, was undergoing the birth pangs of modernization, particularly Yorkshire, site of a flourishing textile industry whose workers were threatened by innovations in machine technology. Gaskell's *Life of Charlotte Brontë* describes the "great worsted factories" and "rows of workmen's houses" that one encountered when traveling the four miles from Keighley to Haworth (3). The length of time it took to travel between major cities in England was cut in half between 1770 and 1830, a development that fueled anxiety in Brontë's literary contemporaries. William Wordsworth, who lived seventy-three miles from Haworth, bemoaned the encroachment of railroads on his beloved and previously remote Lake District. Thomas De Quincey deplored the train passenger's loss of sensory experience, and John Ruskin (born a year after Emily Brontë) declared that "all travelling becomes dull in exact proportion to its rapidity."[22]

In order to adapt to the conditions of rail travel, the historian Wolfgang Schivelbusch writes, "a process of deconcentration, or dispersal of attention, took place in reading as well as in the traveler's perception of the landscape outside."[23] Reading while traveling became obligatory, with book stalls appearing in English railway stations in the late 1840s (*Wuthering Heights* was published in 1847). An 1850 review of Brontë's novel praised its portability. "The volume is compact, and may be slipped into a coat pocket for the railway, so that the traveller may wile away with it the long hours of his journey in grim pleasure."[24]

Elizabeth Gaskell marks the railroad's centrality to the Brontës' lives when she opens her biography by describing the path of the Leeds and Skipton railway past a "slow and sluggish stream" (1). The railroad runs in and out of Gaskell's account of the Brontës. She notes that Branwell worked as a clerk on the Leeds and Manchester Railway, and she describes a journey to Brussels during which Charlotte's train from Leeds to London arrived at Euston Square too late for her to seek out the Charter Coffee House where she planned to stay. Gaskell recalls that when Anne Brontë was dying, she and Charlotte embarked on an ill-conceived train journey to Scarborough, and that Anne died in Scarborough before Charlotte could transport her back home. Soon after Anne's death, Gaskell notes, Charlotte fretted about the depreciation of railway shares she had waited too long to sell.

When I thought about the Brontës, I imagined them in a state of technological isolation, in the kind of rural remove that informs the punch line of a *New Yorker* cartoon that depicts courting couples strolling across a heath. The caption reads: "This moor got a great Yelp review."[25] However, Emily Brontë wrote as new forms of technology delivered new modes of distraction, provoking related concerns. A year after Emily's death, Gaskell tells us, Charlotte was having trouble corralling her thoughts into correct discipline. "They are idle, and keep taking the train down to London," she wrote (358). The postman's call, too, contributed to Charlotte's lack of focus. She denied herself the pleasure of writing letters too frequently because she dreaded the temptation of "centring all her thoughts upon this one time, and losing her interest in the smaller hopes and employments of the remaining hours."[26]

Wuthering Heights was first translated into Japanese by Yamato Yasuo in 1932; over the following decades, nineteen more translations have appeared, four since 2001.[27] (Manga versions, too, have multiplied—five since 2003.) Walter Benjamin wrote of how translation "is charged with the special mission of watching over the maturing process of the original language and the birth pangs of its own." "For just as the tenor and significance of the great works of literature undergo a complete transformation over the centuries," Benjamin wrote, "the mother tongue of the translator is transformed as well."[28] A translation produced in the early Shōwa era (1926–1989) might not be the optimal translation for the present moment. But Yamato's translation still circulates in Japan alongside newer, more accessible versions. In one of my favorite scenes in Brontë's novel, the interloper Lockwood, stranded by a snowstorm at Wuthering Heights, falls asleep in "a large oak case, with squares cut out near the top, resembling coach windows."[29] There, scratched into a ledge, he notices "a name repeated in all kinds of characters, large and small—*Catherine Earnshaw*, here and there varied to *Catherine Heathcliff*, and then again to *Catherine Linton*." When Lockwood wakes from a doze, a glare of white letters start from the dark. "The air swarmed with Catherines," Brontë writes. Just so did Japanese literary culture seem to be swarming with *Wuthering Heights*es.[30]

The multiple Japanese versions of *Wuthering Heights* led me to think about the *lack* of English versions—or even translations—of Japanese literary works. My bookshelf sagged with Japanese novels that were not available in English, books that I would purchase in fits of optimism.[31] I leaned on English-language versions of Japanese literary works, such as A. Lloyd and M. Lloyd's version of Ozaki Kōyō's *Konjiki yasha* (*The Gold Demon*), which a Japanese friend recommended because it tells the story of an orphaned boy who falls in love with the daughter of his adopted family, and who, after that daughter enrages him by marrying a rich man, goes off and becomes a rich man himself. Ozaki's story was the *Wuthering Heights* of the Meiji period, I hoped, but in encountering it through the English-language version of A. and M. Lloyd, I relied on what they described as a *Gold Demon* in English dress, one that had been "re-written rather than translated."[32] A. Lloyd wrote in an introduction to the volume, "A few of the earlier chapters are translations, but the rest are abbreviated reproductions of the original." It was as if the Lloyds had started translating only to fall into a slough of despair. "Ozaki's greatest charm is his language," A. Lloyd wrote, before continuing sadly, "and that charm cannot possibly be reproduced." He continued, "His immense power and beauty of language enables him to take the Japanese reader through mazes of minute description which, under the guidance of a less skilful pen, would be tedious in the extreme."[33] I was counting on the Lloyds to take me through the mazes of Ozaki's description; I imagined them as Edwardian travelers in 1905 Japan, making their way through the narrow alleys surrounding Shinjuku station, but my confidence in the Lloyds as tour guides diminished as they went on to confess that they had curtailed Ozaki's descriptions, and condensed Ozaki's soliloquies, and, "in a word, [made] the book a little more Anglo-Saxon."

How isolated I am on my island of English where literary translations rarely wash ashore, I thought. The Japanese have twenty or so translations of *Wuthering Heights*, but there is not even one English translation of Okuizumi Hikaru's *Mushiki ongaku shū* (which I translate, too literally, as "Tree Insect Music Collection"), a novel that, a Japanese friend advised me, was inspired by the work of Kafka.[34] Nor is there an English translation of Okuizumi's *Shinki* (The three sacred treasures), reportedly inspired by the work of Melville. Okuizumi writes novels that engage challenging Western novels. Western publishers return the compliment by publishing only a single Okuizumi novel in translation, his Akutagawa Prize-winning *Ishi no raireki* (*The Stones Cry Out*). Similarly, the major novelist Mizumura Minae's first novel, in which she boldly writes an ending to Natsume Sōseki's unfinished *Light and Darkness*, is unavailable in English. And how about all the Sōseki novels for which there is only one translation? Even when a masterwork of Japanese literature *has* been translated into English, it has often only been translated by one translator. What if that lone translator was incapable of registering the linguistic nuances that make Sōseki Sōseki?

When I first started learning about *Wuthering Heights* in Japan, I was most interested in adaptations: the transformation of Brontë's novel into a manga, a stage production, or a contemporary novel.[35] These new versions I could begin to understand, whereas the myriad translations were more imposing, requiring a full command of Japanese.[36] I first set out to master *Wuthering Heights*, and then I set out to master the Japanese language. Of course, both goals were unattainable, but also, for reasons this book will explore, well worth pursuing, however hopelessly. I write this book from a way station between two languages, lacking complete command of the second one. There are drawbacks to this vantage point—for example, a danger of romanticizing Japanese culture or reducing it to those parts which seem most foreign to a foreigner: geisha and samurai, love hotels and eel pie. (*Wuthering Heights*, too, has been romanticized and abridged, transformed into an anodyne version of the original vicious novel.) Japanologists, striding across the peaks of their scholarly domain, may reasonably look askance at someone who has not crested its summit.[37] But there are advantages to my approach as well. Matsumoto Kazuhito writes fondly of the condition of being lost between languages, a linguistically clumsy state of mind that can cause panic and uncertainty.[38] "One of the pleasures of learning a foreign language is to be led out of our own language into some unknown realm unconfined to either of the languages, whose virtue is that even an absolute beginner can experience it," he writes.[39] Tawada Yoko, a Japanese writer who lives in Germany, celebrates this in-between status: "I would rather find the poetic ravine separating two languages, and descend into its depth."[40] I set out to write about the Japanese *Wuthering Heights*. I ended up writing about the wayward tendencies of scholarly investigation and about the thwarting of a sincere endeavor. That is, I wound up writing about love, loss, and longing.

In the pages that follow, I seek out Emily Brontë in Japan, taking the reader across a landscape in which *Wuthering Heights* appears with surprising frequency. The journey begins at the Tokyo Imperial University, where the English poet and critic Edmund Blunden convinced his Japanese students that *Wuthering Heights* is one of the three greatest tragedies in the English language. The second stop is the Yokohama Bay Sheraton Hotel, where Koshiro Miyako, retired star of the all-female Takarazuka theater company, explains how Heathcliff changed her life. Along the way, Miuchi Suzue, the creator of *Garasu no kamen* (Glass mask), one of the most popular manga series in Japanese history, describes how her manga's heroine came to play Catherine in a drama school production of *Wuthering Heights*. I visit the resort village of Oiwake, site of Mizumura Minae's rewriting of *Wuthering Heights* (*Honkaku shōsetsu* [*A True Novel*]), a novel that takes place during the Japanese festival of the dead, during which a ghost Catherine shows up wearing a summer kimono. All the while, Catherine's most famous sentence—"I *am* Heathcliff"—rises above the novel like the high note of a station guard's whistle. I ponder why this sentence is impossible to exactly replicate in Japanese, and I explore why, nonetheless, Brontë's novel has become a staple of the English-learning curriculum. The book's coda focuses on my status as a late-in-life foreign language learner, and on my attempt to document my semimastery by passing the intermediate level of the Japanese-Language Proficiency Test. In this final chapter, I recall how I found myself clutching a fistful of number 2 pencils in a classroom full of anime fans, in whose company I realized the error of my ways.

Soon after I first arrived in Japan, I tried to buy five boxes of chocolate in the food hall of a department store, and could not understand why the shop attendant seemed reluctant to carry out the transaction. In Japanese, she pointed out that some of the chocolates I had selected contained sake, and in Japanese, I communicated my agreement with this observation. In Japanese, she said something else sake-related, and in Japanese I (falsely) assured her that I understood what she was saying. It was as she was wrapping up candy boxes, and after we had carried out small talk circumscribed by my knowing only how to communicate what I ate, where I lived, and what I studied, that the shop clerk was emboldened to explain in English that I'd asked for chocolates for five-year-olds, rather than five boxes of chocolate. She was afraid I would give sake-laced candy to kindergarteners.

By the end of my Brontë project I could speak Japanese well enough to ask for directions and to mostly understand what people said in reply. If I was uncertain about whether I was taking the right train, I would dart into the nearest *kōban* (police box, often situated next to a train station entrance) and request guidance, pleased that I understood the policeman's mentions of platform numbers and express trains. I ultimately learned enough Japanese to orient myself in the swirl of Japanese reimaginings of *Wuthering Heights*, but I will never totally comprehend them, and this state of affairs is not entirely regrettable. Attempts at mastery often entail efforts to render something less complex, to make it bend to one's superior understanding. As we set out, let me acknowledge the limitations of my perspective. Once, when I was riding a bullet train from Tokyo to Osaka, I looked out at a distant mountain that was fleetingly visible through a scrim of fog. No matter how intently I gazed, trying to determine whether the ghostly mountain I briefly glimpsed was Mount Fuji, of that I was never certain.

CHAPTER ONE

Let Me In—Let Me In!

> Most of us can remember the strangely moving power of passages
> in certain poems read when we were young, irrational doorways as
> they were through which the mystery of fact, the wildness and the
> pang of life, stole into our hearts and thrilled them.
> —William James, *The Varieties of Religious Experience*

> I called out: Who's there?
>   Whoever it was
>   In snow
> Still knocks at my gate.
> —Kyorai Mukai (trans. Peter Beilenson and Harry Behn)

I can't remember the first time I read *Wuthering Heights* because I knocked
on its door several times without passing over the threshold. I checked
Emily Brontë's novel out of my grade school library, but returned it un-
read; I cracked it open during high school but stalled on the tedious first
paragraph about someone visiting his landlord. Not until graduate school
did I understand that Brontë's novel was *deliberately* holding me at a distance by having Lockwood serve as narrator. It is only by means of Lockwood, a preening interloper, that we gain access to Catherine and Heathcliff's love story. Lockwood visits Wuthering Heights seventeen years after
Catherine's death, at a moment when Heathcliff is living with his sullen
daughter-in-law Catherine Linton (the daughter of Catherine and Edgar)
and with Hareton Earnshaw, the benighted son of Hindley Earnshaw. In
my earliest thwarted readings of *Wuthering Heights*, Lockwood stood at
the door like an obnoxious party guest blocking access to the canapés.

From its first publication in England, *Wuthering Heights* encountered
readers, who, like me, found the novel off-putting. When Emily Brontë

died, among the scattering of papers found in her writing desk were five published reviews of *Wuthering Heights*. None of them included the undiluted praise that an aspiring author might hope for. Among the more enthusiastic reviewers was the *Examiner* commentator who began by stating, "This is a strange book," before going on to call Brontë's novel "wild, confused, disjointed, and improbable."[1] Other reviewers felt moved to note the one-off nature of Brontë's writing—"His work is strangely original," wrote the *Britannia* reviewer of the novel, assuming a male author.[2] The critics seemed unhappy about the hold *Wuthering Heights* had taken over their minds; they attributed to the novel a creepy sensibility to which they did not want to be attached. "His narrative leaves an unpleasant effect on the mind," continued the *Britannia* reviewer, writing, "There are no green spots in it on which the mind can linger with satisfaction. The story rushes onwards with impetuous force, but it is the force of a dark and sullen torrent, flowing between high and rugged rocks." The reviewer for *Douglas Jerrold's Weekly Newspaper* complained, "In *Wuthering Heights* the reader is shocked, disgusted, almost sickened by details of cruelty, inhumanity, and the most diabolical hate and vengeance."[3] "It should have been called *Withering* Heights," wrote another reviewer, "for any thing from which the mind and body would more instinctively shrink . . . cannot be easily imagined."[4]

There are many memorable first sentences in nineteenth-century literary history, including Dickens's magisterial "It was the best of times, it was the worst of times" (and so on), or Tolstoy's oft-quoted "All happy families are alike; each unhappy family is unhappy in its own way." The first sentence of *Wuthering Heights*, by contrast, is entirely forgettable, conveying the bland quotidian activity of a faintly misanthropic narrator. The novel begins, "1801—I have just returned from a visit to my landlord—the solitary neighbour that I shall be troubled with."[5] Emily Brontë starts her novel by making readers suffer the awkwardness of Lockwood's intrusion into the Wuthering Heights household; her first paragraph gives us Lockwood's misguided point of view. "A capital fellow!" he calls Heathcliff with forced jauntiness. His proliferating exclamation marks collide with the glowering figure of Heathcliff himself, whose "black eyes withdraw . . . suspiciously under their brows" (3). Lockwood misinterprets Heathcliff's response so as to make of it a reflection of his own state of mind. "I felt interested in a man who seemed more exaggeratedly reserved than myself," says the man who has just forced himself on his neighbors.

Before Lockwood enters Wuthering Heights, he pauses on the threshold "to admire a quantity of grotesque carving lavished over the front, and especially about the principal door" (4). Brontë's description of the threshold is full of baffling details. "Among a wilderness of crumbling griffins, and shameless little boys," Lockwood detects the date "1500" and the name "Hareton Earnshaw." Why Brontë chose to give the house an origin in 1500, and to imagine some original householder with the same name as the child of Hindley Earnshaw and his short-lived wife Frances, I didn't pause, in my earliest readings, to contemplate. It was only when I slowly reread the first chapter under a Japanese tree of an unfamiliar phylum, and while experiencing a weather front that I knew as Indian summer, but which in Japanese is called *koharubiyori*, or little spring—it was only in this foreign setting that I lingered over the crumbling griffins and the inscribed name. Then I soldiered on, willing myself to contemplate Lockwood's entrance into the Wuthering Heights "penetralium," a word Emily Brontë pedantically used to reference the home's interior. (In so doing, she earned the derision of Jorge Luis Borges, who added Lockwood's comment—"I had no desire to aggravate his impatience, previous to inspecting the penetralium"—to his treasury of terrible lines from literature).[6]

In Japan, thresholds are marked by the *genkan*, a foyer where you leave your shoes before stepping inside. The word *genkan* brings together the Japanese character *gen* (玄), which connotes something mysterious or occult, with the character *kan* (関), which evokes a barrier or gateway. That is, the word *genkan* suggests the same liminal quality that is written into Western depictions of thresholds, such as when, in Samuel Taylor Coleridge's poem *Christabel*, a mysterious lady must be lifted up, "a weary weight / Over the threshold of the gate," in order to enter a castle. The *genkan* of a Japanese dwelling enforces the barrier between inside and outside, between private and public space, between family and visitors. In the first chapter of *Wuthering Heights*, Lockwood effectively barges right through the *genkan* without removing his shoes.

The title or threshold page of Brontë's novel in its first edition is a model of obfuscation, holding the reader at arm's length.[7] It announces the work of Ellis Bell "in three volumes," even though the third volume is taken up by Acton Bell's *Agnes Grey*. Acton, Currer, and Ellis Bell were Anne's, Charlotte's, and Emily's pen names. "Ellis" was less eager than "Currer" to let readers into their literary domain. *Wuthering Heights* was preceded by the sisters' 1846 *Poems*, published despite Emily, who displayed not the slightest interest in seeing her poems ushered into print. She had to be harried into action by Charlotte, who harbored outsized ambitions for the volume. The 1846 *Poems* of Currer, Ellis, and Acton Bell is a strong contender for the lowest-selling book of all time; it eventually drove a humbled Charlotte to send gift copies to famous literary men, claiming in her cover letters that she hoped, before the sisters' edition would be transferred "to the trunk-makers" (that is, come to serve as lining paper for suitcases), to acknowledge the "pleasure and profit" she had "often and long derived" from these men's work.[8] But really, of course, she hoped that one of them would praise or promote the sisters' poems. Emily never tried to ingratiate herself to Coleridge's son or to Walter Scott's son-in-law. As self-contained as a cat, she let Charlotte carry out the doomed self-publishing project, and turned her own attention to writing *Wuthering Heights* with its uninviting foyer pages.

Wuthering Heights was not the first English-language book to cross over into Japan. That honor belonged to Samuel Smiles's 1859 *Self-Help*. The so-called "Bible of the Meiji era" (it was translated into Japanese in 1871), Smiles's work consisted of edifying stories of humble people who transcended their circumstances.[9] Nor was *Wuthering Heights* the first Brontë novel to be translated into Japanese. A version of *Jane Eyre* was published serially in the *Bungei kurabu* (Literary club) magazine in 1896 under the Japanese title *Riso kajin* (An ideal lady).[10] The translator Mizutani Futo reduced to a five-line summary the scene in which Mrs. Reed banishes Jane. Commenting on his compression of Jane's life at Lowood, Mizutani wrote, "I am afraid these tedious details may bore my readers before they reach the main part of this novel." He promised readers that if they would put up with one more chapter, "a beautiful flowery garden will be waiting for them," but his *Jane Eyre* translation ended with this installment. According to the Brontë scholar Iwakami Haruko, the readers of this serial *Jane Eyre* were left hanging after "Jane meets Rochester unexpectedly and they enjoy a blunt, but lighthearted conversation."[11]

But at least Charlotte Brontë's novel had a Meiji-era translator to shepherd it into Japan, albeit piecewise and imperfectly. Emily Brontë's novel had to wait several more decades for its first Japanese translation; *Wuthering Heights* warded off translators in the same way that its characters repelled outsiders. Heathcliff enters the household under cover of darkness and under Mr. Earnshaw's great coat. "A dirty, ragged, black-haired" orphan found on the streets of Liverpool, he immediately gets marked as a foreigner when he first touches down in the Earnshaw household, and "only stared round, and repeated over and over again some gibberish that nobody could understand" (36–37). Mrs. Earnshaw, asking how her husband "could fashion to bring that gipsy brat into the house," is ready "to fling it out of doors."

Heathcliff is the first of several visitors who cross over the Wuthering Heights threshold to their own detriment; the house seems toxic to outsiders. Hindley's wife Frances arrives at Wuthering Heights with Death flicking his scythe in her direction—she seems predisposed for the consumptive decline that soon claims her. Old Mrs. Linton pays several visits to Wuthering Heights, attempting to "set things to rights," ordering and scolding the householders, before transporting the convalescent Catherine to Thrushcross Grange. Brontë writes, "But, the poor dame had reason to repent of her kindness; she and her husband both took the fever, and died within a few days of each other" (88).

In *Wuthering Heights*, "Boundaries and barriers receive unusual attention," notes Elizabeth Napier, one of several critics to focus on scenes in which characters pass through doors and windows, most famously the scene in which the ghost waif Catherine taps on Lockwood's lattice window, but also the moment when Catherine and Heathcliff hang from the Lintons' window ledge as they spy on their neighbors, and the time when Heathcliff enters Wuthering Heights through a window as Hindley waits inside with pistol drawn.[12] In Heathcliff's death scene, rain from an open window pours onto his corpse and bedclothes.

"Almost every character in *Wuthering Heights* tries to get across a threshold," I told my husband as we stood in front of the vending machines at the Takanodai train station near our temporary home in Japan. I, who was beginning to recognize every third or fourth Japanese character on posters in train stations, informed my husband that we were looking at an advertisement for a business that catered to children and involved someone standing up and brushing something. My husband could not recognize any Japanese characters, but he often stopped me from stepping onto the wrong train. As I debated whether I had time to purchase a green tea ice cream cone, I was feeling calm and powerful because I had already mastered the vending machine's payment system. And also because I thought I had discovered how *Wuthering Heights* was first introduced into Japan. "It all started with Edmund Blunden," I pronounced, as my husband studied the scrolling train alerts, posted in alternating Roman and Japanese characters, the former of which I ignored so that I could reinforce my Japanese.

The English critic and poet Edmund Blunden took over the professorship of English literature at Tokyo Imperial University in April 1924 at age twenty-seven after surviving active combat in World War I. Sometime over the course of his three-year tenure at what is now the University of Tokyo, he made an important pronouncement that set the course for Brontë studies in Japan. He confidently averred that the three greatest tragedies in the English language are *King Lear*, *Moby Dick*, and *Wuthering Heights*, a decree that was preserved by one of his students, Abe Tomoji, in a critical biography of Herman Melville.[13]

Blunden was beloved by his students. Abe called him Japan's best friend, and a special issue of *Today's Japan* presents a "homage to Edmund Blunden," with former Blunden colleague and Keats scholar Saitō Takeshi recalling the six hundred lectures Blunden delivered in post–World War II Japan, his "performing [of] prodigious work with almost superhuman energy far in excess of what his duty laid upon him."[14] The chairman of the English Literary Society of Japan, recalled, decades later, how Blunden's "quiet lectures . . . sunk deep into the hearts of the students."[15] Blunden espoused a different view of his lectures' impact. "Next term approaches & I shall be preaching my unreal gospel to the 150 unfortunate wretches who 'have ears & hear not,'" he wrote in a letter to his editor.[16] But for Saitō Takeshi he reserved special praise, describing him as a "scholar, gentleman and Christian of the first quality," and visiting him during a 1950 return to Japan (fig. 2).[17]

I combed the tributes penned by Blunden's students and colleagues, looking for mentions of *Wuthering Heights*. Blunden lectured in Japan soon after the Great Kanto Earthquake of 1923; it was a time when, as Sone Tamotsu recalls, "Hardly a week passed without tremors, oftentimes of considerable severity."[18] When a strong earthquake interrupted Blunden's lecture on *King Lear*, causing a cloud of glass fragments from a broken skylight to rain down on his assembled students, he responded with aplomb, reemerging from under his desk "with a puzzled smile on his face."[19] I wished Blunden had been lecturing on *Wuthering Heights* when a tremor hit; although his students made frequent references to his comments on Thomas Hardy and James Joyce, they neglected to mention the specific words he spoke about *Wuthering Heights*.

Imagine the Brontës' arrival in Japan as a map of the Tokyo railway system with Edmund Blunden as the giant station of Shinjuku. A smaller ancillary station might be assigned to the novelist Natsume Sōseki, whose role in the Brontës' reception history was more difficult for me to pin down. Sōseki read *Jane Eyre* in the original in 1896, four years before the Japanese government sent him to study in Great Britain as Japan's first

Claire + Edmund Blunden
Fumiko + Takeshi Saitō

Tokyo Woman's Christian College, 13 Feb. '50

Fig. 2. Edmund and Claire Blunden with Saitō Takeshi and Saitō Fumiko,
© National Portrait Gallery, London.

Japanese English literary scholar. A blue plaque in Clapham marks one of the four lodging houses where he, miserably, stayed. "The two years I lived in London were the unhappiest two years of my life," Sōseki recalled. "Among the English gentlemen, I was like a lone shaggy dog mixed in with a pack of wolves; I endured a wretched existence."[20] He immersed himself so fully in reading that a rumor spread that he had gone mad. I had not yet established that Sōseki read *Wuthering Heights* during his period of lunatic reading, but I hoped that I would one day be able to do so. I felt an affinity for Sōseki, who bemoaned his inability to attain the difficult intellectual goals he set for himself. "I compared the number of books I had managed to read with the number I still needed to read—and was shocked at how little progress I had made." He brought back with him to Japan a stack of notebooks, "five or six inches tall" and "written in tiny script the size of a fly's head," the record of what he saw as his failure to pass his eyes over any more than 60 percent of classic literary works. "It was quite regrettable," he wrote, "that, given my innate stupidity and lack of scholarly ability, I had not attained any mastery of foreign literature."[21] In his pursuit of mastery, Sōseki was emulating his English tutor Professor William James Craig, whose lifelong quest it was to compile a Shakespearean dictionary, to which end he filled ten blue-covered notebooks with references he collected "like a miser storing away small coins."[22] Professor Craig died without completing his glossary, it was chastening to note. And Sōseki's academic career took a swerve.

Upon his return from London, and twenty years before Blunden would assume a similar role, Sōseki took up an academic post at the Tokyo Imperial University, where he became the first Japanese person to teach English. He stepped into a position previously held by the writer Lafcadio Hearn, who transmitted Japanese folklore, sometimes inaccurately, to the West. (Hearn was raised in Ireland and France, and lived in Cincinnati before moving to Japan.) When Sōseki assumed Hearn's position, students "felt that his objective, Western-style analysis, in contrast to Hearn's more emotive 'Japanese' approach, was like taking a scalpel to things of rare beauty," according to the translator Jay Rubin.[23] That is, the Japanese Sōseki was faulted for a teaching method that seemed insufficiently Japanese when compared to that of Hearn, a man of Greek and Irish ancestry.

If you walk across the University of Tokyo campus today, you will see a pond shaped like the Japanese character for heart (心) and named after the eponymous protagonist of Sōseki's novel *Sanshirō*. Sanshirō travels by train from the hinterlands of Japan so that he can enroll at Tokyo Imperial University, and, encountering more cosmopolitan travelers, is abashed by his unworldliness. Sanshirō keeps a copy of Francis Bacon's *Essays* on his lap during the journey. "Now, here is a question few Japanese readers may have bothered to ask:" the novelist Mizumura Minae writes, "Is the book a translation or the English original?"[24] The reason few Japanese readers would bother to ask this question is because a present-day reader, "long accustomed to the idea that every important book from the West has been rendered into Japanese, is likely to assume that it's a translation." Mizumura goes on to point out that during the time period in which *Sanshirō* is set (the latter part of the Meiji era [1868 to 1912]) translations of Western books were rare. If we picture Sanshirō perusing a book in English, Mizumura writes, "We can expect this novel to be about bilingual intellectuals of the Meiji period in whose lives reading Western languages, particularly English, played a central role."

I had never bothered to consider whether the Bacon edition that Sanshirō carries is a translation or the English original, but not because I assumed that all important Western works have been translated into Japanese. I had not thought about the translation issue because, as a native English speaker, I could easily access all of Bacon's works; it had not occurred to me that the book on Sanshirō's lap stands as a mark of his intellectual ambition, of the heavy lifting he's done in order to read English. But when I started reading about the generation of Japanese intellectuals who immersed themselves in Western literary works, all of these issues rushed to mind. As Mizumura notes, Japanese writers applied themselves to reading foreign literary works with extraordinary energy: Akutagawa Ryūnosuke, the father of the Japanese short story, read *War and Peace* in English translation in just four days; the novelist Nakazato Kaizan was an avid reader of Victor Hugo in English.[25] Mizumura writes, "Of all the male Japanese writers born in the nineteenth century, each one a pioneer in his way, the number who attended Tokyo Imperial University . . . and thus were bilinguals, if not polyglots, is astonishing."[26]

When Edmund Blunden arrived at Tokyo Imperial University, he was not bilingual, and while there he learned only basic conversational Japanese. "The Japanese speech is a long way beyond me yet, though I have a few phrases which I bring out regularly as opportunity comes," he wrote, in one of many mentions of his linguistic deficit.[27] He was pleased with the success of his lectures—"My lecturing goes on like the train between Mark's Tey [a village in Essex] and Cambridge," he wrote—but he required

the assistance of a Japanese secretary, Hayashi Aki, to carry out his affairs.[28] Hayashi eased Blunden's passage across the threshold of Japanese
society and became, for a brief period, his romantic partner. By the time he
left Japan in 1927 the passion had grown one-sided, Blunden's biographer
Barry Webb reports, but Blunden dutifully installed Hayashi in a London
flat. Blunden wrote, "I will not sacrifice Miss Hayashi who was so perfect
in her devotion to me in Japan. I am aware that she is in love with me, as
other Japanese women seemed in danger of being—one came to the boat
at Kobe in tears, who had seen me at school lectures two or three times,
and would have gone to the gallows for me!"[29] Blunden's wife accused him
of bringing a geisha girl back with him from Japan, and although his sexual
relationship with Hayashi ended, he continued to view her as his minion.
He wrote admiringly, "The Japanese women are in such a tradition that it
is almost incredible that one or two of them, like her, achieve such culture,
freedom of thought and skill of action."[30] He assumed Hayashi's considerable gifts would be deployed in his service. When there was uncertainty
about whether Hayashi's permit to remain in England would be renewed,
he considered resuming his career in Japan, in which case, he wrote, "A.H.
would see to it that I was not starved, ill, or without buttons on my small-
clothes," going on to say, "I am her unalterable admirer, as I am of Mrs.
Barbauld or Queen Victoria." It's hard to imagine, however, that Blunden
would have asked those eminent British women to reattach his buttons.

Blunden supported Hayashi financially for thirty-four years, during
which time she served as his research assistant. Blunden's biographer Barry
Webb describes her sublimating her affections in an intense schedule of
work, chasing references for him at the British Museum or the Newspaper
Library at Colindale for the next thirty years, but not without complaining
about her situation. In a 1932 letter, Blunden criticized her possessiveness
as he got ready to take a new wife. "I may ask you to be absolutely content
with working for me, and with having my friendship and my continued
care and trust," he wrote, going on to stipulate a code of behavior that
she should follow: "to avoid all attempt at a love affair with me; to behave
quietly and respectfully towards me, as a secretary should; to expect that I
shall not visit you alone as much as I have done."[31]

To his students and Japanese colleagues though, Blunden was a great
man. They took seriously his statement that *Wuthering Heights* was
among the three greatest tragedies in the English language. One of them,
Yamato Yasuo, in 1932 published the first Japanese translation of *Wuthering Heights*; another, the same Abe Tomoji who recorded Blunden's pro-

nouncement about the three greatest English-language tragedies, would, thirty years after Yamato, publish his own *Wuthering Heights* translation. Both of them, like all subsequent Japanese translators of Brontë's novel, gave their translations a title that can be traced to Saitō Takeshi, whose library Blunden drew on for his research.[32]

More than one Japanese person has attributed the popularity of *Wuthering Heights* to the genius of the Japanese title, *Arashi ga oka*, or, as it is written in Japanese, 嵐が丘. Saitō's title phrase contains the kanji for *arashi* (嵐 stormy) and *oka* (丘 hill) separated by the *hiragana ga* (が). *Ga* usually serves as a particle, that is, as one of a category of sentence parts that communicate the relationships among words in a sentence.[33] The particle *ga* often marks the subject of a Japanese sentence, but in the case of the title *Arashi ga oka*, or so I was assured by one of my Japanese friends, the *ga* derives from the symbol ケ, which is often used to indicate the possessive, especially in place names, so that the title means "the hills of the storm," or "stormy hill." Edmund Blunden's student Saitō Takeshi, when he came up with the name *Arashi ga oka*, gave it a title that evoked Japanese place names like *Jiyū ga oka* (the name of a neighborhood in Tokyo), and so managed to capture the vague rootedness of "wuthering heights." Lockwood describes "wuthering" as "a significant provincial adjective, descriptive of the atmospheric tumult to which its station is exposed in stormy weather" (4). Unlike the Japanese title of *Little Women*, another Western literary work that holds a special place in the hearts of Japanese women readers, and whose Japanese title, *Wakakusa monogatari*, translates back into English as "a story of young grass," *Arashi ga oka* hews closely to Emily Brontë's original title. Brontë's choice of the unusual words "wuthering" (as opposed to "windy") and "height" (as opposed to "mountain") gives the English title a literary quality matched by the evocativeness of the Japanese title.[34]

I had an opportunity to talk to one of Saitō's students—"Saitō's *last* student," declared Professor Iki Kazuko, whom I met at an academic conference. I asked her how Saitō came to give *Wuthering Heights* its Japanese title. She recalled that Professor Saitō gave many Western literary works their Japanese names.[35] "So he was kind of the go-to person for titles," I said, thrilled to encounter someone who could have touched the sleeve of Saitō. Professor Iki nodded.

My theory that Blunden had ignited the *Wuthering Heights* fire in Japanese people, or, at minimum, kindled a small votive flame, was eventually undermined by the blank stares with which Japanese people greeted my mentions of his name. Once, while I was having dinner with some Japanese friends, the conversation turned, as it always turned, since I was gripping the steering wheel with the force of a long-haul trucker, to *Wuthering Heights*. We had settled on our restaurant after several minutes of delicate negotiations on the food floor of a Japanese vertical mall. The mother of the family had wanted me to choose which restaurant we entered, but she had also noted twice that a nice sushi restaurant was an option. Before too long we were unfurling hot towels with relief. When the patriarch of the family started crying "Heathcliff . . . Heathcliff," and gesticulating in a theatrical manner, a woman at an adjoining table stared for a moment and then quickly averted her eyes. Even as I was having trouble grasping sashimi with my chopsticks, I understood that he was performing an early scene of the film version of *Wuthering Heights*, in which Lockwood's sleep is interrupted by a banging shutter and by the cries of Catherine's ghost.

William Wyler's 1939 film stars Laurence Olivier and Merle Oberon as the first celluloid Heathcliff and Catherine, if you don't count a silent film *Wuthering Heights* that has been lost to history.[36] Although nominated for twelve Academy Awards, the 1939 *Wuthering Heights* debuted in a year that saw the premier of more great films than any other year in American film history; filmgoers could watch *Gone With the Wind*, *The Wizard of Oz*, *Stagecoach*, *Dark Victory*, *Mr. Smith Goes to Washington*, and *Of Mice and Men*, among other celebrated films. *Wuthering Heights* won only the Academy Award for Cinematography, but it made an impression on Japanese audiences when it finally opened in Japan in 1950, the eleven-year delay caused first by war censorship, and then by whatever market vagaries determined that *Dark Victory* would premiere in Japan in 1948 and *The Wizard of Oz* would open in 1954.[37] According to Hiroshi Kitamura, the film was originally approved for screening in 1947, and when it was finally released it was considered as having "reorientation value" by the Civil Information and Education Section of the U.S. Occupation.[38] Kitamura describes the thousands of Japanese fans who flocked to the first Hollywood movies that were screened after the war. The year before *Wuthering Heights* was belatedly released, Japanese moviegoers were urged to "weep at the rose-colored chronicle" of *Little Women* (1949), and to participate in "four-sisters" contests.[39] Louisa May Alcott's novel was already familiar to Japanese readers, and the film was marketed as a "literary and artistic" work, its Victorian context emphasized.[40] "No other film is as fantastic, moving, and romantic," its promoters claimed, perhaps helping to build an audience for *Wuthering Heights* when it was released in Japan the following year.

These days, one can buy a DVD of Wyler's film with Japanese subtitles for five hundred yen, or less than five dollars. A banner across the DVD case advertises the film's inclusion in Mizuno Haruo's list of world masterwork films. Mizuno Haruo, a round-faced man with a moustache, gazes out of a little porthole frame on the front cover of the DVD, just beneath the more serious faces of Laurence Olivier and Merle Oberon. Before his death in 2008, Mizuno was a movie director, movie critic, and *tarento* (high-profile celebrity). When I slipped my DVD of the Japanese imprint of *Wuthering Heights* into a DVD player, I hoped to see Mizuno explain why he listed *Wuthering Heights* as the number ten pick in his world masterwork film list. I imagined him as a modern-day Blunden who would fill in the gaps of Japanese viewers' understanding of nineteenth-century England. But the only choice to be made on the DVD menu was one of subtitling language. And when the film began, there was no glimpse of Mizuno, only the opening shot of a farm building with "Samuel Goldwyn Presents 'Wuthering Heights'" in a distinctive font with serifs that looked like whale tails. I wondered if Japanese people were as flummoxed by this ornamental typeface as I am by stylized kanji. I once saw a Japanese record sleeve on which *arashi ga oka* was written as if it was passing through a wind tunnel.

Wyler's film opens with Lockwood's arrival, his stumbling through a snowstorm in order to barge without permission through the door of Wuthering Heights. Lockwood fights off a dog that attacks him upon his entrance, and then walks directly into another room in which the members of the household are assembled. The camera lingers as they stare at Lockwood as if he is responsible for bringing a noxious smell into the room. Heathcliff, who is standing by the fireplace, also glowers at Lockwood. Isabella cranes her head around the wing of an armchair so that she, too, can stare. The director Wyler tracks everyone's displeased glances so slowly and deliberately that a viewer of any cultural background is able to read the scene.

The film's Japanese subtitler does not render the English speech exactly. Heathcliff's brusque greeting of Lockwood at the beginning of the film becomes even more rude in Japanese, since Lockwood speaks in the polite language one would use if one were speaking to an elder or a stranger, and Heathcliff uses language one would use in speaking with a friend or family member. When Lockwood gets attacked by a dog, he says, *Yameru*, which is the plain-form version of the verb "stop" or "quit," but he quickly slips into *desu* (more polite) form when he speaks to Heathcliff. Heathcliff, by contrast, speaks to Lockwood in the manner that Lockwood talks to the attacking dog.

Abé Markus Nornes notes that the Japanese language seems "ready-made for subtitling," since kanji express the maximum amount of meaning in a minimum of syllables.[41] The Japanese tendency to do without subjects and pronouns makes it easy to compress a lot of information into a brief line of text, and since the Japanese language can be inscribed either horizontally or vertically, there is greater flexibility in subtitle positioning. Nornes describes a culture of subtitler celebrity in Japan, where the names of Japanese subtitlers are included in prints of foreign films, and where these subtitlers write books and accrue fans. In the same year (1939) that Wyler's *Wuthering Heights* was released in the U.S., Ota Tatsuo argued for subtitles that would serve as "messenger[s] from a meeting with the Japanese language," and that would "create in Japanese the things that are trying to be expressed in the foreign language."[42] Nornes counters by saying that Ota, writing at a moment when Japan was contemplating the colonization of Asia, called for a domineering subtitling practice, one that would erase difference. Nornes's preference is for what he calls "abusive" subtitling that maintains the strangeness of the foreign.

Ota longed for subtitles that would put audiences at their ease, in the same way that, in the days of silent film, movie commentators known as *benshi* helped Japanese viewers understand what they were watching. The *benshi* narrated what was happening on screen, providing vocal accompaniments to silent films. These narrators became so central and expected a component of the filmgoing experience, and such powerful figures in the film industry, that they retained their roles long after the advent of sound. As Japanese filmgoers watched foreign films whose title shots they couldn't understand and whose actors' lips they couldn't read, the *benshi* provided a form of spoken subtitles.

The correlation between the narratives of the original films and the narratives spoken by the *benshi* was sometimes small. At least one *benshi* found a way to circumvent censorship by means of extreme interpretive license. As Donald Richie recounts, a 1907 French feature about Louis XVI was shut down in Japan because of its incendiary tale of regicide.[43] However, it was replaced by another film, *The Cave King: A Curious Story of North America*, which was exactly the same film with a different *benshi* narrative. In *The Cave King*, set in the Rocky Mountains, Louis XVI became the leader of a robber band who was being resisted by loyal citizens, the same citizens who, in the original French feature, were revolutionaries storming the Bastille.

The *benshi* tradition helps to explain the ubiquitousness of panels of *ekisupāto* (experts) on Japanese television shows, scholars and pop idols (*tarento* like Mizuno Haruo) who join audiences in watching everything from the Olympics to home makeovers, and who have made their way into American culture by way of Iron Chef competitions and assorted Food Network programs. Hiroshi Komatsu and Frances Loden point to the *benshi* as a way of explaining "the Japanese affection for teachers, tour guides, sommeliers, and other conduits for the acquisition of new experience."[44]

The *Wuthering Heights* subtitler dispensed with what was most foreign, and tried, when possible, to place what was happening on screen in a Japanese frame of reference. The subtitler didn't feel compelled to communicate what the film Mr. Earnshaw says when he hands a violin over to Hindley: "Here you go, Paganini." The subtitler deemed this reference to the Italian virtuoso extraneous to a Japanese person's viewing pleasure. The whip and violin that Mr. Earnshaw brings home for his children become for the Japanese viewer *omiyage*, that is, souvenirs of travel. The viewer might reasonably assume that Liverpool, the city from which Mr. Earnshaw is returning, is renowned for its horse whips and violins.

A few minutes into the film I revisited the scene that my dinner partner mimicked when he started moaning "Heathcliff" over his dipping bowl. The film version moves more swiftly than the novel to the moment when Lockwood hears the "teasing sound" of a fir bough brushing against the window, and resolves to silence it (25). In the novel, Lockwood breaks the glass and tries to seize the branch, but grabs instead a small, ice-cold hand, and he hears a melancholy voice sobbing, "Let me in—let me in!" What follows is one of the most chillingly violent moments in the novel. Lockwood sees a child's face looking through the window, and "finding it useless to attempt shaking the creature off," he pulls its wrist on to the broken pane, and "rub[s] it to and fro till the blood [runs] down and soak[s] the bed-clothes." The wraith cries on, and "maintain[s] its tenacious gripe, almost maddening [Lockwood] with fear" (25). The scene dramatizes the novel's main preoccupations: the distance between the living and the dead, the difficulty of traversing that divide.[45] In the subtitled film, Catherine's ghost says, *Naka ni irete*, and then *Onegai*, a verb used to ask a favor. She demands, "Let me in," and then softens the command to something I read as "Please do me the favor of letting me in," but which a native speaker might read as "Let me in. Please."

Gratuitous cruelty, Dorothy Van Ghent called Lockwood's attempt to break the ghost Catherine's grasp; the novel is full of gratuitous cruelty, which the Hollywood version downplayed, and which the Japanese subtitling, by turns, amplified or muted.[46] But even when the subtitles accentuated Heathcliff's rudeness, they in no way prepared me for Yoshida Yoshishige's 1988 film *Arashi ga oka*, a reimagining of Brontë's novel that stands as "a challenge [to] the romanticism of the Hollywood version."[47] Yoshida's film, which transports Brontë's novel to late fifteenth-century Japan, dials up the viciousness and violence of Brontë's novel to samurai level. The film's equivalent of Mr. Earnshaw gets penetrated by an arrow, and the film's Heathcliff (Onimaru) rapes Isabella Linton (Tae), after which she slings her kimono belt over a *torī* (entrance gate) and hangs herself. Yoshida's film depicts the wife of Hindley (Hindemaru) being savaged by bandits, and Edgar (Mitsuhito) cutting his own neck after his house has been invaded by Heathcliff (Onimaru). Onimaru has come to seize the daughter of Kinu (Catherine), a daughter who is also called Kinu, and who is possibly also the daughter of Onimaru since he and the first Kinu had sex in a profane space, a room where menstruating women are confined, before Kinu married the film's Edgar equivalent. The filmmaker Yoshida channels and amplifies the violence and sacrilege that disgusted Brontë's early reviewers. His Heathcliff (Onimaru) not only digs up Kinu's coffin (twice), he hauls it off to the House of the East (Wuthering Heights), where Kinu 2 relegates it to the contamination room; there Onimaru finds it dressed in a kimono and propped up like Norman Bates's mother in Hitchcock's *Psycho*.

Yoshida's version, like the novel, draws firm boundaries between insiders and outsiders, and lingers over the gateways that distinguish separate realms. The Brontë scholar Okumura Maki, who interviewed the director, conveys Yoshida's view of Heathcliff as a variant of the Japanese medieval legend of *Ijin* (a stranger). She describes how, in medieval Japan, strangers were viewed as *oni* (demons), whom people feared.[48] Certainly in Yoshida's film, Heathcliff/Onimaru is a terrifying figure, his hair radiating from his head like a fright wig, his face contorted into a permanent sneer. Even after he gets his hand chopped off by Yoshimaru (Hareton) in a sword fight, Onimaru carries on, leaving behind his sword, with hand still attached, planted in the earth like a flag. In the final scene, Onimaru carries Kinu's coffin over his shoulder as he disappears into the mist.

I admired the Yoshida film's faithfulness to the unsettling aspects of Brontë's work, and also its emphasis on the moment when Catherine suggests to Nelly that she and Heathcliff are one. The scene occurs in a chapter that begins with Heathcliff saving the baby Hareton from certain death (Hareton has been inadvertently tossed over a bannister by the drunken Hindley), and ends with Catherine's marriage to Edgar Linton. In between these exciting events, a disturbed and anxious Catherine seeks out Nelly Dean in the kitchen of Wuthering Heights, and reveals her plan to marry Edgar. Unbeknownst to Catherine, Heathcliff hears her comments, but he moves out of earshot before she speaks the novel's most iconic line. Contrasting her love for Linton to her love for Heathcliff, she cries, "Nelly, I *am* Heathcliff—he's always, always in my mind" (82).

In Yoshida's film, this moment gets anticipated when Mr. Earnshaw (Takamaru) arrives home with the orphan Heathcliff. In the Wyler film version, he brings Catherine a riding whip, but in Yoshida's film, Takamaru gives Kinu a mirror that she uses to catch the light and attract Onimaru's attention in a subsequent scene. In Yoshida's version of the "I *am* Heathcliff" moment, Kinu gazes at her own face in this mirror, while saying, in Japanese, "Onimaru is me" and "I am Onimaru," and then again, "Onimaru is me."[49] In the same scene Yoshida's Nelly chastises Kinu for letting Onimaru get away, but Kinu insists that he is still with her. The mirror reappears again and again, most startlingly when Onimaru exhumes it from Kinu's coffin, where it has been buried with her corpse. With the recurring mirror image, the director Yoshida seems to underscore the importance of the "I *am* Heathcliff" line.

Yoshida's *Arashi ga oka* is not a mainstream film, the critic John Collick reminds us, situating Yoshida's work in the radical cinema movement of the late 1960s and early 1970s.[50] Yoshida's film is less well known in Japan than William Wyler's 1939 version, which has inspired a manga version, on whose cover a man I at first took to be William Wyler sits in a director's chair holding a rolled-up script. His portrait is superimposed over drawings of a bosomy Catherine, wearing a tiara, and a stern Heathcliff, who flashes a piercing gaze. Catherine has big blue 1970s-manga sparkle eyes, and Heathcliff has a floppy hairstyle beloved by Tokyo high school boys. The man in the director's chair is actually Hirokane Kenshi, a manga artist famous for a long-running series about a salaryman, and the editor of the series in which the *Wuthering Heights* film manga is included.

I turned to Hirokane's afterword so as to determine why he oversaw a manga series based on American movies, and why he chose to feature

Wuthering Heights, along with *Charade* and *Casablanca*. Hirokane mentions Wyler's other films, *Roman Holiday* and *Ben-Hur*, before going on to discuss Wyler's audacious elimination of the second-generation *Wuthering Heights* characters, conceding (and here I started losing control of Hirokane's Japanese sentence) that this was an alteration with which some people could not be quite satisfied, before expressing his own judgment, which took into account mainly entertainment value, from which perspective, and in his personal view, Wyler's film was a huge success.[51] Hirokane's afterword is two pages long, but forty-five minutes passed while I deciphered the first paragraph.

Spread out before me was a stack of Japanese translation tools. There was a *Langenscheidt Pocket Japanese Dictionary*, a Canon Wordtank V330, and *The Complete Japanese Verb Guide*. I routinely surrounded myself with dictionaries, settled down to work in earnest, and slowly parsed eight manga frames before getting discouraged and reading the *International Herald Tribune*. In my Japanese reading, Lockwood was perpetually arriving at Wuthering Heights. I looked at the slim manga volume and then I looked at the moat of dictionaries with which it was surrounded.

"I'm Lockwood," I thought to myself.[52]

Brontë's frame story suddenly stood revealed as the history of a person who tries to gain entrance into a foreign country, and who is baffled at every turn. When Lockwood arrives at Wuthering Heights he totally misreads the household situation, mistaking Heathcliff's daughter-in-law for Heathcliff's wife, and a heap of dead rabbits for pet cats. He initially thinks he and Heathcliff have a great deal in common, when nothing could be farther from the case. The Japanese have an expression for people who are unable to read social cues: *kūki yomenai*, or "can't read the air" (abbreviated as KY in text messages). Lockwood's inability to read the air of Wuthering Heights is dramatically heightened in the opening scene of the Wyler film. In the past I'd judged Lockwood to be a loathsome character, but now I felt some sympathy for his awkwardness.

As I continued to slowly read the manga's afterword, I noticed that Hirokane mentions the Japanese titles of *King Lear* and *Moby Dick*. "He's quoting Edmund Blunden," I nearly shouted to myself, pushing my glasses back on my head so that I could see the vertical sentences more clearly. The Japanese phrase meaning "English literature three great tragedies" was clearly legible before me.[53] Blunden's statement about the greatness of Shakespeare's and Melville's and Brontë's masterworks had somehow made its way from a Taishō-era lecture hall to a contemporary manga series, but Blunden himself had been jettisoned along the way. Hirokane didn't acknowledge that he was quoting Blunden. However, in a fleeting moment of triumph, I realized that he was doing just that.

Perhaps I alone, I thought smugly in the quiet of my Japanese dining room, where only the cries of Japanese crows punctured my reverie— perhaps I alone, among the admittedly limited number of people who have purchased a Japanese manga based on an American film based on a nineteenth-century English novel, have registered this connection. In Chinese legend, the gods tie a red cord around the ankles of those who are fated to meet each other in a future situation; the cord may stretch, but it does not break. I had discovered a red cord connecting Edmund Blunden to William Wyler to Hirokane Kenshi to Japanese Brontë fans. Maybe my red cord wasn't as strong as the one that links soon-to-be lovers by their pinky fingers in the manga series my daughters liked to read, but it counted for something.

Do we love hard books more than easy ones? Did the tiresomeness of Lockwood's frame story lead me back to *Wuthering Heights* despite my having more than once halted at the door?[54] As a college student, I read *Remembrance of Things Past* under the tutelage of a courtly old professor who led his bewildered students through the vagaries of Proust's complex mental journey. For a few hours each week, my classmates and I drank cognac on the Left Bank, and then, as Proust acolytes, we went back to counting laundry quarters. When I brought *Wuthering Heights* with me to Japan, I was, unaware, transporting a book freighted with past aspirations. And when I started gathering Japanese versions of Brontë's novel, my aspirations became entangled with the hopes and dreams of Japanese readers, for whom Brontë's novel is a hundred times more difficult to understand than it is for me.

Or maybe it isn't, what do I know? Maybe there are aspects of Japanese literary history that make *Wuthering Heights* seem oddly familiar to Japanese readers. Emily Brontë's novel shocked early reviewers because they were reading it in the context of buttoned-up English novels, but perhaps in Japan Brontë's novel has more frisky bedfellows beside whom *Wuthering Heights* seems tame. Emily Brontë never traveled to Japan, but she might belong there in some greater cosmic sense, I thought, buoyed by the tiny discovery I'd made in my Japanese dining room. Outside my window, two crows quarreled over a half-eaten rice ball, but I paid them no mind, and turned back to my book.

CHAPTER TWO

Heathcliff in Yokohama

"I *am* Heathcliff—"
—Catherine, *Wuthering Heights*

"I *was* Heathcliff."
—Koshiro Miyako, Takarazuka actress (trans. Kurosawa Ayako)

I met my first Japanese Heathcliff at the Yokohama Bay Sheraton Hotel, where she blended in with the other elegant women who had gathered to sip iced milk tea in midafternoon. We sat on upholstered chairs around a low table in a vast high-ceilinged room in which bridal shows sometimes took place. There were giant chandeliers and plinths of oversized flower arrangements featuring calla lilies. Harp music struggled to be heard over the din of chatting women. My first Japanese Heathcliff, whose stage name is Koshiro Miyako, performed the role of Heathcliff in the 1969 Takarazuka Revue production of *Wuthering Heights*.

The Takarazuka Revue was the brainchild of a railroad tycoon who established an all-female theater company in 1913 as a means of drawing visitors to the hot springs resort of Takarazuka, a city near Osaka. There, female actors would play both male and female roles—Rhett Butler and Scarlet, Gatsby and Daisy, Richard Gere and Debra Winger—in melodramatic theatrical productions based on Western novels or movies.[1] The origin of the Takarazuka Revue closely coincides with the beginning of the Taishō era (1912–1926), "Japan's Jazz Age," a moment when stylish young people wore Western clothes and *roido* glasses (spectacles like those of the silent film star Harold Lloyd) while riding bicycles, when "free love" was part of the new revolutionary ethos inspired by the West. Takarazuka fans, disembarking from the maroon train cars of the Hankyu Railway, looked forward to having a thrillingly Western and foreign experience while still safely grounded in Hyōgo Prefecture.

Takarazuka productions often share in common a Byronic hero who looks good in a slim-cut suit and who dies slowly and tragically before the play ends. When my daughters and I attended the Takarazuka production of *Trafalgar*, we saw enacted the military heroics of the British admiral Lord Nelson combined with the romance of his ill-advised affair with Emma Hamilton, all set to music and performed by beautiful Japanese women costumed in British military uniforms and period gowns. After the curtain went down on Nelson's attenuated death, we wandered through the Takarazuka gift shop, fingering souvenir key rings and cast DVDs. Then we noticed that the audience members had started surging, in a well-mannered way, back into the auditorium, so we joined the queue filing back into the theater to watch a musical revue called "Funky Sunshine." The revue featured sunshine-related song-and-dance routines that looked like the work of a choreographer on a sugar high. This was cuteness on a scale that was impressive even for Japan, where you can buy a book to teach you how to turn your child's bento lunch into a panda mosaic. After the "Funky Sunshine" extravaganza was over, the sated audience, made up of mostly middle-aged women, trooped out of the auditorium.

Wuthering Heights, which has been performed twice by the Takarazuka company, first in 1969 and again in 1997–98, might seem an odd selection for a company that capitalizes on swoony romances. Brontë's novel is a compendium of curiously unsatisfying love stories in which attachments are benighted and brief. Hindley Earnshaw marries the flighty Frances only to see her exit the world in a coughing fit. The first Catherine marries the phlegmatic Edgar Linton because she looks forward to being the greatest woman in the neighborhood; the second Catherine marries the neurasthenic Linton so that she can get home to her dying father. And Heathcliff stumbles through Brontë's novel in a sulk of unreciprocated devotion, the whole world "a dreadful collection of memoranda" that remind him that he has lost Catherine. "In every cloud, in every tree—filling the air at night, and caught by glimpses in every object, by day I am surrounded with her image!" Heathcliff cries.[2]

But then again, *Wuthering Heights*, given its portrayal of erotic masochism and power-hungry characters, seems like the perfect vehicle for a Takarazuka production. In the most spontaneously romantic moment in the novel, Isabella Linton, smitten with a man she mistakes for a brooding romantic, elopes with Heathcliff. "I love him more than ever you loved Edgar; and he might love me if you would let him!" Isabella cries to Catherine (102). From that moment forward she inspires Heathcliff's most violent cruelties. He hangs Isabella's springer spaniel from a bridle hook, a gratuitous act of animal abuse that anticipates his lack of sympathy for Isabella herself, whom he views as "a strange repulsive animal, a centipede from the Indies" (106). Isabella's romantic fantasy evolves into a sadistic struggle as Heathcliff coolly dissects her misperception of him. "She abandoned [her friends and family] under a delusion, picturing in me a hero of romance, and expecting unlimited indulgences from my chivalrous devotion," he notes (149). He imagines "turning [her] blue eyes black, every day or two" (106). Belatedly disabused of her fantasy version of Heathcliff, Isabella writes to Nelly, "I assure you, a tiger, or a venomous serpent could not rouse terror in me equal to that which he wakens" (144).[3]

In Brontë's novel, Heathcliff, "an arid wilderness of furze and whinstone," is an ominous microclimate into which others venture at their peril (102). But the Takarazuka Heathcliff, who has the big hair and delicate features of a boy band idol, presents a more temperate erotic fantasy zone. Koshiro Miyako, the first Takarazuka Heathcliff, brought to the Yokohama hotel a large envelope containing photos of herself as a young star, and let me pick out a *buromaido*, a signed souvenir photograph of the kind that fans sought out during the golden era of the Hollywood star system. In *Sunset Boulevard*, the aging film star Norma Desmond busies herself with signing head shots of her younger self. In the *buromaido* (the word derives from "bromide," the chemical used to process photographs), Koshiro's beautiful eyes were accentuated with eyeliner drawn in the slightly cat-eye manner of the 1960s. Her eyebrows, too, were heavily penciled, and she wore pink lipstick. In my favorite publicity shot, Koshiro, dressed in a velveteen suit and holding a martini glass, directs a sultry gaze at the camera (fig. 3). She turns a frank but gentle eye on the viewer, her hair a confluence of comb-over and ducktail, with a spit curl thrown in for good measure. It must have been easy for Takarazuka fans to take the erotic excess of their secret dreams—fantasies that could not easily be grafted onto salaryman husbands—and attach them to Koshiro and the other dashing female actors. Describing the impact of a Takarazuka performance, one of the fans in a Takarazuka documentary recalls, "My heart had never felt like that before. From head to toe I felt an electric shock. My mind just exploded."[4]

I tried to meet an actual Takarazuka fan—the friend of the wife of a Japanese friend—but she demurred, offering instead a stack of Takarazuka fan magazines like the one my daughters and I purchased at the *Trafalgar* performance. The fan magazines featured casual shots of the stars in re-

Fig. 3. Takarazuka star Koshiro Miyako. Courtesy of Koshiro Miyako.

hearsal, but they also displayed the women-playing-men in glittery louche glamour shots. An actress playing the Scarlet Pimpernel held a sword over her sequined shoulder; the bedazzled star of *Classico Italiano* struck a disco pose. Both of them aimed come-hither gazes at the reader.

The Takarazuka Revue first staged *Wuthering Heights* when Koshiro Miyako was an ingénue coming up through the company's training program. Takarazuka trainees get divided into *otokoyaku* (performers of male roles) and *musumeyaku* (performers of female roles), with the *otokoyaku* cutting their hair short and learning masculine gestures and speech patterns. Taller girls are selected to play male roles so that they can tower over their romantic partners. Since this is a country in which an American teenage girl of average size looks like Gulliver alongside her Japanese classmates, an *otokoyaku* Rhett Butler represents a bit of stage magic that enables a tiny Japanese woman to evoke a swashbuckling blockade runner. Wearing trousers with cuff straps pulled over elevator boots to accentuate the length of her leg, she will mimic the physical mannerisms of Elvis Presley or Marlon Brando, both of whom serve as models for *otokoyaku* in training, perhaps because of their hyped-up versions of masculinity, perhaps because at their most iconic moments (the young Elvis gyrating on stage, the young Brando bellowing for Stella), their "rampant male sexuality" allows for alternate interpretations.[5] The *otokoyaku* fans may register these performers as both male and female, as exuding a male sexuality made safe by its containment in a female body. Or perhaps the erotic performances seem more dangerous because of the way the female bodies tip male sexuality out of kilter. The gender theorist Judith Butler might say that the *otokoyaku* are able to shift the relationship between ground (their sexed bodies) and figure (their stage identities), and in so doing "create erotic havoc of various sorts."[6] That is, they are not simply replicating the terms of heterosexuality, they are putting a new spin on them. Whatever the case, over the course of their Takarazuka education, aspiring *otokoyaku* are transformed from junior high school girls in knee socks to dashing heroes in Chelsea boots.

Settling in with the graciousness and aplomb of a seasoned celebrity, Koshiro took a sip of her tea, and speaking in the kind of low voice that *otokoyaku* cultivate by means of chain-smoking—I would come to identify retired *otokoyaku* by means of the residual baritone—she recalled when her grade school class was taken to a performance by the Takarazuka Revue: "I was so overwhelmed—I loved it. The male star was very, very attractive and cool, and that prompted me to start singing lessons."[7]

This may be the right time to introduce the presence of the interpreter whom I had engaged for this occasion, and who spoke the rough translation of Koshiro's actual words that I am transcribing on these pages. I admired my interpreter for her enviable ability to swiftly navigate back and forth between Japanese and English. A slim, tall woman with a short haircut and a soothing voice, she perched on the edge of a bucket seat, jotting notes on a stenographer's pad as Koshiro talked with great dynamism about how she came to be a Takarazuka star. When Koshiro paused, the interpreter took a deep breath, flipped through many pages of frenetic jotting, and spoke a calm English version of Koshiro's words. Something is always lost in translation, but as Koshiro spoke, she sometimes trained her eyes on me as if willing me to understand her words, and whether because she spoke so expressively, or because I had memorized hundreds of Japanese vocabulary words, I sometimes thought I knew what she was saying even before the interpreter started speaking.[8] But once the interpreter spoke, I realized that I hadn't understood most of what Koshiro said.

"We received power from all the people around us," Koshiro was revealed to have said, once the interpreter read from her scribbled notes. "It was like a family, and you must make it a better family, a better society." Koshiro continued to speak in a rush of words: "If you don't have the power, you can't make it to the top." In order to get to the top, the aspiring actor had to cultivate a fan base because fans voted to determine which Takarazuka actors in training would be allowed to step into starring roles. Aspiring trainees performed in a line dance, which gave Takarazuka fans an opportunity to decide which girls were worthy of bigger roles. As the girls danced, the audience members, in my interpreter's version of Koshiro's words, looked for girls who had "seeds of stardom." When fans decided to follow a particular girl, the Takarazuka management took notice, and let the fans' enthusiasm influence the casting of the all-important *shinjin kōen* (new face or newcomer performance) in which girls who had just completed their school training would replicate the main stage offering.

At this point in Koshiro's history of her ascent through the ranks of Takarazuka training, I worried that we were wandering too far afield of *Wuthering Heights*. Koshiro was a busy woman, the head of a performance company in Hamamatsu. We had only allotted an hour and a half for the meeting, time was passing, and we were still talking about her teen-aged self. But it was clear that, for Koshiro, the *shinjin kōen* moment was the one that had separated her from the other *otokoyaku* wannabes, and made her a star. "I was assigned to be the hero, the main character. That was a big chance—it would determine your destiny!" And then, so that I wouldn't miss the point, she looked me right in the eye, and spoke the word *Burōdowē* (Broadway).

"When did you first come in contact with *Wuthering Heights*," I asked in Japanese, the interpreter restating my question when Koshiro looked puzzled. Koshiro guessed that she'd first encountered the novel in junior high school, at which time she'd only read it as entertainment. "I knew the story," she said, "but not so deeply that I could play the role. As a girl I had no idea that I would grow to become Heathcliff." Koshiro reflected on the Japan of her childhood, in which entertainment options were limited and often featured Misora Hibari, a popular Japanese singer, whose performance as a twelve-year-old in the 1950 film *Tokyo kiddo* (Tokyo kid) served as a morale-booster in postwar Japan.

Later I found a clip of *Tokyo kiddo* on YouTube, and then acquired a recording of the intact movie so that I could see Misora Hibari, whose stage name means "lark flying in a beautiful sky," dance around like a plucky Mouseketeer, singing that she had a dream in her right pocket and gum in her left. In the movie, Misora plays a girl who, after her mother dies, dresses up in boy's clothing and, accompanied by a guitar-playing man, breaks into song. Watching the Misora video brought home to me the obvious fact that Koshiro and I, even though we had both first encountered *Wuthering Heights* as adolescent girls, had read Brontë's novel under the influence of different cultural touchstones. As I sat in the Yokohama hotel and listened as Koshiro answered questions, I didn't yet realize that I couldn't understand the impact on Koshiro of her first exposure to Brontë's novel because I hadn't grown up listening to Misora Hibari. In order to understand Japanese versions of *Wuthering Heights,* I needed to understand the contexts in which Japanese people read Brontë's novel. I would have to practice a cross-cultural version of reader-response criticism, a critical approach advocated by the French literary theorist Roland Barthes, who took it to its extreme in *Empire of Signs*, a meditation on Japanese artifacts. In that work Barthes breezily denies any necessary connection between the Japan he discusses and an actual Japan, acknowledging the "enormous labor of *knowledge*" that would be necessary in order to begin to learn about "the Orient," while evincing no motivation to exert this effort.[9] I found Barthes's insouciance disturbing.

As Koshiro went on to graciously talk about her Heathcliff performance, she repeatedly used the word "dirty" to describe the role, or at least that's the word the interpreter used. In the photographs of Koshiro in her Heathcliff costume, she doesn't look dirty at all, but she explained that, even if one was playing a rough working-class character, the Takarazuka costume department would first make a pristine new version of the character's costume, and then take a scissors to it and apply grime. A defining moment in Koshiro's career, and an important precursor of her Heathcliff performance, came when she was asked to share the role of Curly in *Oklahoma!* with another Takarazuka star. The other star refused to play Curly unless she could have the role to herself, so Koshiro was offered the rougher secondary role of Jud, a character whose image was far different from the one typically projected by Takarazuka stars. "I didn't want to play it," Koshiro recalled. "Jud was a very stout man who was hated by everybody." She thought about the request for an entire week, and then decided to use the opportunity to improve her acting skills. "I decided to get rid of my awareness of being a star," Koshiro recalled, noting that it was the first time that a top Takarazuka actor had played the role of a rival. She threw herself into the role, and decided, "This person is not pretty, but he has a very pure heart."

At this moment in our interview, a harpist started playing "Pachelbel's Canon." I was sitting in the lounge of a luxury hotel in Yokohama, listening to a former star of the Takarazuka Revue recall how she played the bad guy role in a Rodgers and Hammerstein vehicle. And not just any star—Koshiro Miyako had performed back when Takarazuka stars had longevity; she held top billing for over eight years, whereas current-day Takarazuka stars burn out after one or two. If I'd had any distance from the situation—which I did not, so dazzled was I by the hotel ambience and by Koshiro's presence—I might have wondered at the line she drew from Jud to Heathcliff. "Before that I thought that playing the star was something very attractive and pretty and stylish," Koshiro said, "but that was a time when I was awakened to acting." Actually, these words were spoken by the interpreter, and since I've done some grammar fiddling, it may or may not be permissible to place the altered words within the certification of quotation marks. Who exactly am I quoting here? Koshiro herself? The interpreter's necessarily hurried and almost-precise version of her words? Or my own fussy autocorrecting of the interpreter's grammar?

Koshiro was not the only Takarazuka Heathcliff. Wao Yōka played the role in a 1997 Takarazuka production of *Wuthering Heights*. Since then Wao had retired from the Takarazuka theater company, launched a successful solo career, starred in a production of *Dracula*, and, according to the English language version of her website, scheduled a "Live Tour 2012 History."[10] Along the way, she amassed a fan base that included my Japanese friend's ten-year-old daughter, whose eyes lit up when I spoke Wao's name. I had spent several weeks trying to get in touch with Wao, for whom I could find only a fan club address. By e-mail, I implored the fan club secretary to communicate my interest in talking to Wao about her sensational performance. My interpreter, too, approached the fan club officer, but Wao remained elusive. However, Wao's performance, unlike Koshiro's, could be accessed by means of DVD, and even on a small screen, Wao's Heathcliff made a strong impression.[11] Standing in a spotlight of swirling pebble light, Wao spoke soliloquies that I didn't entirely understand, but as Catherine's ghost voice echoed spookily across the stage, and as Wao rolled her heavily-lined eyes and tossed her shiny wig, I could comprehend the intensity of Heathcliff's feelings.

Koshiro, through the interpreter, was speaking. "After I played Heathcliff in *Wuthering Heights*, all the top actors that succeeded me wanted to play this role in their final show before they left Takarazuka, but the producer said, 'I wrote this for [Koshiro] Miyako so no one else can play it,' and so nobody else has played it again." I was confused—what about Wao? Eventually it became clear that the script Koshiro used and the script Wao used were not the same. Also, the second Takarazuka *Wuthering Heights* had been performed in a midsized theater, whereas the first Takarazuka *Wuthering Heights*, Koshiro's *Wuthering Heights*, had been performed, she noted, in the company's larger venue. Koshiro believed her performance was the more authentic one. She described Wao's Heathcliff as *kakkoii*, a phrase used to describe stylish young men. Of her own performance, Koshiro, in the interpreter's version of her words, exclaimed, "I *was* Heathcliff."

Koshiro's sentence floated over our table like a banner dragged across the sky by an airplane. When she said, "I *was* Heathcliff," I felt certain that she was near-quoting Catherine's line. I wanted to fumble in my bag for my copy of *Wuthering Heights*, as bristly with Post-its as a porcupine, and let it fall open to the scene in which Catherine proclaims her oneness with Heathcliff. A waitress ministered to our table, and a lone man wandered through the room looking for his wife, and Koshiro spoke, and the interpreter scribbled, and I wandered into the Earnshaw kitchen where Catherine engages a reluctant Nelly in an existential debate. "What were the use of my creation if I were entirely contained here?" she cries. Something follows about sharing Heathcliff's miseries, and the Universe being a mighty stranger (I really wished I could consult the actual page); Edgar Linton is to foliage as Heathcliff is to rocks, and then—got it!—Catherine says, "Nelly, I *am* Heathcliff—he's always, always in my mind" (82).

Perhaps because the restaurant of the Yokohama Bay Sheraton Hotel was an all-female zone, perhaps because I had been looking at photographs of Koshiro Miyako dressed up for male roles, I thought of Catherine's famous line as a marker of her refusal to behave as she was expected to do. The novelist Mizumura Minae once mentioned to me that the version of Catherine she created in *Honkaku shōsetsu* (*A True Novel*, a rewriting of *Wuthering Heights* set in postwar Japan) was necessarily milder than Brontë's original character. "Yoko is not a strong character like Catherine; it would have looked too Western to have a strong-headed woman," said Mizumura.[12] Yet in Japan no one had any problem with a female actor raging around a stage in the role of Heathcliff. Koshiro the actress had entered so fully into her identification with Heathcliff that, in her view, she had become Brontë's character.

At this point in my meeting with Koshiro, the harpist started playing "Somewhere Over the Rainbow." Later, when I played back the interview recording I heard the interpreter convey Koshiro's commentary on Heathcliff. "Maybe some people would receive it as a cold, aloof, personality; others would think he has many sides and is a very mysterious man," she said. "Still others would think he is somebody who is very passionate at heart and took his whole life to love." But when the interpreter first spoke these words I was anticipating the moment when I would be back in Iowa City. As soon as I heard the interpreter say, "I *was* Heathcliff," the pages I am now writing started organizing themselves around that moment in the novel. I sipped my milk tea and listened to Koshiro talk about her Heathcliff performance, and the interpreter scribbled in her steno pad and summarized Koshiro's comments until I gently mentioned the time so that I wouldn't miss my train. Before we left, Koshiro allowed herself to be photographed standing, and then sitting, and then standing next to me, and then standing next to my interpreter.

In the days following the meeting, when I clicked through the photographs I'd taken of Koshiro in the Yokohama hotel lounge, it was hard to see Heathcliff in the visage of the stately woman who sat with back erect, gazing calmly at the camera. Heathcliff in Brontë's novel is a cipher onto whom other characters project their fantasies. Lockwood describes the fortyish Heathcliff as a "dark-skinned gypsy in aspect, in dress and manners a gentleman" (5), inaugurating a line of speculation about his origins.

"You're fit for a prince in disguise," Nelly tells Heathcliff. "Who knows, but your father was Emperor of China, and your mother an Indian queen, each of them able to buy up, with one week's income, Wuthering Heights and Thrushcross Grange together?" Warming to her subject, Nelly goes on to speculate, "And you were kidnapped by wicked sailors, and brought to England" (58). Nelly tries to convince Heathcliff that "a good heart will help [him] to a bonny face," but a page later in Brontë's novel, Heathcliff dashes a tureen of hot apple sauce into Edgar Linton's face, and dedicates himself to wreaking revenge on Hindley. "I only wish I knew the best way!" he says of his retaliatory fantasies. "While I'm thinking of that, I don't feel pain," he says (61).

I didn't know exactly what kind of Heathcliff Koshiro had enacted because I could only access her performance through a rare recording of one song. "The wind blows at Wuthering Heights and picks up the heath fragrance," Koshiro sings in Japanese on the CD I found in the Diet Library, Japan's Library of Congress. "The wind blows at Wuthering Heights and carries a cold blizzard," she crooned in her deep voice.[13] I carefully copied out the Japanese lyrics of Koshiro's song.

A few days later the interpreter and I tracked down copies of Koshiro's and Wao's *Wuthering Heights* playscripts at the Ikeda Bunko library, where the interpreter used the computer catalog and carried out complicated negotiations with the librarian while I stood in front of the copying machine, puzzling over the operation buttons. The interpreter bustled about, bringing me books and magazines that documented Koshiro's career, and tactfully translating them on the spot when she noticed I was mostly looking at the pictures. The fan photos from the era when Koshiro launched her career reminded me of *Seventeen* magazines from Twiggy's heyday. There amid advertisements for women's "leisure wear," featuring minicoats and miniskirts, Koshiro looked like a 1969 Vassar undergraduate.

It was easy to find the "I *am* Heathcliff" moment in the script used by Wao Yōka because the scenes were titled, and I recognized the word for "kitchen" in one of the scene headings.[14] It was harder to find the scene in Koshiro's script, which included a brief English-language synopsis.[15] The synopsis caused me to worry that Koshiro and I had not been talking about the same literary work. The synopsis reads: "Ellen, who had formerly been a housekeeper for the Earnshaws, was reciting to Charles, a millionaire, just back from London, a sorrowful story involving the Earnshaws." Charles? In the 1969 Takarazuka version of *Wuthering Heights* Lockwood acquires great wealth and undergoes a name change. As the synopsis writer continues, he or she uses the kind of unidiomatic turns of phrase that occur when English gets converted into Japanese and vice versa. Hindley treats Heathcliff "in all malicious ways conceivable for nobody did really know where in the world he was born." Catherine, however, "did ever stand on [Heathcliff's] side." When the synopsis writer gets to the part of the story in which Catherine and Heathcliff peer in the window of the Linton household, the writer describes the Lintons holding a gala dancing party. "Catherine, of course, was invited to the function but, to Heathcliff, who lived in the stable, no invitation arrived."

The language of the English synopsis resided somewhere halfway between standard English and standard Japanese. It was the English of someone who isn't fully conversant in the language and so manages to make English speak in new and surprising ways.[16] Heathcliff *is* treated "in all malicious ways conceivable" although no native English speaker would describe his plight like that. I, too, spoke in an interlanguage that occasionally befuddled listeners, for example, when I'd say I "had" an interest in something, instead of saying I was "holding" an interest in something. I used the word *motsu* (to hold or carry) when I talked about a grocery bag, but Japanese people use the verb in a more capacious sense that allows one to carry an interest in *Wuthering Heights*. When the Takarazuka synopsizer writes that "to Heathcliff, who lived in the stable, no invitation arrived," she puts some English on her English so that it doesn't bounce in quite the way a native speaker expects. Released from the correctness of either English or Japanese, the language resides in an odd and pleasurable space apart from either language.

I was especially interested in the changes the 1969 Takarazuka scriptwriter worked on Brontë's novel. In the novel, Heathcliff and Catherine, caught peering into the window of the Linton household, get attacked by a bulldog while attempting to flee. The scene evokes the disturbing moment in Brontë's biography that Virginia Woolf recalled when she visited the Haworth parsonage, noting the "certain grim interest" of an oblong recess "into which Emily drove her bulldog during the famous fight, and pinned him while she pommeled him."[17] After Catherine is set upon by the Linton bulldog, Heathcliff tells Nelly, "The devil had seized her ankle. . . . I got a stone and thrust it between [the dog's] jaws, and tried with all my might to cram it down his throat." By his account, when a servant arrives and realizes what's happened, "The dog was throttled off, his huge, purple tongue hanging half a foot out of his mouth, and his pendant lips streaming with bloody slaver" (49). The bulldog is just one of the many snarling curs that populate Brontë's novel—if you wave a biscuit over the book's nose, you will draw out a kennel of hounds. Even when Brontë is not writing about dogs, she evokes their presence, as when Catherine, in a revolt against reading, tosses a "dingy volume by the scroop, and hurl[s] it into the dog-kennel" (21).[18]

However, in the Takarazuka synopsis of the window scene, the dog disappears, and Catherine is inadvertently shot by a Linton guard. "The truth was that a guard in the employ of the Lintons had mistaken the lovers for a bear!" reads the synopsis. Why had Utsumi Shigenori, the writer and director, replaced the dog with a bear? And exactly how far did Utsumi stray from Brontë's story line? And what about the "I *am* Heathcliff" scene, of which there was no mention in the brief English synopsis, and which the interpreter could not find in the playscript? I was sure there must be some misunderstanding between us that was preventing her from finding the key scene in Koshiro's script, and I resolved to read the play on my own, or to have my daughter swiftly skim it, so that I could zero in on the crucial moment.

"Everyone is oh my gosh, this kid, his skin is darker," was my daughter's translation of the opening scene of the script, which depicts the moment when Heathcliff arrives at Wuthering Heights. I took notes as she continued to paraphrase. "He doesn't have a name yet, so Mr. Earnshaw is like, 'Oh I don't know what his name is, let's just give him a name, he's like a heath flower, so we'll call him Heathcliff,'" she continued, as I typed. "He's named after a dead child in the novel—are you sure he's named after a flower?" I asked. "Pretty sure, and Cathy is hanging around while Ellen gives him a bath, and she's all curious, and there's one bit that is interesting where Cathy and Heathcliff are talking, and she says she doesn't like guys who say *ore* and *omae*, so he starts over and says *boku* and *kimi*." I typed with greater fervor since she was referencing Japanese pronouns (I and you) that had direct relevance for the translation of "I *am* Heathcliff."

"As I understand it, *ore* is a little rougher than *boku*; is that how you understand it?" I hoped to draw her into a discussion of the pleasing nuances of the Japanese "I" pronoun.

"Yes, yes," she said, distractedly, her eyes darting over the page.

"Have you found the kitchen scene yet?" I asked. She seemed to be losing interest in our project, and had started playing with her phone. "No," and here she started summarizing more hurriedly. "There's a scene where Heathcliff is on Peniston *oka* because he's angsty or something, and someone says something about heath being the flower of happiness, and in another scene Cathy is sneaking out to visit Heathcliff, and he's all like 'Cathy,' and then they hug strongly, and then for some reason they make their way to the Linton house because the Lintons are having a ball, and Cathy is really into it, but Heathcliff keeps saying he is bored, and then Cathy gets shot, and Ben and Cecil show up and say, 'OMG we thought you were a bear.'"

"Who are Ben and Cecil?"

"Not sure. Can I stop now?"

I settled down to slowly translating Koshiro's script by myself. Hindley asks Joseph to bring him sake, and Hindley's wife Frances asks Hindley to lay off the sake. Later, Isabella and Heathcliff seem to bond over whiskey, and then Catherine shows up and tells Isabella she wants to open her eyes. Isabella says, "Heathcliff, let's get married," and Catherine cries and runs out into a rainstorm. Heathcliff says something to Isabella about her hair possibly smelling like heath flowers—a heath flower motif was clearly running through the play—and Isabella shows up at Catherine's deathbed scene. "Catherine is Edgar's thing," Isabella says to Heathcliff, and then begs him to let Catherine die in Edgar's arms, and then Heathcliff says something about his longtime suffering feeling and runs out, and Isabella has a suffering expression, and then Hindley shows up and says something, and then the curtain goes up or down . . . and WTF! There really was no "I *am* Heathcliff" scene. I could not believe it.

I put Utsumi's script aside. The interpreter and I continued to carry out *Arashi ga oka*–related interviews, once showing up for a meeting with two manga artists at the wrong building in the affluent Tokyo neighborhood of Roppongi, and then rushing to a different building where the manga artists were waiting. The interpreter bore the brunt of the social awkwardness that ensued. I was a foreigner; I was forgiven for not knowing the difference between one building and another similarly named building. I was treated as if I were a genius for being able to find my way to Roppongi, or for knowing that the neighborhood existed. The interpreter, like a tardy job applicant, released a torrent of soft-spoken humble verbiage.

Once while the interpreter and I rode a train, she explained the difference between translators and interpreters, translators, in her understanding, being people who translate books and articles, who have all the time in the world to puzzle over complicated English locutions and to transform them into idiomatic Japanese. A translator has to master each sentence. "Interpreters tend to be more outgoing, and less concerned about details," she explained, describing translators as introverted, painstaking types.

A day or two later, I anticipated the interpreter's arrival as I sat in the lobby of the Takarazuka Hotel, where we had arranged to meet Ōta Tetsunori, the director of the second Takarazuka Revue production of *Wuthering Heights*, the one in which Wao Yōka played Heathcliff. I was afraid that if the interpreter didn't show up soon I would have to talk to Ōta on my own in Japanese, but I was also afraid that I wouldn't have to talk to Ōta on my own in Japanese. The lobby of the hotel was lined with light box advertisements in which *otokoyaku* stars of the Flower Troupe and the Moon Troupe tipped their hats or lunged across stage. A *musumeyaku* costume—Bo Peep sleeves, gilt-embroidered bodice, scalloped lace hem—floated in a glass case, near where a trio of white satin gowns on headless mannequins were lined up for inspection. As the desk clerk looked on warily, I wandered around the lobby, stopping before a scale model of the Hankyu railroad line made out of sugar or some other substance whose name I couldn't read. As I stared at the unfamiliar kanji on the train signage, the interpreter walked through the hotel entranceway and I relaxed. At that same moment an older man walked up and identified himself as Ōta.

We stood in the hotel lobby for a few moments, with the interpreter making introductions. One commentator has called an interpreter's presence a "necessary evil," and compared a skilled interpreter to a *tomei ningen* (transparent person).[19] But there was nothing evil about the gracious woman who presented Ōta and me to each other so decorously that, as we moved from the lobby to the hotel restaurant, we might have been heads of state processing in a cortège. After we were seated at a table, the interpreter easily engaged Ōta in a discussion of his directing career with a particular focus on the Takarazuka *Wuthering Heights* he had directed. Then, as Ōta began to answer one of my questions, I took my eye off the interpreter, and she receded into the restaurant decor. Ōta warmed to his subject, discoursing on Heathcliff's name—"His name is very obvious: Heath Cliff; he is the personification of the moorland, of a nature that exists beyond the human ethics and values"—and saying that Brontë's novel was a family saga rather than a romance.[20] "So there's no sense in ending with only the first half," he remarked. Ōta went so far as to wish that Brontë had continued the story beyond Heathcliff's death, at which point I pushed a noodle across my plate in order to mask my disagreement. I liked the Japanese practice, borrowed from William Wyler's 1939 film, of slicing Brontë's novel in half like a melon and discarding the mushy second-generation story.

When I talked to the first Takarazuka Heathcliff, Koshiro Miyako, she emphasized that the actors were in charge during the *Wuthering Heights* rehearsal process. Of herself and the actress who played Catherine, she recalled, "Both of us had to dive deeper down in the roles . . . and then act together to find each scene. And in this process the producer had nothing to say." But when I asked what role he played in shaping Wao Yōka's Heathcliff performance, Ōta used the word *zenbu* (all, entire, whole, or altogether). "We are the teachers and the performers are our students. . . . We know, we can just imagine how each player will act, and when we build each role, we think about the capability of each student to play the role. . . . We know exactly what each actress can do and cannot do." Just as Koshiro had done, Ōta noted that Heathcliff is different from the typical Takarazuka hero. "Traditionally the main male role has to be very stylized and handsome, and [Heathcliff] cannot be." "He's such a complex person," Ōta noted. "I told Wao Yōka not to define him in a single way."

My interpreter had told me in advance that she wasn't going to eat much because she couldn't do her job if she was chewing, but I felt awkward eating a dish whose name she had helped me read on the menu while she barely had time to drink iced tea, so I tried to field an Ōta question about my home state without her help. I told him that there were more pigs than people in Iowa, an observation I'd been making a lot since I'd learned the Japanese grammatical construction for comparisons. Ōta brought up the movie *Field of Dreams*. "The concept of coming up with a dream out of an ordinary cornfield is very difficult for the Japanese," Ōta said, as I solemnly nodded. "They have to depend on the translation," he continued, "so the quality of the translation is very important." I told him that most of the corn in Iowa had been dying because of bad weather conditions, which was a bit of an exaggeration, but I didn't know how to express the corn farmers' weather problems more moderately. I tried to indicate that the temperature had risen to 110 degrees, and then Ōta said, in English, "110 in the shade" and "Katherine Hepburn," alluding (I much, much later realized) to the 1963 Broadway production of *100 Degrees in the Shade* in which Hepburn starred. I blankly nodded. "Everyone in the world is suffering from abnormal weather. Something is wrong," Ōta said, and we both sat in silence for a few moments, as the interpreter sipped.

Ōta recalled reading Brontë's novel, or an abridgement of it, for the first time when he was in junior high, but he was not impressed with Brontë's artistry. "The story meanders. I found it difficult to follow." He characterized Emily Brontë as an author who "did not know who to depend on to tell the story." "She didn't have a clear conception of the whole story at the beginning," a shortcoming Ōta went on to associate with other British novelists, reinforcing his point with reference to Dickens. "He started out writing, then, as the story proceeds this character gets a lot of attention. For example, in *A Tale of Two Cities*, Sydney Carton was a bystander but then he got into the story because he was so popular," Ōta said.

I had last read *A Tale of Two Cities* when I was fourteen, so I tried to steer Ōta back to Brontë by asking him about Catherine's most famous line. Ōta described Catherine's "I *am* Heathcliff" line as the central occurrence in his production, linking it to the Bunraku (puppet play) tradition of Chikamatsu Monzaemon (1653–1725). "I think Japanese people have a cultural background of accepting the notion of one person being identical to another between the lovers because we have the tradition of double suicide," Ōta said, talking about the author of works known in English translations as *The Love Suicides at Sonezaki* and *The Love Suicides at Amijima*, an author whose plays were performed in the early eighteenth century as Bunraku or Kabuki productions, or as both. In Donald Keene's translation of the *Sonezaki* play, a young orphan merchant named Tokubei falls in love with the courtesan Ohatsu, and in one exciting scene, Ohatsu hides Tokubei under the train of her mantle, and communicates with him by means of her foot. The play's narrator says, "She pretends to be talking to herself, but with her foot she questions him [Tokubei]. He nods, and taking her ankle, passes it across his throat, to let her know that he is bent on suicide."[21] In the final act, Tokubei binds Ohatsu to a tree and stabs her with a razor, and then thrusts the razor into his own throat. In the *Love Suicides at Amijima*, Jihei Kamiya, a paper merchant, stabs the courtesan Koharu with a sword—"He twists the blade in the wound, and her life fades away like an unfinished dream at dawning," Chikamatsu writes.[22] Jihei then hangs himself from a tree. "These lovers have to kill themselves in order to fulfill their love in heaven. [That's] how the relation between Catherine and Heathcliff can be understood from a Japanese perspective," Ōta said as we turned down a waitress's offer of dessert. Although Catherine and Heathcliff don't die together, "When one dies, that person lives in the other person" and "In order to be together again, the other person has to die," Ōta said.

"Let there be no tears on your face," Jihei tells Koharu in one of the most famous lines in *The Love Suicides at Amijima*.[23] It was a little unclear to me why this line was so famous. Jihei also cries, "May we be reborn on one lotus!" Reading the lotus line, I kind of understood why Ōta thought of Chikamatsu's suicide plays when I asked him about the "I *am* Heathcliff" line. I imagined Catherine and Heathcliff floating off into eternity together on a large flat leaf.

After I said goodbye to Ōta, I wandered to a coffee shop across from the Takarazuka hotel without my interpreter. The London Cafe was devoid of customers, but four staff members were lined up ready to serve. I drank coffee from a cup on which was embossed a royal guard wearing a bearskin hat and holding a baguette. Another bear. I inspected the tiny guard who was high-stepping it across the cup's porcelain side, the bearskin towering atop his head. I pulled from my bag the playscript that Koshiro Miyako used when she played Heathcliff, the script from the Takarazuka production in which a guard shot Catherine Earnshaw, mistaking her for a bear.[24] In the English synopsis of Koshiro's script, and in my daughter's hurried summary of this scene, the guard's action seemed inexplicable, but in the actual script scene, which I attempted to translate for the second time—my coffee cooling as I drew kanji with my dictionary stylus—someone notes that a baby bear has been captured near the gate, and that its mother, for that reason, sometimes appears nearby. A bear had wandered in from somewhere in the Takarazuka playwright's mind and taken up residence in Emily Brontë's plotline, for better or for worse, I did not know.

On the other side of the room, three café workers tried to decide where to hang a framed photo of themselves. One of the workers held the framed photograph up to the wall, and the other two considered the photograph's placement with serious regard. A second worker held the photo on the wall so that the first worker could inspect the placement, and then a woman wearing a kerchief held the picture hook while a third man drove a nail into the wall. Then one of the café workers saw me watching them, and hurried over to ask if I wanted more coffee.

For the longest time, I continued to sit in the Takarazuka City café pretend-sipping my already finished coffee, thinking about the director Ōta and the actress Koshiro and their separate experiences of *Wuthering Heights*. "We are living in a time when love and passion are not considered to be persistent," Koshiro responded when I asked her why *Wuthering Heights* is so popular in Japan. "Because cherishing one love with such attachment is something that people long for," Koshiro had said in the interpreter's swift approximation. "Probably we have very little to do with the world of *Wuthering Heights*, but we long for that passion." And then Koshiro and the interpreter and I had nodded as if in perfect agreement.

CHAPTER THREE

Catherine Earnshaw's Japanese Girlhood

Even in Kyoto—
hearing the cuckoo's cry—
I long for Kyoto.
—Bashō (trans. Robert Hass)

The Kyoto International Manga Museum is a repurposed school building that has been transformed into an academy of reading pleasure. Sprawled on staircases and draped over benches, Japanese schoolchildren devour contemporary manga series like *Naruto* or *One Piece*, while older readers scan the shelves for classic manga like *Astro Boy*. I went to the Manga Museum in order to find a popular manga series in which *Wuthering Heights* gets staged. Miuchi Suzue's *Garasu no kamen* (Glass mask) tells the story of Kitajima Maya, an unprepossessing thirteen-year-old who longs to become an actress, and who performs the role of Catherine Earnshaw in one of her first ventures on stage. I'd brought my daughters along to help me find the series; they fanned out across the museum. Left alone, and gazing over all the silent readers around me, I was overtaken by a wave of nostalgic longing. As a child, I raced through comic books, gobbling up the inane and repetitive adventures of hapless goofballs. But now I applied myself to manga as if I were working out geometry theorems, snagging on grammar constructions whose perfect translation was in no way necessary for understanding the story lines.

"You know Donald Richie never learned how to read or write Japanese," I told my husband on more than one occasion, drawing sustenance from the illiteracy of the man who'd written many authoritative books on Japanese cinema. Donald Richie, who used a job with the American occupation force in the aftermath of World War II as a means of escaping Lima, Ohio, claimed that his initial inability to understand Japanese (he later became a fluent speaker of the language) made him an especially observant

51

student of film, a visual medium in which words are less important than images. If Donald Richie could write authoritatively about Ozu Yasujirō, the most Japanese of Japanese film directors, I could write about Miuchi Suzue, I wanted to believe. In the Kyoto International Manga Museum, two boys tugged at the same manga volume, then one of the boys held out a closed fist, and they rock, paper, scissored until one of them laughed and grabbed the book.

In January 1976, Miuchi Suzue, who was to become one of the best-selling manga artists of all time, published the first chapter of *Garasu no kamen* in the pages of *Hana to yume*, a semimonthly magazine aimed at girls. Like many Japanese magazines pitched at female readers, *Hana to yume*, whose title in English means "Flowers and Dreams," comes shrink-wrapped with *furoku,* or promotional swag: calendars or manga antholo-gies or *shitajiki* ("pencil boards" that are placed under a sheet of paper for writing). A single edition of *Hana to yume* is the size of a metropolitan phone book, and like a phone book, seems like a throwback to an ear-lier era. While you still see young girls paging through manga magazines in Japanese bookshops, you more often see them peering into cell phone screens. Miuchi's chapters have been compiled in forty-nine volumes over thirty-seven years, with a fiftieth and final volume hotly anticipated.

To Miuchi's manga can be traced a legion of *Wuthering Heights* enthu-siasts. For Miuchi's original readers, now stepping into their sixth decades, *Garasu no kamen* served as a portal into *Wuthering Heights*, and it contin-ues to serve that function to this day. When, in 2002, the Shinbashi theater in Tokyo staged *Wuthering Heights*, the actor Matsu Takako, who played Catherine, said that she had longed to perform in *Wuthering Heights* ever since reading *Garasu no kamen*.

I wasn't sure which of the series' forty-nine volumes encompassed *Wuthering Heights*, but the International Manga Museum's open shelves (a separate scholarly archive was closed to casual readers) made it possible to flip through all the volumes. I was counting on my daughters' manga familiarity and superior Japanese comprehension to help them spot the *Hana to yume* publishers' logo (a girl's head made up of a lollipop swirl of hair), and scan *Garasu no kamen* until they found the drama school production of *Wuthering Heights*. Once they located the right volumes, I'd pull a Richie and study the pertinent pages with keen observational acuity.

I gazed uncomprehendingly over the shoulder of a boy with whom I was sharing a library bench; he was reading a tank manga. In Japan there are manga for readers of every age, gender, and predilection. There are *shōnen* manga aimed at a young male audience, *josei* manga aimed at late-teen and adult female readers, and *seinen* manga, a broad category that encompasses both works written for adolescent boys and for older male readers. There are manga that center on school life and *robotto* manga that showcase robots and big machines. There are historical manga, such as Yamazaki Mari's popular *Thermae Romae*, in which a Roman architect gets swept down a drain pipe only to surface in a modern-day Japanese bathhouse. And there are erotic manga depicting sexual encounters of every permutation: between two men (*yaoi*), between two women (*yuri*), between an adult and a young girl (*lolicon*), between an adult and a young boy (*shotacon*), and involving a female character with male genitalia (*futanari*).

There are also *Wuthering Heights* manga, six by my count. There is Iwashita Hiromi's Heathcliff-centered manga, which captures the mean-spiritedness of Brontë's male protagonist.[1] In the first pages, the child Heathcliff glowers from beneath Mr. Earnshaw's bundled clothing, and on a final page, the dead Heathcliff bares his teeth in a ghoulish grin. There is Hanabusa Yōko's *Arashi ga oka*, in which Catherine Earnshaw's story is compiled with those of Anne Boleyn, Madame Pompadour, and Queen Nefertiti. Hanabusa's *Arashi ga oka* begins with an image of Catherine standing in the middle of the heath, arms spread out to embrace the surrounding wilderness (in Japanese, the heath gets translated as *kōya*, that is, "wilderness" or "prairie").[2] There is Sakurai Mineko's *Arashi ga oka*, in which Mr. Earnshaw's affection for Heathcliff causes marital tension with his wife, who darkly imagines Heathcliff falling into a stream, and who promptly falls into this body of water herself and drowns.[3] In Sakurai's version of Brontë's story, the grief-stricken Mr. Earnshaw visits the child Heathcliff in his bed. In other words, the manga *Wuthering Heights* editions emphasize Heathcliff's malevolence or Catherine's longings or Mr. Earnshaw's incestuous tendencies. The spirit of Brontë's twisted melodrama is mostly conveyed even as the manga artists occasionally step beyond her story line and venture into odd backstreets.

Every now and again a manga artist will zoom in on minor scenes so that random details loom larger than they appear in my rearview memory. In the 1989 "Famous Love Comics" version of *Wuthering Heights*, for example, Suzuka Reni devotes a frame to Catherine's reminder that Mr. Earnshaw will bring Nelly apples or pears from Liverpool, a detail that takes up half a sentence in Brontë's novel, and which I didn't recall reading.[4] But just as often, the manga versions compress or lop off scenes in order to meet the constraints of the comic book format. For the Japanese there is nothing antithetical about turning a hefty Western literary classic into a slim comic book. The Japanese turn everything into manga: self-help books, Steve Jobs's biography, Thomas Piketty's economic manifesto.[5] But inevitably, when Brontë's novel undergoes manga transformation, its long and carefully constructed nineteenth-century sentences fall by the wayside. When Catherine describes her love of Heathcliff to Nelly, she explains, "If all else perished, and *he* remained, I should still continue to be; and, if all else remained, and he were annihilated, the Universe would turn to a mighty stranger."[6] You cannot fit that sentence into a speech bubble, nor are you likely to find that kind of pleasing parallel construction within a speech bubble's confines. In Morizono Miruku's manga version, Catherine says, in Japanese, "Even if all the world perishes, if only Heathcliff remains, I will continue to exist."[7] Morizono is a *josei* manga specialist—her other works have titles like *Bondage Fantasy* and *Let's Go to Bed*. Following the Wyler film version, Morizono's Catherine, when she returns from her visit to the Lintons, rips her dress from her shoulders and strides into Heathcliff's arms. In a two-page afterword to her manga, Morizono imagines herself in Catherine's situation. "If this story took place nowadays I would probably choose Heathcliff [over Edgar]," Morizono writes, going on to say, "The reason is I have a job, Heathcliff would have work, and life wouldn't have trouble."[8]

Before I started studying Japanese, I would have sneered at the kind of radical truncation most of the manga artists enacted on *Wuthering Heights*. Once when my younger daughter was happily reading an abridged edition of *Little Women* she'd pulled from her grandmother's bookshelf, I kissed her on the head and hovered over her armchair like a storm cloud. "That's much better in the *original* version," I declared, plucking a Barbara Pym I'd given my mother-in-law from its place between *The Reader's Digest Book of Home Remedies* and *Dr. Atkins' New Diet Revolution*. My daughter, calmly ignoring me, continued to enjoy the March sisters' abbreviated adventures.

But now that I routinely devoted fifteen minutes to deciphering a Japanese book jacket advertisement, I was in no way opposed to abridgement or simplification. I longed for a Tanizaki aimed at sixth-graders. I would have killed for a remedial-reader Sōseki! In his classic, consolatory work, *Making Sense of Japanese*, the Harvard professor and Japanese translator Jay Rubin writes of the daunting visual quality of Japanese text, and describes the linguistic pleasure "stimulated by the sheer satisfaction of making [one's] way successfully through an orthographical garden, the gathering of whose fruits is only becoming possible . . . after years of disciplined study."[9] After years of disciplined study, I still tripped over vines.

A museum docent picked up an abandoned manga and restored it to its shelf. I inspected a nearby *shōjo* display. *Garasu no kamen* (Glass mask) is credited with playing an instrumental role in the origin of *shōjo*, that is, manga aimed at teenage girls. Literary historians place *Garasu no kamen* at the center of the *shōjo* form's modern development, which they date to the period from the 1960s to the 1980s (the first girls' weekly magazine, *Shōjo Friend*, began publication in 1963). Hiromi Tsuchiya Dollase traces the girl culture of *shōjo* magazines back to the first decade of the twentieth century, when Western works like *Little Women* and *A Little Princess* were first translated into Japanese (*Little Women* in 1906 and *A Little Princess* in 1910).[10] In a preface to *Little Women*, Kyōtei Ōson writes of Alcott's March family: "This family is warm as spring. Sometimes, unbearably sad events hit their minds with the severity of wind, frost, and drought. However, the four girls' warm hearts, like a fire in the fireplace, protect each other from the outside."[11] Publishers of the Japanese translations of Louisa May Alcott's and Frances Hodgson Burnett's work presented their stories as cozy depictions of domestic tranquility, but Japanese girl readers derived other lessons. As Dollase writes, "Jo's young and free spirit fascinated the Japanese girl audience and mentally released it from the suffocating reality of old fashioned conventions and expectations."[12] The word *shōjo* in Japanese refers simply to a young girl, usually one who is between 7 and 18 years old, but Dollase associates the word with an escapist mental state that allows girls in this age group to temporarily take leave of reality.

I hoped that when my daughters found the *Garasu no kamen* section in the Manga Museum—where were they? had they started reading *other* manga?—I would be able to detect this escapist tendency in the *Wuthering Heights* passages. I opened an English-language brochure that I had picked up at the building entrance, studying the Manga Museum's mascot, a mushroom-shaped character named Mamyu who had a manga pen sprouting from his head and a *furoshiki* (wrapping cloth) tied around his neck. "It's full of manga from around the world," the brochure said of Mamyu's wrapping cloth cravat. Most of the manga in the Kyoto International Manga Museum were Japanese manga because Japan is the manga colossus of the world; other countries' puny comic book offerings pale in comparison to the scope and artistry of Japanese manga. If Mamyu sought out comic books in other countries' bookstores he would find mostly Japanese manga in translation.

"*Glass Mask* is that row of red-and-white ones," said my older daughter, pointing, as she wandered by my bench. "*Wuthering Heights* shows up in volumes 7 and 8." A covey of girls scattered as I approached the *Garasu no kamen* shelving area and pulled out the first volume of the series. The "glass mask" of the title refers to the fragile masks actors wear when they take on different personae, and also, perhaps, to the performative aspect of gender roles.[13] On the book jacket of the first volume, Maya holds a sparkly mask in front of her face. A line of writing running alongside (sort of) reads, "Thousand masks holding girl." Maya is the girl of a thousand masks.

In her pursuit of thespian greatness, Maya throws herself into her roles Method-acting style, and infuses even minor parts with great emotion. Her acting skills are nurtured by Tsukikage Chigusa, a stage diva who becomes Maya's acting teacher. Celebrated in her younger days as a brilliant actress, Tsukikage was burned in an onstage accident which involved a lamplighter and which left her face scarred. This explains why she wears her long black hair in a Veronica Lake curtain that conceals half of her features. Looking like a cross between Norma Desmond and the Phantom of the Opera, Tsukikage subjects Maya to a series of acting challenges—at one point demanding that she play a chair. I had learned this much about *Garasu no kamen* in advance of my visit to the Manga Museum by watching the anime version and by reading fan sites.[14]

I pulled out volume 7 of *Garasu no kamen*, and studied its pages as observantly as I could. In volume 7, Maya is performing on stage with a baby doll strapped to the back of her kimono when, all of a sudden, the baby's head pops off and rolls across the stage. The audience looks on aghast, as another girl, clearly Maya's rival, smiles malevolently. For a few frames, Maya stands in panicked mortification, but then she brushes the baby head off and reattaches it to the top of her baby carrier, saying, in Japanese, "Truly, being a nursemaid is not easy."[15] An onlooking teacher (I think), declares Maya no ordinary girl, and suggests she should be a candidate for a role in *Kurenai tennyo* (Crimson goddess), a play in which Tsukikage once starred, and the acme of theatrical aspiration.

I shut the book for a moment, pleased with my progress. It was warm in the Manga Museum. I paged less observantly through volume 8, relaxing a bit; now that I'd identified the *Wuthering Heights*–related volumes, I could buy my own copies and study them at my leisure. It had been two years since I'd embarked on my *Wuthering Heights* research, two years during which I'd completed second- and third-year Japanese classes, and announced to anyone who would listen that I was writing a book about

Japanese versions of *Wuthering Heights*. No, not *translations*, I would reply to the inevitable next question, making a distinction between translations and adaptations. But surely the manga versions were translations, some more faithful than others, each with its own interesting idiosyncrasies. Vaguely unsettled, I wandered through the old school building in search of my daughters.

When we got home to the short-stay apartment in Nakano where we were spending part of the summer, I typed *Garasu no kamen* in an Amazon Japan search box and placed my order, choosing the convenience store pickup option. A few days later, I walked into a Family Mart, marching confidently up to the store clerk, who pointed in the direction of an ATM-like machine. From that service kiosk one could do a number of things that did not seem to have anything to do with Amazon Japan, such as purchase tickets for baseball games and museum exhibits. I punched buttons uncertainly, and whenever anyone got in line behind me, I bailed out, and studied the stationery rack, pondering the purchase of tiny scissors until the adept person finished. As I stepped up to the machine for the third time, the clerk came over and coaxed the receipts I needed from the machine, and carried out a flurry of receipt stamping before he handed over an Amazon mailer.

As I walked back to the short-stay apartment, stabbing the shrink-wrapping with my tiny scissors, and pulling the books free of cardboard as I went, the face of Maeda Atsuko gazed at me from shop windows and hoardings. Maeda, star of the J-pop group AKB48, whose phalanx of members dance in tartan kilts or vegetable costumes, had revealed in March that she was going to "graduate" from the group; the long hot summer was one long hot windup to her official farewell, scheduled to take place at a Tokyo Dome concert in August. So devastating was the news of Maeda's imminent departure that a University of Tokyo student was rumored to have committed suicide in response. As I walked home from the convenience store, flipping through the pages of *Garasu no kamen*, Maeda's sweet bland face, smiling on billboards, loomed over the metropolis.

Back at the short-stay, as we tried to eat beans and rice my husband had made after a miscommunication in the grocery store, I showed off my new manga.

"Cool," said my younger daughter, carefully extracting rice grains from the beans.

"I'm going to contact the artist. Will you help me write a message to her in Japanese? I already found her website."

"Mom!"

"I'll write it. I just need you to double-check it for me."

We chewed and cleared our plates. We were living in a 2DK—the Japanese classification for a two-bedroom apartment with combined dining room and kitchen and with no LR. The D was debatable; there were four chairs and a table in the kitchen, but to clear a path from the door to the bedroom you had to push the chairs up against the sink. After dinner we watched TV, a Japanese home makeover show in which an elderly couple's house was redesigned with special respect for the old man's hideous massage chair. The chair was going to have a room of its own.

"Miuchi Suzue is really famous," I said. "She probably doesn't respond to e-mail, but maybe she'll reply to a foreign academic who is writing a book about Japanese versions of *Wuthering Heights.*"

"What?" said my husband. The TV architect was taking measurements as the elderly man triggered his retractable footrest.

"Maybe Miuchi will talk to me because I'm an academic and I'm only in Japan for a short while," I said, standing by the TV.

In a television commercial, an adorable child was eating pudding, but I refused to be distracted. I headed straight to a bedroom, opened my laptop, and drafted a message to Miuchi. Then I wrote some questions I wanted to ask if she agreed to meet with me. And then I pestered my daughter to check my work.

"My Japanese is not much better than yours."

"That's OK," I said, "you'll catch the worst mistakes."

Miuchi responded to my message courteously, proposing a location for our meeting, and asking if I would provide the questions I wanted to ask her in advance. I showed the questions I had written to my friend Yoko. "What are you trying to say in English?" she asked, and then she wrote my Japanese questions in new ways, adding layers of politeness like buttercream piping. By the time Yoko finished I had trouble reading the questions, and so I checked to make sure that my interpreter was available to accompany me on my visit with Miuchi.

My interpreter and I met Miuchi Suzue at a restaurant belonging to Miuchi's husband, and located in a stylish neighborhood of Tokyo, which I knew for its Mister Donut shop and for the miniature dachshund puppies that could be viewed in a pet store nearby. The restaurant was a cool-jazz, new-age kind of place with rough-hewn tables and a canoe out front. With little prompting, Miuchi talked about the moment when she first encountered Emily Brontë, whom she recalled reading about, when she was sixteen or seventeen, in a postscript to *Jane Eyre*. "Unlike Charlotte, Emily stayed in the heath as long as she lived; that made a strong impression on me," Miuchi recalled.[16] She later spotted *Arashi ga oka* in a bookshop. "Around that time—I don't know what was first—I saw the 1939 film by Wyler," Miuchi recalled. "The movie version was rearranged so it was easier for me to understand that version; it was quite hard to read and understand the Japanese translation." She picked up a Japanese *Wuthering Heights* edition that the interpreter had placed on the table, and commented on how much easier it was to read than the translation she had read as a girl. The interpreter and Miuchi spent a few minutes discussing the new *Wuthering Heights* translation together as I observed them closely and listened for familiar words.

In advance of my meeting with Miuchi Suzue, I hadn't, strictly speaking, finished reading the entirety of the two pertinent *Garasu no kamen* volumes, but not for lack of trying. I glassily masked my partial ignorance by asking questions about the images, and about the Western literary works she had embedded in her story line. As a Japanese singer wailed a plangent ballad on the restaurant's sound system, Miuchi recalled the versions of *Wuthering Heights* she encountered as a schoolgirl. "As I look back, we grew up with translations of *Wuthering Heights*," she said. "They were always there on the bookshelf, although it was never mentioned in conversation." I leaned in with my yellow legal pad, drawing a little too close, as she continued unperturbed. "I have a feeling that there were very few people who actually read them, but they were always there, the abridged version and the translations, in the elementary school library, the junior high library, the high school library, and the local library in Osaka. *Wuthering Heights* was available always as one of the novels in world novel series."

I nodded encouragingly.

"When I look back on those versions, they seem too simplified," Miuchi continued. She noted, "A reason why I took up *Wuthering Heights* [as one of the plays within *Garasu no kamen*] is because Maya is a teenager and . . . this was the first time she tried out for a romantic play and I didn't want her to play an adult love."

An instrumental version of the *Titanic* theme song played softly in the background, pennywhistle dominant. Miuchi continued, "I wanted to depict Catherine as a girl and . . . I wanted to focus on episodes that led to the love between Heathcliff and Catherine." As Miuchi spoke, and as the interpreter transformed her comments into English, I glanced nervously at my Zoom recorder to see if its digits were still turning over. I sensed Miuchi was about to provide some essential insight.

"As I made the episode with *Wuthering Heights*, I read the original novel over and over again. I got the feeling that Heathcliff and Cathy had only themselves in this vast moor background.... I got this sense that they needed [only] themselves; they were the only ones to play with, to be around."

I leaned in closer.

"There is this line, I'm not sure if I read this in the novel, or if it just felt this way, it's kind of ambiguous," Miuchi was saying. "Catherine tells Heathcliff: I am you and you are me."

"Yes, the 'I am Heathcliff' line," I interrupted.

"I think this is the greatest love that can be expressed. I'm no longer sure—it's mixed up in my mind, whether it's in the novel or whether I made it up—but that's the interpretation that I have."

Miuchi started to talk about *Kurenai tennyo* (Crimson goddess), the play treasured by Tsukikage, the scarred diva. The interpreter said something about a plum tree spirit and a monk. Only later, when I played back the recording, did I realize that Miuchi was talking about an actual Noh production of the fictional *Kurenai tennyo* that she had invented in her manga.[17] "It has a scene where Akoya, the spirit of the plum tree, tells her lover the monk, 'I am you and you are me,'" Miuchi said. "This is the original line that appears in *Wuthering Heights* [and] this character says the same thing to her monk lover."

"In the [Japanese] translation it says the soul of Heathcliff and myself are identical; the version I read as a high school student was very difficult," Miuchi continued, growing more somber. "I'm sixty-one years old, and when I look back right now, I feel that it's unthinkable how the characters hurt people around them. Catherine hurts her loving husband who cherishes her so much, and also Heathcliff marries Isabella, the sister of Catherine's husband, just for revenge." Miuchi also noted, "Love that makes others unhappy is not acceptable in Buddhist teaching. It's considered to be rather selfish. In *Wuthering Heights* love destroys people, making them really unhappy—it's something that's hard to accept."

I thought of the chapter in which Heathcliff levels a "shower of terrific slaps" on the head of the second-generation Catherine, whom he has imprisoned at Wuthering Heights while her father is dying at Thrushcross Grange (271). "Had I been born where laws are less strict, and tastes less dainty, I should treat myself to a slow vivisection of those two, as an evening's entertainment," Heathcliff says of Catherine and Linton (270). In the serene restaurant where I was seated with Miuchi, a waiter watered a fern.

"For me, I could not dive into that world," Miuchi said. "Personally I prefer *Jane Eyre* because of its dynamic and rhythm."

I snapped to attention, hearing Charlotte Brontë's novel being given preference over Emily's masterwork.

"The translated version that I read of *Jane Eyre* was done by a literature researcher called Abe somebody—he's from a long time ago. His composition was very eloquent and very easy to read and created a lot of feelings that made me feel interest." Miuchi was talking about Abe Tomoji, who, I recalled, had studied with Edmund Blunden at the University of Tokyo in the 1920s, and who had gone on to translate *Wuthering Heights*. Abe was not the first translator of *Wuthering Heights*, but his translation had an unusual staying power; I owned a 1992 reprint of his 1961 translation, purchased in a used book shop for four hundred yen (less than four dollars).[18] Up until Miuchi made this observation about his translation of *Jane Eyre*, Abe existed for me as the *Wuthering Heights* translator and the *Wuthering Heights* translator only. I imagined him as that novel's loyal vassal, deliberating over how to translate the more difficult long sentences in *Wuthering Heights*, for example, the one in which Isabella stirs porridge. (She says, "It racked me to recall past happiness, and the greater peril there was of conjuring up its apparition, the quicker the thible ran round, and the faster the handfuls of meal fell into the water" [141]). I did not know that Abe, before he translated Brontë's novel, had translated Melville's *Moby Dick* (Japanese title: *Hakugei*, or "white whale"), Percy Shelley's poems, Shakespeare's *As You Like It*, and Agnes Smedley's *The Great Road*, as well as publishing short stories and essays of his own devising, including books entitled *Genbaku to bungaku* (The atom bomb and literature) and *Shōsetsu no yomikata* (How to read a novel). And five years before he translated *Wuthering Heights*, Abe had translated *Jane Eyre*, and apparently done a better job of it. "The *Wuthering Heights* translation was very stiff and rigid," Miuchi said.

Signaling that our meeting was coming to an end, Miuchi asked me about my interest in *Wuthering Heights*, and I spoke of *Arashi ga oka* as a door into Japanese culture, and mentioned my daughters and their manga reading. Miuchi said that she had started to draw manga when she was my younger daughter's age. "It has been thirty-seven years since I started to draw *Garasu no kamen*. I was expecting it to last no longer than two years," she said. "Because I ended up drawing plays and players, it got longer and longer and longer." I imagined Miuchi's entire *Glass Mask* series rumbling behind her like an overloaded librarian's cart, one final volume missing. "It's very intricate so it takes me a lot of effort; it will take double or triple time to do it," Miuchi said.

I asked Miuchi to autograph my volume of *Garasu no kamen*, and she looked around for a signing pen—a felt-tip was provided by the restaurant's bartender. On the end paper of volume 7 she drew the head of Maya: a wave of hair, a tiny nose, gigantic sparkly eyes. Miuchi took her time with the eyes, drawing out a hint of iris and full eyelashes with practiced scrawls of ink. The interpreter and I looked on as she finished off the drawing with her signature, and then we both applauded.

At the restaurant entrance Miuchi and the interpreter chatted for a few minutes in Japanese. Then I bid them both farewell and walked briskly to Kichijōji station, barely glancing in the puppy store window where a lone sausage dog took a roll in cedar shavings. The station was teeming with people, all of us heading home after a productive day, I thought, as I nodded at a station guard.

Tadaima (I'm home), I called unnecessarily, as I entered the short-stay. *Okaerinasai* (Welcome home) replied a bored voice from the kitchen, into which I charged. My daughter, reading, looked up and blinked like an owl.

"She first started drawing manga when she was your age," I told her, unpacking my bag and showing off my Miuchi signature. She feigned interest and turned back to her manga.

"How can you read that without a dictionary?" I asked. "What happens when you don't know a kanji?"

"I skip it."

That kind of laissez-faire attitude was fine for a casual manga reader, I thought as I hauled my bag into the bedroom. I, however, couldn't risk such a slapdash approach. I applied myself to *Garasu no kamen* with a renewed discipline, inspired by Miuchi's career-long dedication to her craft, and fired by a notion that I would read her entire opus. When Miuchi finally brought out her final, long-awaited volume I would be among the ardent readers who had read to the forty-ninth volume and idled there like passengers on a stalled train. But first things first. I balanced my dictionary on a pillow, and turned to the second half of *Garasu no kamen* volume 7, in which Kitajima Maya prepares to play Catherine in *Wuthering Heights*.

Maya considers Catherine so "passionate, obstinate, headstrong, and wild" that she can't at first imagine how she can make Brontë's character her own. Recalling Catherine's house alone on the moor,

Maya thinks, "She had nothing but the wind for company. . . . She can only turn to Heathcliff for company." Then Maya thinks, "I can do it." In Japanese, she says, *Atashi wa Kyasarin ni nareru*, or "I can become Catherine."[19]

The bedroom of the short-stay was the size of a bed. *Semai*, I thought, the Japanese word for "narrow" floating into my consciousness, as Japanese words sometimes did, not often when I needed them. I typed the word into my Japanese dictionary so that I could see its kanji meanings: cramped, narrow, contracted, tight. I consulted the list of other words that begin with the same kanji as *semai*: heart attack, angina, stenosis, narrow-minded. From a single kanji rose a world in which bigots succumbed to vascular disease in capsule hotels.

"We're leaving," called my daughters from outside the bedroom door. Jolting up, I stumbled into the hallway.

"Where are you going?"

"Nakano Broadway."

"Have you got your train pass?"

"Yes, Mom."

"Money?"

"*Yes.*"

My daughters put on their shoes in the meter-square *genkan* where our shoes were piled next to a cabinet full of foreign slippers.

"I saw a *Wuthering Heights* reference in *Aoi hana*." My younger daughter balanced on one foot and maneuvered her other foot into a shoe.

"What's *Aoi hana*?" I asked.

"It's a manga about schoolgirls; their drama club performs *Wuthering Heights*."

"Are you sure?"

"Mom—read it yourself! It's in the kitchen."

Aoi hana, or *Sweet Blue Flowers*, as it is known in English, is a *yuri* (lesbian-themed manga) by Shimura Takako. I turned its pages, looking for the drama club performance. There it was: a swift interlude between Nelly and Lockwood, followed by Nelly's account of the orphan Heathcliff, and then fast-forward to Catherine telling Nelly about Edgar's proposal. But just before Shimura segues from the boy Heathcliff to the kitchen scene, she includes a shot of the audience that includes a dad of one of the drama club girls. This performance is a Takarazuka-like thing, says the dad, and so pleased was I to catch his reference I did not bother to iron out my bad translation, but rather turned directly to Catherine's heart-to-heart discussion with Nelly, and her famous line. "Heathcliff is myself, the very thing," Catherine exclaims, in Japanese, in Shimura's version.[20]

I felt vindicated in my belief that *Wuthering Heights*, more than other Western literary works, had insinuated itself into Japanese culture, with *Garasu no kamen* providing an opening wedge, and also in my preoccupation with Catherine's "I *am* Heathcliff" line. Not only had Miuchi Suzue introduced Brontë's novel to millions of manga readers, but she had inspired other manga artists to follow her lead, I thought in the kitchen of the short-stay, opening the rice cooker lid hopefully. Then I retrieved my *Garasu no kamen* volumes from the bedroom and spread them out on the kitchen table with a bowl of leftover rice and a pair of chopsticks.

I turned the pages of *Garasu no kamen* to an early rehearsal scene. Miuchi draws Maya with her head tilted back and her mouth open in a giant smile, rays emanating from her head, the entire image framed by daisies. In a subsequent frame, an embarrassed Maya is encircled by laughing onlookers (fig. 4). "Why a cheerful Catherine?" asks an actor.[21] Part of the appeal of *Garasu no kamen* seemed to lie in the timid Maya becoming a force with which others must reckon. As I read on, I watched Maya's transformation. In one scene, Maya responds spontaneously when the actor playing Heathcliff gets injured in a scuffle and starts bleeding on stage. What would Catherine do, Maya thinks to herself, and then swiftly rips a piece of fabric from her skirt to wipe away the blood (fig. 5). A boy in the audience is so disturbed by Maya's intensity that he walks out in the middle of a scene. Two girls comment on her severe facial expression and on the harshness of her demeanor.[22]

A riffle of marimba tones interrupted my reading: my phone alarm. I was right on the edge of something, but it slipped away. I assembled my *Garasu no kamen* volumes, my *Wuthering Heights* edition, my electronic dictionary, my phone, my notebook, my wallet, my train pass, my short-stay keys, and a tea towel embroidered with a map of Iowa, and stuffed it all into a tote bag. I was scheduled to meet a Japanese friend at Kokubunji station; if conversation allowed, I wanted to direct her attention to my research.

I walked from the short-stay to Nakano station and, carried along by a mob of commuters, entered the station. All around me schoolchildren were dashing from one gate to another. Weighed down by *randoseru* (square leather backpacks), jaunty in sailor blouses and Gilligan hats, two girls waved their travel cards at a guard as they passed through a wicket. As I boarded the train, a girl the size of an American kindergartener, water

Fig. 4. Miuchi Suzue, *Garasu no kamen* [Glass mask], vol. 7, p. 104. Courtesy of Miuchi Suzue, © Miuchi Suzue.

Fig. 5. Miuchi Suzue, *Garasu no kamen* [Glass mask], vol. 7, p. 176. Courtesy of Miuchi Suzue, © Miuchi Suzue.

canteen dangling from her backpack, squeezed into a half-seat between two salarymen and glanced at her cell phone.

As we started moving, I assessed the seating situation; the train was crowded but not packed. I might be able to slip into a seat soon to be vacated by one of a trio of middle-aged women, their handbags contained on their laps, their feet tucked under their seats. The women were carrying out minute physical adjustments in anticipation of the next stop. One of them eyed me up and down as I rummaged one-handed (my other gripping a support bar) in my tote bag; I was feeling for my dictionary so that I could read the headlines on a newspaper a nearby businessman had folded into a long thin rectangle that he held up to his face.

Angling myself into position, I stood as close to the trio of women as I politely could. At the next stop, two of them stood up and bid the third goodbye. The remaining woman waved at them as I plopped heavily down beside her, my tote bag knocking her leg. She suffered my disturbance without comment. On the back of the businessman's newspaper, there was a photograph of the soon-to-be graduating member of the AKB48 girl band. In the weeks that followed, the sweet face of Maeda Atsuko, so often seen on billboards, would be supplanted by coarser photos. Maeda would be caught leaving a drinking club in a state of inebriated dishevelment, and being hoisted into a taxi by a male friend. A photograph of the young man carrying the bare-legged Maeda as if she were a sack of rice would become an Internet meme: the photoshopped pair would trudge across a bridge in a Hokusai print and climb Mount Fuji and face down tanks at Tiananmen Square.

All through the train car, readers were absorbed in books, their titles concealed by the brown paper jackets with which Japanese bookstore clerks wrap newly purchased volumes. I wondered what everyone was reading. To my left a college student pulled a book from his backpack and found his place in an unwrapped *Guretto gatsubi*, the Murakami Haruki translation.

I opened *Garasu no kamen* volume 7 to the scene in which Maya, performing as Catherine, stuns onlookers with her theatrical audacity. In the scene just before she rips a strip of fabric from her skirt, she thrusts herself between Hindley and Heathcliff, shouting at Hindley and pummeling him with her fists. She demands that he stop his cruelty, and she calls him stupid. At least that's what I think was happening; it was impossible for me to consult my dictionary without jostling the woman next to me.

A *gyaru* clattered onto the train, laden with shopping bags, and trailing her boyfriend. The Japanization of the word "gal" is used to describe a certain kind of fashion-conscious young woman. The *gyaru* on the train had bleached blond hair and fake eyelashes as thick as pastry brushes. She took out a compact and examined her makeup, and then contoured her cheekbones as her boyfriend pawed at her knees.

A thought whisked back into my head. Catherine might represent an escape hatch from societal norms for Japanese women readers, especially those of a certain age. In an insightful introduction to *Wuthering Heights*, Beth Newman writes of how Catherine seeks to transcend gender conventions. "What Cathy seeks is the wholeness denied all of us when we must fit into rigidly differentiated—and, especially for women, oppressive—gender identities."[23] The *gyaru* was slapping her boyfriend's hand and laughing. *Dame* (not allowed), she shrieked as he ran his hand up her thigh. In the few minutes since she'd boarded, the girl had broken five rules of Japanese train etiquette, namely by:

1. Talking too loudly
2. Applying makeup in public
3. Taking a cell phone call
4. Eating (shrimp crackers)
5. Engaging in public displays of affection

Was the *gyaru* transcending gender conventions or just being a brat? It was hard to decide. I projected onto the woman sitting next to me a judgmental response, and joined her in silent disapproval.

In prior readings of *Wuthering Heights*, I'd never thought of Catherine as an especially transgressive character. Juliet Barker calls the novel's complete lack of any moral purpose "a quality almost unique in Victorian culture," but Catherine's obstreperousness had not made a particular impression on me.[24] Across the train car aisle, the *gyaru* looked me up and down, her eye lingering for a moment on my clodhopper walking shoes. I pulled out my Penguin Classic, searching for Catherine scenes, which I'd marked with blaze orange Post-its.

I turned to the scene in which Catherine remembers locking herself into her bedroom and throwing herself on the floor. "I couldn't explain to Edgar how certain I felt of having a fit, or going raging mad," she says. "Oh, I'm burning! I wish I were out of doors—I wish I were a girl again, half savage and hardy, and free . . . and laughing at injuries, not maddening under them!" (125) The female manga artists, I recalled, highlighted the novel's love story, but also Catherine's emotional outbursts.

The *gyaru* started berating her boyfriend, her nasal cries racketing around the train car. I strove to keep reading.

"Why am I so changed? why does my blood rush into a hell of tumult at a few words?" Catherine asks Nelly. When Nelly refuses to open a window, the invalid Catherine throws open the window and leans out, "careless of the frosty air that cut about her shoulders as keen as a knife" (126).

The train rolled to a stop. The *gyaru* gathered her shopping bags and stepped through the exit door just as a warning whistle sounded. The boy lunged for the door, but it surged shut before he made it down the aisle. Outside, the girl banged on the glass. *Iyada, iyada* (No, no way), she screamed. The boy cursed at the automated door as the train started to move. Then he sloped back to his seat, a sulking Heathcliff in skinny jeans.

I closed my book, and watched out the window as the train picked up speed and zipped by several smaller stations—Musashi-sakai, Higashi-koganei, Musashi-koganei.

Catherine is scrappy and forceful, I thought approvingly, remembering how, in defiance of Joseph, she sets out for "a scamper on the moors" (22). But then I was brought up short by a memory of Heathcliff berating Catherine on her deathbed, giving the sick woman no quarter. "I have not one word of comfort—you deserve this," he savagely proclaims. When Heathcliff starts to leave, Catherine shrieks, "Oh, don't, don't go. . . . Heathcliff, I shall die! I shall die!" (164). She clings fast, gasping, with "mad resolution in her face," but Heathcliff leaves to stand sentinel under some larch trees outside. While he is absent, Catherine gives birth to her namesake and, soon after, dies.

Ever since I began my study of *Wuthering Heights* I had avoided being diverted by Brontë family history. I will not pour *Wuthering Heights* through the colander of biography, I resolved, striving to keep my focus on the pages of Brontë's novel, rather than on the cut of her sleeve or the breed of her dog. But now I recalled the tutor Monsieur Héger's reference to Emily's "strong imperious will," a comment handily available in the introduction to the Penguin Classics edition.[25] The train emptied; I shifted my tote bag to the seat beside me, and ran a finger down the book's preliminary pages, looking for the foreign name. "She should have been a man—a great navigator," Héger said. "Her powerful reason would have deduced new spheres of discovery from the knowledge of the old; and her strong imperious will would never have been daunted by opposition or difficulty." It was easy to read Catherine as Emily's alter ego; I felt myself succumbing to the tidal pull of Brontë anecdotage, and stepped back from the waves.

After the *gyaru*'s boyfriend sat back down, the woman next to me relaxed her posture a little. I palmed through the pages of *Wuthering Heights*, stopping at angry Catherine scenes—her "ears red with rage," pinching Nelly "very spitefully on the arm," boxing Edgar's ear "in a way that could not be mistaken for jest" (71–72). Perhaps Japanese women wouldn't want to sit next to Catherine, but they might thrill to her foot stamping in the cotillion line of nineteenth-century heroines. Even Charlotte Brontë felt conflicted about Emily's unlikable characters. "Men and women . . . trained from their cradle to observe the utmost evenness of manner and guardedness of language, will hardly know what to make of the rough, strong utterance, the harshly manifested passions . . . of unlettered moorland hinds," Charlotte wrote, before going on, ludicrously, to call Nelly Dean "an example of constancy and tenderness."[26] Ha! I thought, remembering Nelly's cold response to Catherine's illness. "Far better that she should be dead, than lingering a burden, and a misery-maker to all about her," thinks Nelly, the only other woman in Catherine's death chamber (164). The train pulled to a stop at Kokubunji station. Exiting, I got distracted by a flower show poster, and a logjam of commuters formed behind me until I realized what was happening and stepped aside.

Nelly is wrong, I thought, headed to a cake shop in the upper reaches of the station's vertical mall, but dallying for a moment in the OIOI department store. ("OheeOhee," I called it.) Catherine is entitled to her feelings; Nelly is not nearly so judgmental of Heathcliff, the biggest misery-maker of all. He has a "blackness of spirit that could brood on, and cover revenge for years; and deliberately prosecute its plans, without a visitation of remorse" (223). Yet even though she calls Heathcliff "selfish and disagreeable," she is still "moved with a sense of grief at his lot" (212).

I wandered around a display of decorative handkerchiefs, and then, double-checking my bag for the Iowa tea towel, I headed to the station escalator. Slowly ascending, I thought about Maya in *Garasu no kamen*, and how she revels in the role of Catherine. Miuchi Suzue, by whatever means she had accessed Brontë's novel—through reading the difficult, old translation, or through watching the more accessible Wyler film—had understood the story's fundamental melodrama. Not being able to read Brontë's novel in the original English had not prevented Miuchi from conveying its emotional theatrics.

When I got to the cake shop my friend was late, and I loitered next to the cash register as other women arrived in twos and threes. A waitress bustled by, and I pressed my back against the wall, trying to constrain my tote bag's bulk. There I stood for a few minutes, studying the cakes in a refrigerator case, and reading their names. *Su-to-ro-be-ri—ku-ri—mu*, I slowly sounded out.

When my friend arrived, she apologized with passion. "My God, how thoughtless of me to keep you waiting," the excessive nature of her regret a result of her effort to translate Japanese into English. As a hostess guided us to a table, I strove to forgive her just as ardently in Japanese.

"It was no problem; I like to look around the OheeOhee."

"OheeOhee?"

I made a little circle and stick with my fingers and marched them step-wise in front of my face to mime the store name's repeating characters.

My friend stifled a laugh as the waitress arrived to take our orders, and I ordered the exact same tea and cake set as my friend did.

"I think you mean the Marui," she said.

"What?" I said, but more politely, in Japanese.

"The store name—it's *Marui*."

And then she explained that OIOI is a visual pun, evoking the Marui company name (*maru* is the Japanese word for circle) as well as its 0101 phone number.

Normally, this kind of misunderstanding would have cast a shadow over my day. I would move swiftly from a reminder that I still missed basic Japanese cues to a suspicion that my research project was doomed. If I wasn't observant enough to detect the visual puns in famous Japanese brand names, I would never be able to understand all the twists and turns that *Wuthering Heights* took on its journey into the hearts of Japanese readers, I'd conclude. By my focus on *Wuthering Heights* in Japan I had boxed out 99.95 percent of Japanese literature and culture, yet I still had not mastered the 0.05 percent that remained.

This was true, but still I felt happy to be corrected by my friend in the fancy cake shop, the waitress arriving at our table with individual tea accouterments: a sugar bowl the size of a shot glass, a thimble of milk. How fortunate I was to benefit from the superior cultural knowledge of my capable friend; how kind she was to suffer my confusion! Remembering the gift in my tote bag, I pulled out the tea towel made from a flour sack and inscribed with a map of Iowa. I said something disparaging about the tea towel, trying to remember how to offer a gift in Japanese. Just then I noticed that the map's Davenport marker had wandered north of that city's actual location. I started to mention this but then stopped. My friend was, or appeared to be, or anyway said she was, pleased with the gift.

The café grew cozier as the sky darkened outside the window, and we looked out at the rooftops of adjacent buildings. Far below, a snarl of rail lines converged at Kokubunji station, some of them running alongside each other, others swerving off onto sidings. Did my friend see what I saw when she looked out the window? I don't know. We admired the view companionably for a moment or two. Then, in English and in Japanese, with wayward grammar and inadequate verbs, we discussed Brontë's ugly sprawling novel, and ate tiny slices of strawberry cake.

CHAPTER FOUR

Wuthering Heights and the Return of the Dead

> Over the deepest
>   Darkest river,
>   The fireflies
> Are flowing slowly
>   —Shiyo (trans. Peter Beilenson and Harry Behn)

Mizumura Minae, the most compelling Japanese novelist Americans have never read, was born in Tokyo in 1951, and moved to the United States with her family as a young girl, transferring from the Keisen Junior High School for Girls in Tokyo to Great Neck North Junior High School on Long Island. The most renowned graduates of Great Neck North High School are Mizumura Minae and the performance artist Andy Kaufman, but such is the impoverished state of literary translation in the United States—only two of Mizumura's novels have been translated into English— that Kaufman's Foreign Man character (who told unfunny jokes with a vaguely Eastern European accent) has achieved a larger measure of fame than Mizumura's novels, the fourth of which, *Honkaku shōsetsu* (*A True Novel*), is a rewriting of *Wuthering Heights*.[1]

I first encountered Mizumura's writing when, as a graduate student, I read a retrospective essay she wrote on Paul de Man.[2] Mizumura studied under de Man at Yale, the final stop on an educational itinerary that included the School of the Museum of the Fine Arts in Boston, where she studied art, and the Sorbonne and Yale, where she studied French. Her immersion in French was an act of cultural assertion. "My knowing the much revered language would allow a small, insignificant Asian girl to look down upon the big, white, almost invariably uncultured, monolingual Americans," she recalls.[3] The time she spent at Yale, by Mizumura's own account, encouraged a strain of experimentalism in her work, eventually emboldening her, in her first published work, *Zoku meian* (Light and dark continued), to write a sequel to Natsume Sōseki's unfinished classic novel. Mizumura capped off her graduate studies by publishing the essay on de Man in a tribute issue of *Yale French Studies*, and then took up visiting lecturer posts at Princeton, the University of Michigan, and Stanford.

Mizumura is not the only Japanese woman writer who has been inspired by Emily Brontë's novel. The celebrated short-story writer Kōno Taeko wrote an essay about her pilgrimage to Haworth Village and a playscript of *Wuthering Heights*; her debt to Emily Brontë manifests itself as well in the sadomasochistic themes and casual violence of her short stories, the most famous of which, "Toddler-Hunting," features a narrator who is obsessed with little boys.[4] The novelist Miura Ayako, too, in her 1964 best-selling novel *Hyōten* (which I accessed in Hiromu Shimizu and John Terry's translation *Freezing Point*), evokes Brontë's work when she has her main character read *Wuthering Heights*, mention Heathcliff's line ("The entire world is a dreadful collection of memoranda that she did exist, and that I have lost her!"), and visit a place called "Arashigaoka hill."[5] Miura also reveals her debt to Brontë by writing a revenge saga in which a man (Keizo) tricks his wife into raising the child of their own child's murderer, and in which the vengeful man's son falls in love with the orphaned girl. Keizo admits, "Even though I wouldn't want others to discover it, I still have a feeling that I would like to continue to keep bugging my wife Natsue till the bitter end" (419), a sentence that perhaps menaces more in the original Japanese—"bugging" doesn't capture the nastiness of Keizo's action and its tragic fallout. Miura, her biographer notes, wrote a melodramatic story of love and revenge when she was only in fifth grade; in *Freezing Point*, she writes from within the shadow of Brontë's novel and deploys its vengeful energies to great effect.[6]

Mizumura Minae, more than these other writers, however, most exactly replicates the structure and story line of *Wuthering Heights*. Mizumura's *Honkaku shōsetsu* (which I read in Juliet Winters Carpenter's translation *A True Novel*) stands as both an homage and a retort to *Wuthering Heights*. If there were anyone who could explain to my satisfaction the reason why *Wuthering Heights* is so popular in Japan, it would be the woman who turned Catherine and Heathcliff into Yoko and Taro, and transported them to "a twentieth-century Japan crowded with small houses," a place distinct from nineteenth-century Yorkshire, "with its empty heathland."[7] And Mizumura, uniquely of these writers, meditates upon the relationship between Japanese literary innovation and the Western literary tradition.

I'd nearly crossed paths with Mizumura ten years earlier when she passed several weeks in Iowa City as part of a contingent of foreign writers invited to spend a residency at the International Writing Program. Mizumura arrived at a time when the comings and goings of writers from Nigeria or Portugal or South Korea impinged on my consciousness not at all. Even though the distance between the guesthouse where the foreign writers stayed and the building where I taught could be traversed by a louche student in the course of smoking half a cigarette, I was oblivious to their presence.

The International Writing Program describes itself as "a unique conduit for the world's literature, connecting well-established writers from around the globe," and as a force for "bringing international literature into classrooms," and it does serve these functions well.[8] But in order to participate in the IWP, a writer has "to possess sufficient proficiency in English to profit from the Iowa experience," a requirement that, if you pause to think about it, is entirely antithetical to the organization's internationalist aspiration—if an organization in Japan were trying to foster fellowship among foreign writers, it could not stipulate that the writers it gathered from all parts of the world be conversant in Japanese. Of the inflated currency of her English-speaking ability Mizumura was acutely aware. When invited to speak at a foreign university, she said, "More than likely I am invited not because the host read and liked my novels, but because I conveniently speak English." She noted, "Foreigners, even those who teach Japanese literature at a university, cannot read novels written in Japanese with any ease."[9] It was just this kind of pronouncement that made me fear Mizumura before meeting her. Would she scorn me for my Japanese illiteracy?

In advance of her trip to Iowa City, Mizumura, her imagination fired by Agatha Christie audiobooks, anticipated sojourning at a quaint hotel with a window view of soothing scenery. She writes, "I pictured myself in a tweed skirt that fell just below the knees and low pumps—things I never actually wear—looking (apart from my decidedly Japanese features) like a behind-the-times middle-aged English lady."[10] However, upon her arrival in Iowa, she was housed in a brick compound next to, but with little view of, the Iowa River. The Iowa House, with its whiff of grilled meat from the adjacent Student Union, turned out to be a disappointing setting for a Miss Marple whodunit.

When the gathered writers boarded two minibuses to take a tour of the Iowa countryside, Mizumura recalls, "The Westerners headed toward one, and shortly afterward, Asians with uniformly black hair began trooping toward the other."[11] On the bus, a Lithuanian poet leaned toward Mizumura and asked, "Do you know bonsai?" She writes, "It had never occurred to me that the pastime of elderly Japanese bending over to trim dwarf pine trees had reached all the way to the youth of a country I couldn't even locate on a map."[12]

At the time Mizumura visited Iowa, I didn't know that I would, in the not too distant future, seek to understand why *Wuthering Heights* is popular in Japan, nor did I anticipate that there would come a day when, if a Japanese writer landed in Iowa City, I would pursue her like a bird-watcher tracking a rare warbler. Back when Mizumura visited Iowa, I kept to my cramped corner of specialization, writing books about British Romantic poets with blithe disregard for how and when their poems had been translated into Japanese, and with no awareness of the Japanese Romantic movement, which I only later came to learn was a thing. My provincial ten-year-ago self stayed pent up in the bomb shelter of the English-Philosophy Building, while just across the empty field where sororities sometimes hold mud-wrestling charity events, Mizumura took up residence at Iowa House, and told people about her novel based on *Wuthering Heights*, and allowed translated bits of it to be posted on the International Writing Program's website. Luckily for me, during the ten years that had passed since that time, Mizumura's entire novel was published in English translation, so I could now see how she had rewritten Brontë's famous scenes, or, rather, how Mizumura's translator, the Michigan native Juliet Winters Carpenter, had conveyed Mizumura's scenes to readers of English.

Mizumura transforms the most famous scene in *Wuthering Heights*, the moment when the interloper Lockwood, while lying in an oak closet that was once Catherine's childhood sleeping chamber, is vexed by a fir bough that touches the window lattice. When he knocks his knuckles through the glass, Lockwood feels the grasp of a child's ice-cold hand, and hears a voice, "I'm come home, I'd lost my way on the moor!" (25). It was a scene to which I kept returning since it resurfaces in different guises, for instance in the Ali Project's 1993 Japanese single *Arashi ga oka*, which begins with the lines: "One night dancing, like a fire of love that will not vanish, I am calling your name, on the Wuthering Heights."[13] In Mizumura's rewriting of this scene in *A True Novel*, her version of Lockwood (Yusuke), an editor at a Tokyo publishing firm, while stranded overnight in a strange setting, encounters a child ghost.

Brace yourself—not for the ghost child, who, for the moment, I leave hanging in the air—but rather for a brief excursus on the complicated structure of Mizumura's novel. *A True Novel* takes the Russian nesting doll structure of *Wuthering Heights* and adds another ring of narration based on Mizumura Minae's personal biography. In Brontë's novel, Catherine and Heathcliff's story is conveyed by Nelly Dean by way of Lockwood. In Mizumura's *A True Novel*, Yoko and Taro's story gets conveyed by Tsuchiya Fumiko (Mizumura's Nelly) by way of Kato Yusuke (Mizumura's Lockwood), *and* Yusuke's story is communicated by a narrator named Mizumura Minae (I'll use this narrator's first name, Minae, to distinguish her from the author Mizumura). One day Minae, who is struggling to write a novel while teaching at Stanford, is met at her office door by Yusuke, who wants to talk about their mutual acquaintance Taro (Mizumura's Heathcliff). It's as if Emily Brontë described Lockwood showing up at the door of the Haworth parsonage, wanting to share stories about their mutual friend Heathcliff.

By inserting details of her own biography into her rewriting of *Wuthering Heights* (the fictional Minae shares Mizumura's Long Island upbringing and peripatetic academic career), and by naming her novel *Honkaku shōsetsu* (*A True Novel*), Mizumura evokes a Meiji-era controversy over Japanese novelists' engagement with the European realist tradition. As Mizumura points out in the frame story of *A True Novel*, the opening of Japan to the West corresponded with the golden era of the European novel. Many Japanese writers viewed these literary works, in which fictional worlds were presented by impersonal authors, as ideal realizations of the novel form. But a half century into their infatuation with this form, some Japanese writers began to argue that novelists should write truthfully about themselves. They innovated the *shi-shōsetsu*, or "I-novel," in which events correspond to events in the author's life, and they suggested that such writing was imbued with the soul of Japan, where, as Mizumura notes, "The diary has been an esteemed literary genre for over a thousand years" (*A True Novel*, 161).

Honkaku shōsetsu (real or true novel) is the name given to novels that were "true" or faithful to the European tradition of a transcendent remote subject, but were not true in the sense of recounting the actual experiences of an actual person. *Shi-shōsetsu*, or "I-novel," is the name given to novels that recounted an author's personal experiences and that were written from the point of view of the author's own subject position. When Mizumura gave the name *Honkaku shōsetsu* to her rewriting of *Wuthering*

Heights, she recalled the Meiji-era critical debate. But when her novel's title was translated into English, the reference to Japanese novelists' tense engagement with European realism was lost on most readers.

I could see how Brontë's novel anticipated I-novel plots, which according to the critic Yamanouchi Hisaaki, typically feature a hero who becomes alienated from and defeated by society, and who avenges himself on the world. His initial moral vision "assumes Satanic immorality," Yamanouchi writes, calling to mind the transformation of Heathcliff into a vengeance-seeking missile.[14] Yamanouchi was not impressed by the I-novelists' efforts; he faulted one for serving up trivial details of his private life "as if on a tray for all to stare at," suggesting that the result was less a work of art than "a spectacle fit for public consumption like an animal in a zoo."[15] Mizumura had written a hybrid work that was part I-novel (based closely on her own experience) and part true novel (based on Emily Brontë's *Wuthering Heights*).

But back to Yusuke and the ghost. Vacationing with a friend in Karuizawa during Obon, the Japanese festival of the dead, Yusuke crashes his bike into a hedge in the village of Oiwake. When an older woman named Fumiko emerges from a cottage to investigate the accident, Yusuke recalls an old tale he'd read as a child. "A traveler seeking shelter at the end of a long day's journey sees a faint light in a distant field and walks toward it, until at last he reaches a hut where a woman reluctantly lets him stay the night. In the morning, though, he finds only a pile of bleached bones on the floor and hears the wind howling through the bamboo lattice-work of crumbled walls" (173). Yusuke feels like he has been thrust back into the Japan of an earlier generation, "somewhere he knew from the coarse grain of old black-and-white photographs, newsreels, and movies" (174). As he stands under a small circle of light in the kitchen, surveying a tin-lined sink and an electric rice cooker with Bakelite handles, the word "postwar" occurs to him. Mizumura writes, "The term recalled the Japan of the years before his birth, a country still shabby and poor and slightly ludicrous when outlays of money were made" (175). When Yusuke discovers that he's lost his friend's house key in the bike crash, Fumiko (Mizumura's Nelly Dean), offers to let him stay overnight in a shed behind the cottage.

As Yusuke settles in, "moths had flattened their powdery white wings against the windowpane" of the shed. Mizumura writes, "They seemed to be pleading to be let in. His nerves were still fragile: the sight was suffocating" (204). A little later, "Motes of dust rose and danced in the air around the doorway, illuminated in the still, transparent rays. No more than a few seconds could have gone by—yet it felt longer, as if he were watching images projected in slow motion" (206). Yusuke turns off the bare bulb in the shed and, lying in the dark, recalls passing a rustic graveyard where, mingling with "extravagant new granite tombstones," were humble older graves, "little more than piles of roadside stones" marking the graves of the unknown (205). Because of the Obon festival, "someone had placed fresh flowers even on those forsaken graves." And then the door of the shed blows open and a ghostly girl appears wearing a summer kimono. Mizumura writes, "With her frizzy hair flaring out around her head, she stared up at Yusuke on the top bunk, her eyes wild, her tiny fist tightly clasping a round festival fan" (206). As the sounds of "Tokyo Ballad," a traditional Obon festival song, float through the air, the girl shouts something at Yusuke, and then flees, "her long sleeves fluttering in the air" (206).

When Catherine's ghost seizes Lockwood's hand in *Wuthering Heights*, he reacts with horror: "Finding it useless to attempt shaking the creature off, I pulled its wrist on to the broken pane, and rubbed it to and fro till the blood ran down and soaked the bed-clothes" (25). Once Lockwood manages to snatch his hand back through the hole in the windowpane, he "hurriedly pile[s] the books up in a pyramid against it," and stops his ears for "above a quarter of an hour." In contrast, when Yusuke sees a ghost, he scrambles down from his bunkbed and runs outside in pursuit of the apparition. He sees "something white wander through the gate and veer off to the right," and recalls seeing "something similar pass in front of him just when his bicycle crashed into the hedge." But when he runs out past the gate, he sees only "the tall fronds of pampas grass [shining] silver and ghostly in the moonlight" (206).

Mizumura's ghost wears a *yukata* (summer kimono) "with bright scarlet koi, like giant goldfish, swimming this way and that against a white background" (189). In a *New Yorker* profile of a kimono painter, Judith Thurman describes the kimono's enduring status in Japanese culture: "Last summer, at rush hour in the Tokyo subway, there seemed to be about one passenger taking dainty steps in a kimono to every three hundred in Western street wear."[16] The kimono perfectly emblematizes the clash of Japanese and Western cultures. In Ozu Yasujiro's 1953 film *Tokyo Story*, a pair of grandparents kneel on tatami mats in their kimonos as their neglectful children go about their busy lives in Western wear. In Tanizaki Junichiro's *The Makioka Sisters* (1943–48), three sisters are distinguished from each other by their apparel, with the most modern sister dressing in Western garb, and Yukiko, "the most Japanese," appearing in kimono.[17]

These days, for a foreign visitor, an authentic kimono sighting in the To-kyo subway system is a delightful occurrence. As Thurman writes, "Above the symphonic rumble of a moving crowd, the entrance of a kimono pro-duced to my ear a soulful trill—like that of an archaic flute."[18]

Mizumura recalls turning her back on the English language and spending her teenage years reading Japanese novels her uncle had given to her mother (Brizuela interview). Her narrator Minae, while stranded in a Long Island suburb, pines for the Japanese past:

> I would sit on one end of a sofa bracketed by a pair of lamps with pale silk shades—lamps made of Satsuma vases that, in my pas-sion for things Japanese, I had pestered my mother to buy at the Takashimaya department store in the city—turn on the light closer to me, and lose myself in one of the Japanese novels our parents had shipped out for us, reading until it got dark, while my sole compan-ion, an overweight collie named Della we'd brought with us on the plane, lay quietly at my feet. (6)

Satsuma earthenware, which is manufactured on Japan's southernmost main island, was originally made of a plain dark clay. However, begin-ning in the nineteenth century, elaborately decorated ivory-colored Sat-suma vessels began being marketed to Western consumers. The lamp that Minae pesters her mother to buy as a reminder of their Japanese heritage emblematizes how Japan was transformed by encounters with the West. When I finally met up with Mizumura, the very lamp mentioned by her novel's narrator, its base embellished with leaves and flowers and birds and clouds, cast a soft light in the corner of her dining room, having traveled from Japan to the United States and back to Japan.

My meeting with Mizumura was preceded by epistolary trepidation. I'd recently sent a query to Kōno Taeko, she of the Brontë-inspired dis-turbing short stories: no reply. The stakes were higher in querying Mizu-mura. More than the manga artists, and the Heathcliff enactor, and the theater director, and the Japanese readers with whom I'd been discussing *Wuthering Heights*, Mizumura, a native Japanese speaker who had spent nearly twenty years in the West, was uniquely qualified to explain why *Arashi ga oka* had become a floating signifier in Japan, so that even people who haven't read Brontë's novel recognize its Japanese title. If Mizumura didn't reply, my book about Japanese versions of *Wuthering Heights* would have a sinkhole at its center toward which the other chapters would slide, clutching their small revelations like rope shards and broken pickaxes. I acquired Mizumura's e-mail address from a staffer at the International Writing Program, revised my message six times, and hit the send button. I needn't have worried; Mizumura wrote back with alacrity, and we arranged to meet in Oiwake, the small village near Karuizawa in Nagano Prefecture that is the setting of *A True Novel*.

Because of the efficiency and range of the Japanese rail system, it is possible to travel extensively in Japan without having a firm sense of orientation. Nagano Prefecture is part of Honshu, the largest of the four main islands, and the one that contains Tokyo and Kyoto. If you find Tokyo on a map of Japan, and then move your finger diagonally northwest, you will land on Nagano before your finger falls into the sea of Japan. Mizumura's travel directions were dauntingly detailed. I was to take the Shinkansen (bullet train) from Tokyo station to Karuizawa. I was to get off the Shinkansen, follow the other travelers, and take the escalator to the exit. I was to turn left and walk for twenty meters, after which I was to find an entrance to the Shinano Tetsudo line, and purchase a ticket from a vending machine near the train entrance, or, if the vending machine was too difficult to negotiate, from a person at the ticket window. I would have thirteen minutes between my exit from the Shinkansen and the departure of the Shinano line train that I was to take to Shinano Oiwake station, where, waiting for me, would be a taxi with a driver who was familiar with Mizumura's cottage. If something went awry I was to call Mizumura, but should not expect her to pick up the phone; I was to talk to her machine, at which point she would pick up the receiver.

The directions made me feel like a child in a Victorian children's book who steps through a wardrobe into an alternate realm. So too, did the idea of a summer cottage, or *besso* in Japanese, a word that unites the kanji for "other" and for "house." Mizumura lives for most of the year in Tokyo, but because it was August, and because she is vulnerable to *reibōbyō*, an inability to tolerate air-conditioning, I was visiting her other house. It's possible to translate *reibōbyō* into the English phrase "air-conditioning sickness," but in the United States when office workers shiver in their cubicles they do not complain of air-conditioning sickness. Mizumura's malady hinted at the limits of translation.

Looming in the distance when my train pulled into Oiwake was Mount Asama, an active volcano that rises eight thousand feet above sea level, and which, for three months in 1783, tossed rocks and ash into the air. Emily Brontë could have read about the volcano in Isaac Titsingh's

1822 *Illustrations of Japan*, which included a sensational account of the 1783 eruption. According to Titsingh, the seismic event caused bears and hyenas to flee from the mountains and to devour the inhabitants of nearby villages. He also described the torrent of sulfur, stones, rocks, and mud that swelled rivers and laid waste the countryside. "The number of persons who perished was immense," noted Titsingh, describing mangled carcasses and floating houses.[19]

On the day I pulled into Oiwake, the distant mound of Asama seemed no more imposing than the miniature loaf of Mount Asama sugar bread that I purchased in the Shinkansen terminal. It was the year after the year of the Fukushima disaster; all over Japan, air-conditioning was being kept to a minimum. The stations through which I passed on my journey to and from Oiwake were maintained at a temperature that made me long to jump into a cold lake. Mothers fanned their babies; a little boy refused to eat rice from a bento box in the shape of a bullet train. Even the bottled water I pulled from a convenience store cooler was tepid.

Japanese people were flocking to Karuizawa for the Obon holiday, the three-day festival of the dead. The Obon tradition evolved from the story of a Buddhist disciple who discovered that his dead mother was suffering in the realm of hungry ghosts, and who was advised by the Buddha to make offerings to monks who had just completed their summer retreat. In so doing, the disciple became aware of his mother's sacrifices and his own past selfishness. Whether because of the monks' intercession or his own change of heart, his mother was released from her suffering, and the disciple danced for joy. Current-day Obon revelers wear summer kimonos and carry out regionally specific dances, sometimes waving small towels or clicking wooden clappers. They light paper lanterns so that their dead ancestors can find their way back home, and, on the last day of the festival, they float these lanterns down local waterways as a way of guiding their loved ones back to the realm of the dead.

In a pleasing coincidence that Mizumura pointed out, I was visiting Oiwake on the very day on which the ghost child in *A True Novel* appears to Yusuke during his Obon holiday vacation. Yusuke describes the paper lanterns hanging along the road through Karuizawa, and the shrine where "a ring of people wearing T-shirts and sneakers danced clumsily to the beat of the big *taiko* drum and music from loudspeakers" (205). I sat with Mizumura on the back deck of her cottage, overlooking a casual assemblage of flowering bushes. Blue butterflies swirled around us; one landed in my hair. When I listen to the recording of our conversation, I hear the sound of cicadas, and recall the small shield-shaped bug—a *kamemushi*, or turtle bug—that crawled across the arm of my chair. Before the afternoon was over, I took a photograph of Mizumura standing next to a flowering bush under which her mother's ashes were buried. I thought of my own mother's grave in a Florida cemetery that my sisters and I seldom visited. If we were Japanese, we would light candles so that she could find her way back to us.

Even as Mizumura seemed perfectly at home in Oiwake, I couldn't help but contemplate the peculiarity of her position as one of the few people in Japan who return from extended stays in the United States. There is a special name in Japanese for schoolchildren who return from a sojourn in a foreign country—*kikokushijo* (returnee)—and there is a special difficulty that attaches itself to these boundary crossers, whose exposure to foreign cultures makes them seem less Japanese. When Mizumura returned for good to her native country, she had spent more years in the United States than she had lived in Japan. Having never felt entirely at home in the United States, she must also have felt at odds in a country that was no longer the Japan of her childhood. She was temporally, as well as geographically, displaced. "It's hard to escape America, isn't it?" says the fictional Minae in *A True Novel* (62).

In a poignant scene in the novel, Japanese workers at the American branch of a Japanese optics company gamely attempt an American-style New Year's party. The moment they try to behave like Americans, however, "Everything about them—their figures, faces, expressions, gestures, their speech, even their voices, which struggled out of their narrow chests and spindly necks—betrayed all too clearly the fact that they were not 'real' Americans and made their efforts seem comic, if not pathetic" (70).

I was most interested in talking to Mizumura about a scene that takes place in her narrative counterpart Minae's bedroom. Minae's bookshelf holds the multivolume *Girls' Library of World Literature*, "translations of Western classics, done in a simple prose style" (53). The series was one of several Western literature compilations that lined the classrooms of Japanese schoolchildren who grew up in the 1950s and 1960s. I was fascinated by these series because they presumed a literary ambitiousness that was entirely lacking in my own childhood classrooms, whose bookshelves contained spotty Nancy Drew holdings. American girls, as far as I knew, had never been the target audience for a series of translated Eastern literary classics—say, *The Tale of Genji* or the Ming-era classic *The Golden Lotus*—rendered accessible to sixth-graders. The Japanese literature series included authors that any girl might read (Louisa May Alcott, Lucy Maud Montgomery, Hans Christian Andersen, the Brontës: both Charlotte and Emily), authors an ambitious girl might tackle (Shakespeare, Sand, Tolstoy, Stendahl), as well as authors that only a girl exiting a midcentury time capsule would recognize (Pearl S. Buck, William H. Hudson, Olive Higgins Prouty, the 1939 Finnish Nobel laureate Frans Emil Sillanpää).[20]

Mizumura recalled the girls' series fondly. "I remember every single one. They were important for women readers of a certain age," she said.[21] "My parents were not rich enough to get the whole collection, but I've still kept some of them." Mizumura reminisced about the story of an all-girls school at which a nun commits suicide, a book I later identified as *The Child Manuela* by Christa Winslow. "It takes place in Long Island," Mizumura said before I nudged her back to Yorkshire. "Was that your first introduction to *Wuthering Heights*?" I asked. "Yes," she said. "It was an abridged version, but it was quite well done."

In *A True Novel*, the narrator Minae recalls in particular one Western novel that "never failed to make a disturbing impression on me every time I read it, a literary classic set on the wild Yorkshire moors" (158). *Every time I read it!* Minae the character and Mizumura Minae, who was asking if we'd like to step inside the cottage for lunch, had both read *Wuthering Heights* over and over.

"I read all of the [*Girls' Library of World Literature*] books before I was twelve," Mizumura was saying. "After I was twelve I read Japanese classical literature. The [*World Literature*] books were written for girls up to junior high. I was linguistically advanced—they were too easy for me."

"Do you have a memory of the Brontë novels being especially important in your reading history?" I asked hopefully.

"*Jane Eyre* certainly was," Mizumura disappointingly replied, before going on to mention *Little Women* and *Little Lord Fauntleroy*.

"*Little Lord Fauntleroy* was one of the first English novels to get translated into Japanese," I said, but Mizumura was talking about how she identified as a child with Amy in *Little Women*.

"Do you have any sense of why *Wuthering Heights* has become popular in Japan?" I asked. "Because it's not realistic," Mizumura replied. "Even *Jane Eyre* has more realism. It's just plain plot—I always think of it as being like Greek tragedy. I can imagine *Wuthering Heights* being translated into any language," she said. "Also, it's a romance. *Jane Eyre* is very romantic but you have the middle section where she wanders around—that part is absolutely not interesting to Japanese readers." I thought for a moment about the middle section of *Jane Eyre*, my mind flitting from Jane walking across the countryside to the actor Mia Wasikowska walking in the film version. That scene was better in the movie than in the original novel, I thought, but kept my own counsel as the conversation moved on.

Mizumura was talking about Jane Austen and Natsume Sōseki, stressing the difficulty of translating Jane Austen's novels into Japanese. "He understood English literature like no other person of his age," Mizumura said as some Japanese birds screeched in the distance. Of Sōseki's novels Mizumura had written, "They're bursting with questions regarding Japan's place in the world. Those passages strike a powerful chord in Japanese readers even today. But those are the very passages that are untranslatable."[22] Even the Japanese title of Sōseki's novel *Wagahai wa neko de aru* (*I Am a Cat*) contains within it an untranslatable joke, since *wagahai*, as his translators point out, is a ridiculously lordly way for a stray kitten to refer to itself, but this pompousness is in no way conveyed by the simple declarative sentence of the English title *I Am a Cat*.[23] But Sōseki's translators were not nearly as pessimistic about the successful conveyance of Sōseki's work to other countries as Mizumura was. "I doubt that it's possible to translate Sōseki in such a way that he can be fully appreciated by non-Japanese readers," she had once said to a Japanese interviewer.[24]

Now a gentle breeze rustled the bushes in Mizumura's backyard. "One reason why I like Sōseki is because he understood Japanese literature. His English is not that good—you can tell that in his commentary on Nietzsche." Mizumura seemed to have entirely absorbed both the Japanese and Western canons so that when she wrote her version of *Wuthering Heights*, she did so with an acute awareness of how she was drawing on and reworking both traditions, and also of the overshadowing of one by the other. By her own narrator's account, she had "to follow the inner logic of the Japanese language and interact with countless Japanese texts of the past, all the while maintaining a keen awareness of the small place the language occupies in a world dominated by English" (159). The strong impression I had while listening to Mizumura talk companionably on the deck of her summer cottage was that her reimagining of *Wuthering Heights* knit together the grand literary traditions of both Japan and the West, and that she was uniquely poised to ponder these separate traditions and how they'd collided.

I was happy to be led inside Mizumura's cottage, where I inspected the Satsuma lamp. She served lunch: shrimp cocktail and potato soup and roast chicken with eggplant. "I'm always frustrated by Japanese writers who are not very conscious of history," Mizumura said, as she moved calmly around the table, setting out dishes. "We have experienced such an interesting historical change that it's worth writing it down. Only Tanizaki was an exception," she said. I recalled the several times when, despite the translator Edward Seidensticker's helpful list of characters, I'd stumbled over the opening paragraphs of Tanizaki's *The Makioka Sisters*, confused by the flurry of Japanese names. Mizumura mentioned that she'd used too many "Y" name characters in her novel; Mizumura's Catherine is named Yoko, and she has a sister named Yuko. "My husband said to write it down in Roman alphabet and think about how it would look," she laughed. "But I said, 'Nonsense.'" Japanese readers have no difficulty distinguishing the two sisters from each other because, when written with kanji, the names Yoko and Yuko look entirely different from each other. Mizumura also mentioned the Shigemitsu and Saegusa families, her Japanese Earnshaws and Lintons. The *mitsu* in Shigemitsu signaled a distinguished family history. "It sounds like a samurai class name," Mizumura said, adding, "That's all lost in translation."

As a friend of Mizumura drove us back to the station at the end of my visit, Mizumura pointed out the tourist attractions of Karuizawa, a popular resort area ever since an asthmatic Canadian ventured there in 1866. "Looking for a place to escape the intense summer heat of the city, a missionary discovered this locale, deep in the mountains, often veiled in mist and fog, far above sea level," Mizumura writes in *A True Novel* (235). In the decade that followed, vacationing expatriates constructed Western-style cottages, hotels, restaurants, and churches. Mizumura's version of Wuthering Heights and Thrushcross Grange in *A True Novel* are the Shigemitsu and Saegusa houses, side-by-side dwellings in the nineteenth-century Western style of architecture. Mizumura writes, "With their peaked roofs, both were three stories high, but they looked less grand than timeworn" (245). When I asked Mizumura if the houses in her novel were based on actual houses, she replied that they were amalgamations of houses in Karuizawa. "They're being demolished," she said, referring to small Western-style houses being replaced by larger Japanese-style edifices. We passed the Mampei hotel, where the emperor of Japan met his future wife on the tennis court, and where John Lennon and Yoko Ono sometimes stayed. As we traveled down narrow roads that cut through groves of spindly trees, Mizumura pointed out a building site where a gargantuan dwelling, rumored to be the future home of Bill Gates, was under construction. Then Mizumura and her friend dropped me off at the train station and drove away. Or maybe they walked me inside—the changeover from my sojourn in Oiwake to the Japanese transit system seems abrupt in memory, but perhaps that was because it felt like I was departing Mizumura's novel as well as her town.

After my encounter with Mizumura, I was put in contact by a scholar friend with the Brontë scholar Iwakami Haruko, who had read both Mizumura's novel and its English translation. Both of the scholars agreed that Mizumura's Japanese was distinctive. "Her Japanese itself is not the same as ours," one of them noted. "She learned her Japanese from books, so it is extremely beautiful."[25] For the first time I realized that Mizumura might seem to other Japanese people like a visitor from an earlier Japan. Iwakami mentioned missing elements in the English version. "Her idea of translation is to create something very readable," Iwakami said of the translator Juliet Winters Carpenter. "Some things just get omitted because they don't make sense in English."[26]

Carpenter, an American Midwesterner who teaches in Japan at Doshisha Women's College of Liberal Arts, studied with Edward Seidensticker, the translator of my *Makioka Sisters* edition. When I caught up with her briefly in Kyoto, she criticized slavish translations that wind up sounding odd in the target language. She recalled giving Japanese students a Snoopy cartoon to translate, and then being puzzled when the final frame of every student's translation had two periods. "I thought that must mean something in Japanese," Carpenter recalled, but when she asked her students to explain, they said that the original cartoon had two dots at the end.[27] "There was a period followed by a smudge," Carpenter laughed, "They were retaining a smudge in the original." For Carpenter, the Snoopy cartoon story epitomized the tendency of bad translators to adhere unquestioningly to tiny details, even if the details have no meaning. "If it doesn't mean something in Japanese, why would you bother reproducing it," she asked.

Translators have long argued about how faithful they should be to the works they transport into new languages. Vladimir Nabokov, a fan of strict translations, frequently commented on all that is lost in translation, writing, for example, that for readers of *Don Quixote* in translation, the "Breughelian side of the book is as dead as cold mutton."[28] Nabokov did not believe that the impact of Cervantes' structural devices—his use of quotes from ballads and popular sayings, his plays on words—could be conveyed to readers of translations. "We are unable to palpate the original text through the alien layers of translation—no matter how good," he sadly declared.[29] Jorge Luis Borges, by contrast, suggested that a translator who takes liberties with vocabulary and grammar is more likely to have success. "If you are going to translate Shakespeare," he said, "you must do it as freely as Shakespeare wrote."[30] Of a French translator's version of *The Thousand and One Nights*, Borges said, "Word for word, [Antoine] Galland's version is the most poorly written of them all, the least faithful, and the weakest, but it was the most widely read. Those who grew intimate with it experienced happiness and astonishment."[31]

Carpenter chose not to read *Wuthering Heights* in advance of translating Mizumura's novel, but when Mizumura visited one of Carpenter's classes, she gave her students an excerpt of Brontë's novel with two translations.[32] "I happened to pick the scene just before Cathy gives birth, and she's throwing feathers, and it really gives you the chills. What Brontë accomplishes is amazing," Carpenter said, her enthusiasm mounting. "You read it and think: could you write this? You couldn't—it's really something. The way she delves into character—what an amazing moment!"

The scene takes place when Edgar insists that Catherine must choose between Heathcliff and her husband, and Catherine flies into a rage, "dashing her head against the arm of the sofa, and grinding her teeth, so that you might fancy she would crash them to splinters!" (118). She retreats to her chamber, where she is haunted by morbid thoughts of her own death. Nelly reports that Catherine "increased her feverish bewilderment to madness, and tore the pillow with her teeth, then raising herself up all burning, desired that I would open the window" (122). As the scene goes on, Catherine seems "to find childish diversion in pulling the feathers from the rents she had just made, and ranging them on the sheet according to their different species." Brontë writes, "Her mind had strayed to other associations." Catherine catalogs the feathers she surveys: turkey and wild duck and pigeon. "Ah, they put pigeons' feathers in the pillows—no wonder I couldn't die!" she cries (122).

Brontë alludes to a folklore belief that the soul cannot free itself if a dying person has been laid on a bed made of pigeon feathers. "Instances are on record of pigeon feathers having been placed in a small bag, and thrust under dying persons to hold them back until the arrival of some loved one," writes Richard Blakeborough in his account of the folklore and customs of northern Yorkshire.[33] "The meeting having taken place," he goes on to write, "the feathers were withdrawn, and death allowed to enter."

Why hadn't I seized on this passage in my past readings and found it as arresting as Carpenter did? I wondered. "Is it more exciting in Japanese?" I started to ask, but Carpenter was mentioning a prize that her translation of Mizumura's novel had won.[34] "The question I get from people is how do they know it's a good translation," she said. "But they don't have to judge it as a translation—it's the best translated book. They're not judging on whether it's close to the original, just asking, 'Is it a good book?'" Carpenter went on to recall her mentor Edward Seidensticker asking his students, "So what did you do with it?" when discussing their attempts at translation. "You don't just get a dictionary out. It's like in cooking," Carpenter said. "You have tofu, but what did you *do* with the tofu? There are a million choices and there's no one choice that is the best—as in life!"

I said goodbye to Carpenter and walked around a nearby park, the grounds of an ancient imperial palace. I passed an elderly man sitting on a park bench near the entrance, and then, fifteen minutes later, I passed a different elderly man as I walked toward a different entrance, paused, and turned around, realizing it was not where I had entered. I stared at a park map for a few minutes, and then strode purposefully toward a third entrance, telling myself it didn't matter whether I exited in the same place I entered.

In the weeks and months that followed, I revisited the ghost scene in *Wuthering Heights*, thinking about Lockwood's unhinged reaction to Catherine's ghost, his frantic sawing of her arm against the broken windowpane. Japanese people, by contrast, seemed untroubled by ghosts. They expected the spirits of their dead family members to linger for forty-nine days after their deaths, and they welcomed them home each summer for the festival of the dead. "It's not surprising for Japanese people that the souls of the dead return," the manga artist Miuchi Suzue had said.[35] "When they go to the other world, they will come back during Obon." She recalled how, as a child, she and her family had thanked a spirit for visiting and expressed hope that he would come again. If Lockwood were Japanese, I thought, he would burn incense for Catherine, and the smoke would help her find her way back to the spirit world.

"Do you know how to identify a Japanese ghost?" a Japanese professor asked when I mentioned the ghost topic between sessions at an academic conference. We were picking up lunch items at a convenience store. "They don't have legs!" she proclaimed. "Japanese children are told to look for legs if they think they are encountering a ghost. If it doesn't have legs, it's a ghost." As I unwrapped a tuna rice ball, I recalled Japanese drawings in which the bottom halves of human figures dissolve into a swirl of smoke.

I immersed myself in Japanese ghost stories, or at least those that had been transported to the West by Lafcadio Hearn. Hearn was a problematic source of ghost stories since in disseminating Japanese folklore to the West he seems to have invented some of his stories. Nevertheless, in pursuit of his tales, I ventured into the book stacks of the University of Iowa Main Library, waving my arms over my head so that movement sensors would kick the lights on. It was a little frightening in the crepuscular stacks, where only an occasional student worker broke the solitude, and she was listening to her iPod and so couldn't be counted on to hear someone if that someone screamed. Undeterred, I proceeded to the shelving unit where could be found the *kaidan* (ghost stories) of Lafcadio Hearn.

Hearn's *In Ghostly Japan*, published in 1899 by Little, Brown, and Company, is a beautiful volume, its blue cloth binding festooned with cherry blossoms, its pages deckled. I ran my eye down the table of contents as muffled music leaked from the student's earbuds in the next aisle: Adele. In "Furisodé," Hearn conveys the story of a long-sleeved kimono said to have caused the Great Fire of Meireki, a blaze that in 1657 destroyed more than half of the city now known as Tokyo. In Hearn's telling, the kimono was modeled after one worn by a handsome stranger with whom a young girl becomes smitten. "She would suspend it in her room, and try to imagine the form of her unknown beloved within it," Hearn writes.[36] After her death, the kimono is worn by three subsequent girls, each of whom sickens and dies. And when an attempt is made to burn the robe, first a temple and then an entire city is set afire. Hearn also relays the story of a ghost divorcée whose husband rides her corpse, but the kimono tale, recounting one of the greatest disasters in Japanese history, seemed to have the greater cultural resonance. Unfortunately, it did nothing to clarify my ghost speculation, and seemed, rather, to be leading me on a kimono chase.

"I think I'm just flailing around," I complained to my husband over grapefruit gimlets at an Iowa City restaurant that was really quite as good as anyplace we'd eaten in Tokyo, we told ourselves. "Mizumura's ghost child seems so much more cheerful than Catherine's ghost. She has koi fish on her kimono, for Pete's sake." I recalled for a passing moment the overfed koi that swam under a footbridge near where we lived in Kodaira. I missed Japan.

"I spent the whole afternoon reading Hearn's 'The Story of the Futon of Tottori' and 'The Story of a Tengu,' but I'm not sure Hearn is a good source of Japanese ghost story information." I eyed the last piece of tempura perch on the plate we were sharing. "Before he went to Japan, he wrote about murders in Cincinnati; and when he went to Japan, he changed his name to Koizumi Yakumo and started wearing a kimono." "What's a tengu?" asked my husband, dipping the perch in aoili. I looked sadly at the empty plate, and then, without preamble, unspooled Mizumura's plotline.

"The novel is set during the Obon festival, and before Yusuke sees the ghost, Fumiko unstitches a child's kimono that has koi swimming across the fabric like giant goldfish."

"Who is Fumiko?" my husband asked.

"She's Nelly Dean," I said, carrying on. "And Heathcliff is Taro, a poor orphan who lives in a shack behind the home of Yoko—that's Catherine. Taro was born in Manchuria to a Japanese woman who was raped by a Chinese bandit. Yoko is a member of the Saegusa family; she's only allowed to play with him because she's being raised by her grandmother, a former geisha, and by Fumiko."

"Nelly Dean," said my husband, pleased with himself. The bartender tallied our bill and wiped the rings left by our water glasses. I felt pressure to move things along.

"Yoko and Taro are separated when Yoko's family moves to Hokkaido, but they communicate secretly and have a secret rendezvous in Oiwake. Then Taro leaves Japan to seek his fortune in the United States. He meets Minae on Long Island, where she's moved with her family from Japan."

"Minae? The author?" my husband asked.

"No, the narrator who has the same name and background as the author. While Taro's gone, Yoko marries a son of the Shigemitsu family who own a house next to the Saegusa sisters' summer home in Karuizawa—you know, the two houses are kind of like Wuthering Heights and Thrushcross Grange. Taro becomes a venture capitalist and gets rich; he secretly acquires the Saegusa house—like Heathcliff taking over Wuthering Heights from Hindley."

"What happens to Fumiko?" asked my husband. We put on our coats as another couple hovered near our bar stools.

"I can't tell you; it would ruin the surprise."

In the Long Island frame story of *A True Novel*, a Japanese woman visits America and stays with the family of her father's business associate, Mr. Goldberg. Mizumura captures the exaltedness of Miss Sone's expectations by describing her luggage.

Though she only planned to stay three weeks in the States, she brought with her two large suitcases, containing not only [a] magnificent set of kimono and obi . . . but the entire assortment of precious and cumbersome items required to get dressed in a *furisode* [formal kimono]: a braided cord to tighten and support the obi and a scarflike piece of material to adorn it; a double-layered under-kimono; two rolls of under-obi and several strings to hold the kimono and the under-kimono in place; a pair of white *tabi* [with split toe] socks; and matching gold purse and sandals—all in silk except the fine cotton *tabi*.

(30–31)

One weekend, Minae's mother receives a telephone distress call from Miss Sone, and they go and pick her up at the home of Mr. Goldberg. Minae recalls, "But as soon as we were in the car and on our way, out poured a torrent of words describing the misfortunes that had befallen her in the past week" (27). In exchange for the many kindnesses her father had shown the Goldbergs in Japan—inviting them to see chorus girls dance at the Mikado in Tokyo, and to see geishas sing at the Ichiriki in Kyoto—the Goldbergs treat Miss Sone as a subaltern, asking her to clean the house and do the laundry. The elaborate kimonos, one of which she leaves behind for Minae and her sister, come to evoke cultural disconnection. Even if Miss Sone had been treated by the Goldbergs in the manner she expected, an extravagant kimono would have been out of place, as it will continue to be in the Mizumura household. Minae describes the gift kimono, with its "long-hanging sleeves for unmarried girls," as being "one so expensive [her] mother would never have dreamed of buying it for her daughters" (29). It's hard to imagine a 1960s Long Island social event at which a kimono would serve as suitable attire.

Still a kimono plays a key role in the fantasy life Minae creates to escape her life on Long Island. She romanticizes literary travelers, particularly the heroine of Arishima Takeo's *A Certain Woman*, a novel that reworks Tolstoy's *Anna Karenina* in a Japanese setting. "Having read it over and over again," Minae says, "I dreamed of growing up to become someone like its heroine, a woman named Yoko traveling alone on a voyage across the Pacific. I would dress in an elegant kimono, and my sudden but carefully timed entrance into the ship's dining room would make everyone turn to admire me" (20–21). We might regard Mizumura's Miss Sone as a rewriting of Arishima's Yoko, a rewriting which forecasts the future that may lay in store for a Yoko who stays in America rather than having a florid affair with a ship's purser and returning to Japan. When Arishima's Yoko packs for her voyage to America, she chooses a set of "best" kimonos to suit each of the four seasons, and once on board she deploys kimonos like artillery. In one scene, the eyes of the ship's doctor are drawn irresistibly to Yoko "in the dazzlingly brilliant kimono she had chosen for the occasion."[37] But in America, Miss Sone's kimono and its accouterments—cords, rolls, strings, *tabi* socks—lose their magic.

Time passed. I met up with Mizumura for the second time in 2014 at a French restaurant on an upper floor of a large department store in Shinjuku station. The dining room was packed with women of a certain age eating *cotes de porc* and choosing tiny beakers of mousse from dessert trays, all the while speaking animated Japanese. I had asked Mizumura to bring family photos and she complied; we leaned over the photograph of a small girl wearing a kimono and grasping a fan in her fist. The tiny geisha gazing up at me from the bistro table was Mizumura's step-grandmother, one of the models for Mrs. Utagawa, Yoko's grandmother in *A True Novel*. "My real grandmother died from the Spanish flu," Mizumura recalled.[38] "My grandfather's concubine then became his real legitimate wife. This is her as a little geisha; she was in training" (fig. 6).

In another photo, the child Mizumura danced in the yard of a house in Japan with her sister and mother (fig. 7). Her mother wears a kimono while the sisters wear mohair cardigans their father brought back from a business trip to New York. As Mizumura and I flipped through the photos, I watched her mother transform from a traditional Japanese woman to a modern American woman. In one photo, she stood in front of the Unisphere, a steel representation of the earth constructed to evoke global interdependence at the 1964 New York World's Fair (fig. 8). "My mother only wore kimonos, and suddenly she was wearing American styles," said Mizumura as we gazed at the slim woman wearing a polka-dot sheath dress and mod sunglasses.

In my view Mizumura was a gifted polyglot who could move comfortably from Japanese to English to French, who had early on achieved the linguistic mastery to which I aspired. But Mizumura viewed herself as a failed English learner. "I never learned anything—it was just noise, total noise," she said of her first years in the United States. "I was totally cut off from the English world; I just kept reading, reading, reading [Japanese novels]," she recalled. "The school was kind enough to provide me with a tutor—it was a very rich school; Great Neck was part of the Gold Coast—but I don't think it helped a lot." A waitperson described our next course options; I ordered fish. "My father had this conception of children that they would pick up languages easily," Mizumura said. "But we had

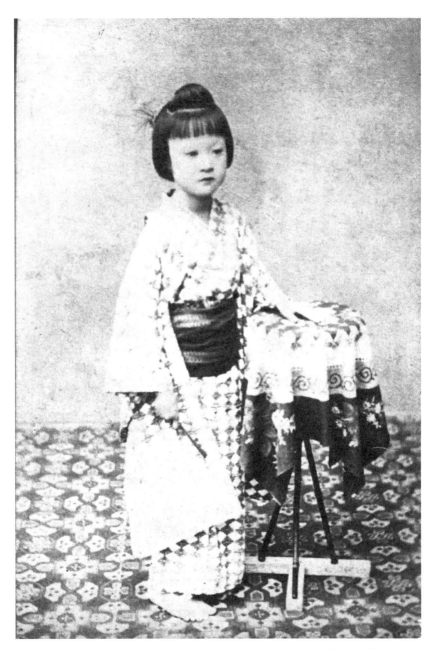

Fig. 6. Mizumura Tomi, the second wife of Mizumura Minae's grandfather, as a child. Courtesy of Mizumura Minae, © Mizumura Minae.

Fig. 7. Mizumura Minae as a child in Japan with her mother Mizumura Setsuko and her sister Mizumura Kanae. Courtesy of Mizumura Minae, © Mizumura Minae.

Fig. 8. Mizumura Setsuko (Mizumura Minae's mother) in front of the Unisphere at the 1964 World's Fair. Courtesy of Mizumura Minae, © Mizumura Minae.

reached an age at which it's very difficult to pick up languages. My father was a maverick; he decided to choose a place to live where there were no Japanese. The junior high newspaper said that we were the first Japanese people to go there." As I chose a fork, my perception of Mizumura shifted slightly, tumblers sliding into new slots.

I asked Mizumura about her new novel, *Haha no isan: shinbun shōsetsu* (*Inheritance from Mother*), which she published serially in the *Yomiuri Shimbun*, and she recalled the most popular newspaper novel in Japanese history, *Konjiki yasha* (*The Gold Demon*), a novel that, because it bears a resemblance to *Wuthering Heights* (orphan boy, thwarted love story), I already knew.[39] When I told Mizumura that I'd read *Konjiki yasha* in the terrible English translation of A. and M. Lloyd, she laughed and said that the original story unfolds in a way that is too sentimental, and then recalled a long description of a kimono that could not be translated into English because English lacks the specialized vocabulary necessary to describe kimono silk. "Also the hairdo," Mizumura continued cheerfully— English didn't have words for that either. I hadn't considered there might be passages of *Konjiki yasha* that defied translation, bulwarks of Japanese that even a reputable translator couldn't breach. No matter how elaborate the kimono fabric, shouldn't one be able to describe it in English?

Fumbling around in my bag, I pulled out a Japanese edition of *Wuthering Heights*, the tenth volume in the *Shōjo sekai bungaku zenshū* (Girls' library of world literature), issued in the 1960s, and the very book, I hoped, that Mizumura referenced in *A True Novel*.

"Is this the *Wuthering Heights* edition you read when you were a child?" I asked.

The book was encased in tissue paper that protected the cardboard book case that protected the book. On the book's jacket a girl wearing a veiled hat attached by a chinstrap was stroking a lyre. As Mizumura turned the volume over in her hands, I spoke admiringly of girls' world literature collections, the ambitiousness of their offerings, the lack of equivalent girls' collections in the United States.

"This is a past thing," Mizumura said sadly. "The craze for Western literature started before World War II and continued until the 1960s. Then as Japan got richer, there was less and less aspiration, less and less desire, because the quality of life had improved tremendously." "A few years ago the box-office sales of Japanese movies exceeded that of foreign movies," she said. "It was unthinkable for my parents' generation. As a child when I went to see a movie, it was always a foreign movie. If you were a middle-class person you always saw foreign movies." I refurled the children's book and moved it to the edge of the table as we paused to make selections from a tray of bijou desserts.

"I gave a little talk in Iowa—I think it was a coffee shop bookstore."

"Prairie Lights!" I exclaimed.

"I was talking about *Honkaku shōsetsu*, and one of the audience members asked if Japanese people would be aware of the existence of *Wuthering Heights*, and an American professor who teaches Japanese literature said, 'They would be more likely than Americans to know about *Wuthering Heights*.'"

"My *True Novel* was recommended by a website called *Three Percent*. Three percent connotes the amount of translated literature that makes up literature published in America. . . . Incredible!"

In *The Fall of Language in the Age of English*, Mizumura writes that translations of Western works end up with a marked style that is distinct from that of works written in Japanese. Japanese readers instantly recognize when they are reading a translation, and easily adjust. "They tend to shift modes of reading, like a driver shifting gears at the wheel of a car," Mizumura writes.[40] During our encounter at the French restaurant, she talked about American editors' intolerance for anything that might be strange or off-putting to readers, their lack of confidence that American readers could inhabit the same kind of transitional space regularly occupied by Japanese readers of Western literary works, a space in which Japanese readers are aware of the oddity of what they are reading, but undeterred by this awareness. Mizumura believed that readers of works translated into English should be expected to carry out the same cognitive shift, that her novel should retain a sense of strangeness when carried over into English. I thought about Japanese readers down-shifting as they confronted the first pages of foreign literary works, while American readers insisted on a smooth frictionless reading experience, unhappy with any grinding between gears.

As the restaurant lunch crowd thinned out, Mizumura brought up the films of Ozu Yasujirō and Kurosawa Akira. "Kurosawa is more translatable," she said. "Ozu is difficult for young people and foreigners to appreciate. But the little details [in his films] tell so much about social structure and social hierarchy—the way people wear kimono reveals so much." Then leaving Ozu's elderly kimono-wearers behind, she returned to the Brontës, calling *Jane Eyre* untranslatable because there is no such thing as a governess in Japan. "You can't change her into a maid; she has to be a governess," Mizumura firmly stated.

When Mizumura published her version of *Wuthering Heights*, she at first included a version of Catherine's kitchen speech, but finally deleted the "I *am* Heathcliff" line, partly because it doesn't sound right in Japanese. "I wanted my book to sound as Japanese as possible," she said. "I'm on the difficult side as a Japanese writer—I use many quaint expressions that young people may not know." In the same way, she wanted the translation of her novel to read *like* a translation of a Japanese work, and, in this manner, to broaden English-speakers' perception of what a novel could be, or perhaps to underscore the differences between English and Japanese.

In the final pages of *A True Novel*, Yusuke revisits the cottage where he once encountered the ghost girl, and finds Taro swinging a hammer over a large cloth, crushing the cremated remains of Yoko and her husband. Fumiko divides the ashes into two containers, the first a little red dish into which she scoops the ashes of Yoko, the second a vase in which she mingles the ashes of Yoko and her husband. Before leaving to take the mixed ashes to a scattering ceremony in Karuizawa, Fumiko gives Taro the red bowl containing Yoko's ashes. As Yusuke watches, Taro "hurl[s] the contents of the bowl at the pale moon with all his might," and "the dust of powdered bones" comes drifting down (849). Could this be Mizumura's version of the "I *am* Heathcliff," moment? I wondered. Was Taro, in a fashion, saying, "I am Yoko," attempting to become one with the dead woman? Or was I imposing the English sentence on a scene that could stand on its own, that could invoke meanings beyond those of Brontë? In *Wuthering Heights*, Heathcliff enlists a sexton's assistance in removing the lid of Catherine's coffin, and strikes one side loose so that, when his corpse is buried next to hers, their dust will mingle (288).[41] In *A True Novel*, Yoko doesn't insist that she is Taro, nor does Taro claim that he is Yoko, and yet they are momentarily joined in the drift of the dead woman's ashes. "As the fine white dust covered him from the head down, he never stirred," Mizumura writes, her Heathcliff poised between the living and the dead (850).

CHAPTER FIVE

As for Me, I Am Heathcliff

A year has gone by
  And still
  I've not yet learned
My new master's name.
  —Raizan (trans. Peter Beilenson and Harry Behn)

It was November when I received the letter from Ichihara Junko, the illustrator of Tamura Taeko's translation of *Wuthering Heights*.[1] Tamura and Ichihara's edition of *Wuthering Heights*, which is the size of an American composition book, comes enfolded in a bright orange dust jacket stamped with a block print of a paisley-shaped flower. Emily Brontë's most famous line—"I *am* Heathcliff—he's always, always in my mind"—is inscribed in a curve of the flower's stem.[2] On the title page, an image of a wintry landscape: clouds drift across the sky, a solitary tree bends in the wind, and a lone house perches on a distant hill. "One may guess the power of the north wind, blowing over the edge, by the excessive slant of a few stunted firs at the end of the house," Lockwood says upon arriving at Wuthering Heights (4). Ichihara's illustration captures this wintry tumult.

A few years before, I had met Tamura and Ichihara in a city near Osaka. Longtime friends, they had collaborated on several projects, and that day they were collaborating on showing American visitors a wonderful time. We ate lunch at an elegant restaurant where waitresses served course after course of *kisetsu gentei* (season restriction, that is to say, seasonal menu) food presented on tiny plates garnished with leaves. We were joined by the students in Ichihara's *inkoku* (seal engraving) class. From the restaurant we proceeded by car to Ichihara's home, where we talked about *Wuthering Heights* while Ichihara's students carved stones in an adjoining room. I had planned to hire an interpreter for the visit, but a scheduling conflict laid waste this plan, so instead I brought along my older daughter. Between

Tamura's English and my daughter's Japanese and everyone's best efforts to communicate—the *inkoku* students showed off their work in progress— the visit went well. At the end of the day, my daughter and I took turns photographing Tamura, Ichihara, and Ichihara's elderly mother—also a Brontë fan—and the women in Ichihara's class, before heading home with a bag full of *Wuthering Heights*–related materials, including gift T-shirts stamped with Ichihara's book cover artwork: the paisley-shaped flower and the famous Brontë line.

I read Ichihara's letter with the aid of my Japanese tutor, who deci- phered the beautiful Japanese handwriting. My tutor had once been my second-year Japanese teacher; now, on every other Sunday afternoon, she helped me practice conversational Japanese, and she helped my younger daughter read a Japanese translation of Laura Ingalls Wilder's *Little House in the Big Woods*, borrowed from the Iowa City Public Library.[3] The cold in Iowa City was already intense. "The earth was hard with a black frost, and the air made me shiver through every limb," says Lockwood of his journey to Wuthering Heights (9). In our backyard, squirrels dug holes in the cold ground, then darted across the yard, their jaws distended by black walnuts. Sometimes the squirrels hid nuts inside the chicken coop, but now the coop doors were locked, and the huddled chickens, their heads retracted, looked like feather poufs.

My tutor's face grew serious as she scanned Ichihara's letter. She waited patiently as I worked out the first sentence, in which Ichihara apologized for taking so long to respond to a letter I'd written to her five months before, a year after my encounter with Tamura and Ichihara, and many months after Ichihara had sent me a New Year's greeting, to which it had taken me weeks to respond. My correspondence with Ichihara had, up until this point, proceeded in the stately manner of nineteenth-century epistolary correspondence; our letters may as well have been conveyed by steamship.

I moved on to the next sentence. "I think she is sending some bad news," my tutor said gently. *More than anything, I have sad news.*[4] I looked up from the flurry of kanji handwritten across the page. "I think her hus- band may have died," I said, recalling that Ichihara's husband had been unwell. My tutor nodded. *Forty days after you came to Kadoma, my hus- band died*, Ichihara wrote. I recalled the cheery New Year's card I'd sent the year before during, I now realized, the aftermath of her husband's death. In Japan, you do not send *nengajō* (New Year's cards) to people who have suffered a loss. "It was not unexpected," I said to my tutor, who gently replied, "I think there is more bad news."

I thought fleetingly of Ichihara's elderly mother, but in the letter Ichihara had already mentioned that she and her mother had moved to a new home. That left only one person about whom she could report sad news. "It's Tamura-sensei, isn't it?" I asked my tutor. She nodded. "Oh noooo," I moaned as my tutor nodded gravely. "She hasn't died, has she?" My tutor looked sympathetic as I explained why Tamura could not have died. "She was so kind to us," I said, as if exceptionally kind people were granted immortal life.

I turned back to Ichihara's letter. *Even now it seems like a smiling Tamura-sensei might show up before us.* Yes, Tamura was always smiling, and she'd passed away before I'd had a chance to read the bounty of *Wuthering Heights*–related materials that she'd transported in a wheeled suitcase to Ichihara's house and handed over to me in a shopping bag. The happy hodgepodge of Japanese Brontë swag that I had hauled through Narita Airport and trundled up the steps to my house, and stowed in a filing cabinet, now assumed a mournful solemnity. Tamura had died. The word for "to die" in Japanese (*naku naru*), when written with a different kanji, can mean "to disappear" or "to be lost" or "to be missing." Tamura had disappeared before I'd had a chance to use the *Wuthering Heights* riches she'd given me, or to achieve a level of Japanese proficiency that would allow me to reread on my own the long polite e-mail messages she'd written in advance of our visit.

My tutor patiently waited for me to continue reading. *Without waiting for Pascoe-sensei's book completion, she passed away,* I translated, maintaining the Japanese tendency to frontload modifying phrases. My younger daughter entered the room, prepared to read her biweekly Japanese installment of *Little House in the Big Woods*, in which Laura and her family live in a log house in Wisconsin. I held her off, my tutor waiting for me to regain my place in the letter. *Without waiting for Pascoe-sensei's book completion, Tamura-san passed away,* I read. *It's too bad,* Ichihara went on, *probably from heaven she's waiting for it.* Probably in heaven Tamura had better things to do, I thought darkly, feeling stricken that I had not finished my book before she'd died suddenly, and to her friends' surprise, of cancer. Ichihara's letter continued, *Certainly, I, too, from my heart, am waiting for it.*

Time was passing. I had led Tamura and Ichihara to expect that I would soon complete my study of Japanese versions of *Wuthering Heights* and send them copies. I had imagined wrapping the books carefully, first in hand-printed wrapping paper and then in white butcher paper, so that they looked like the New Year's gift I'd once received, a box of Yokohama mille feuilles, wrapped first in a map of Yokohama, and then in brown paper. I had pleasurably pondered whether to send the book packages by mail, after bestrewing them with special issue stamps at the post office, or to deliver them in person after the transmission of long difficult-to-write messages in which I suggested assignation sites.

"What is 'head cheese'?" my tutor asked. She and my daughter had started reading. In *Little House*, winter was coming. Pa and Ma and Laura and Mary smoked venison and braided onions as the wind howled outside with a cold and lonesome sound.

I went upstairs to my study, the dog traipsing after me. As he settled himself at my feet, I examined the Japanese stamps on Ichihara's envelope. One had a branch of pine needles tipped with snow; another showed Mount Fuji in a storm. I peered at the light snow dusting the pine branch on Ichihara's stamp, and then looked out the window. Brown leaves still clung to the maple tree in front of my house; a bag of rock salt stood sentry on a neighbor's porch.

Sifting through the papers and books that Tamura had gathered, I came across Brontë lecture handouts, A4-size pages on which were reproduced photos of griffins, Doric columns, and Dorset buttons. Tamura's Brontë stash included booklets commemorating Brontë-related trips upon which she had embarked with members of the Japanese Brontë Society. One contained a photo of Tamura waving jauntily from atop a large chair-shaped rock, the caption reading "sitting on Brontë chair." Tamura had also offered me a Japanese DVD of the 1939 Wyler film, and, even though I already owned a copy of the same DVD, I'd accepted the offer because the shrink-wrapping on Tamura's DVD had some Japanese writing that I hoped would provide a quote-worthy comment. I lingered over a copy of E. M. Attwood's abridged and simplified Graded Reader Edition of *Wuthering Heights* that had been read by the students in a class Tamura taught at the Yomiuri Cultural Center, and I paged through a *Wuthering Heights* translation those students had compiled, a small book on whose purple cover a girl and a boy rode horses across a stained-glass moor.[5] One student in Tamura's class had tackled the sentence in which Catherine describes her love for Heathcliff, saying, "He's more myself than I am." In the student's Japanese, as I translated it, the sentence read, "Not less than me, me he is."

I lingered over Tamura and Ichihara's edition of *Wuthering Heights*, on the front cover of which, Catherine's famous line—"I *am* Heathcliff—he's always, always in my mind"—was partly concealed by a paper advertisement wrapped around the bottom third of the book, an *obikōkoku*, or "kimono sash advertisement." I translated the advertising text on the book's obi. "Wandering around in England's Yorkshire wilderness excessive two people love story," the advertisement sort of said. Tamura and Ichihara's edition was marketed as an easy-to-read version of *Wuthering Heights*. The back of the advertising sash said something about fascinating and ample scenes having been extracted.

Also printed on the paper sash was a Japanese translation of Catherine's line. I stared at the kanji for a few minutes, thinking of Tamura, a thin woman who wore frameless glasses and a pleasant expression. When we'd last spoken, she had been working on a little-known Charlotte Brontë story, one that had never been translated into Japanese. "It's not perfect, I think, but it's a little interesting. It lets us know how she felt at a very young age." When I asked when the translation would be published, Tamura laughed and said, "Before I die!" and then replied more soberly, "Maybe in one or two years."[6] Time had passed quickly. Tamura had died.

A few weeks later, I was sitting in an Iowa City bar with a Japanese friend when she mentioned a television drama based on *Wuthering Heights*. The bar was a dive hung with fading beer posters. My friend pulled out her cell phone so that she could look up the broadcast dates for *Ai no arashi* (Storm of love) and its sequel, *Shin ai no arashi* (New storm of love).[7] "I think it was the 1970s or 1980s," she said, sipping the gimlet she had unfortunately followed my lead in ordering; it wasn't the kind of place where one ordered cocktails. Three men on barstools stared at a TV screen, letting out occasional sports-related whoops. How could I have missed a major *Wuthering Heights* adaptation, which, as it turned out (we finally picked up a wireless connection) had extended to sixty-nine episodes in the mid-1980s and been replicated in a 2002 remake? Someone pumped quarters into the bar's jukebox, and a Taylor Swift song started playing. My friend and I went back to discussing her tango class.

Days passed. I asked a librarian to purchase *Ai no arashi* and *Shin ai no arashi*, and, after the DVDs were cataloged, I sat before an all-zone DVD player, watching and taking notes. During the *Ai no arashi* credits, the characters formerly known as Catherine and Heathcliff wander through an orchard of blossoming cherry trees. In early episodes, Hikaru (Catherine) and Takeshi (Heathcliff) nurse a hurt bird back to health, run off together to Yokohama, and wind up at the home of a geisha who is having an affair with Hikaru's father. In *Shin ai no arashi*, Hikaru and Takeshi, played by different actors, act out similar scenes. It's a baby rabbit rather than a bird that they nurse back to health before they run off to Yokohama, stay with the geisha, etc. At the end of each episode of *Ai no arashi* and *Shin ai no arashi* something exciting happens, and the exciting scene is rebroadcast at the beginning of the next episode, a repetition that I appreciated since neither series had subtitles; I'd gather a few more linguistic breadcrumbs on the second go-round. In one episode, Hikaru's mother discovers the geisha in the bathroom where Hikaru's father is soaking in the bath. I studied the pale long-suffering face of Hikaru's mother as she encountered this unpleasant surprise.

Slowly and attentively, over three days, I watched episodes 1 through 12 of *Ai no arashi* and *Shin ai no arashi*. On the fourth day, I started skipping around, jumping ahead to the episodes in which older actors take over the roles of Hikaru (Catherine) and Takeshi (Heathcliff). In the twenty-first episode of *Shin ai no arashi*, Takeshi is bitten by a snake and Hikaru applies a tourniquet. In the twenty-second episode, a doctor who is caring for Takeshi asks who first treated his snakebite, and Hikaru declares that it was she. In the same episode, a man thrusts a bouquet of flowers at Hikaru, but Takeshi runs after him and throws the flowers out. Two episodes later, I figured out that the man's name is Ogara-san, and I gleaned the extent of his malevolence when I watched him savagely chop a bonsai in half. After three days of binge-watching, I returned the stack of DVDs to the circulation desk.

It was dark when I got home from the library. As I walked from the garage to the back door, something large and brown floated from the chicken coop to the trellis—an owl, I realized, as it rose from a tangle of dead raspberry canes.

Inside the house, the kettle was whistling, and I thought of a rare cheerful scene in *Wuthering Heights*, the Christmas Eve on which Nelly sits alone in the kitchen. She says, "I smelt the rich scent of the heating spices; and admired the shining kitchen utensils, the polished clock, decked in holly, the silver mugs ranged on a tray ready to be filled with mulled ale for supper; and, above all, the speckless purity of my particular care— the scoured and well-swept floor" (55). But then she recalls the dead Mr. Earnshaw and his fondness for Heathcliff and, she says, "From singing I changed my mind to crying" (56).

Upstairs, the Tamura archive, piled on top of a file cabinet, confronted me reproachfully as I entered my study. I picked up the Eichosha-Longman Graded Reader edition of *Wuthering Heights*, abridged and simplified by E. M. Attwood. *Wuthering Heights* is a staple of the Japanese English curriculum, I'd discovered. In Japan I often came across student editions of *Wuthering Heights*, for example, an "English Treasury" edition whose publisher had co-opted the script of a 1939 Lux Radio Theater production of *Wuthering Heights*, starring Barbara Stanwyck and Brian Aherne, and packaged it with a CD.[8] I imagined a Japanese student finding it, as I had done, bargain-priced at a Book-Off in Tokyo, and listening to a long-dead Hollywood film vixen speak the lines of a longer-dead British novelist—all in the service of learning English, a diabolical language whose verb tenses are many times more complicated than verb tenses in Japanese. Opening the Eichosha-Longman Graded Reader, I thought of Tamura and her students applying themselves to Brontë's difficult novel.

On the day we visited, Tamura gave my daughter and me a ride from the restaurant to Ichihara's home. When Tamura turned the ignition, an English lesson blared from the car speakers, and as she inched out of the parking space, I felt a swelling of solidarity. Many had been the times when I had listened to Japanese CDs while driving, and seldom had been the times when those CDs, with their slowed-down versions of idiosyncratic Japanese sentences, prepared me to communicate with actual Japanese people. One can't converse with native speakers unless one gets beyond the kind of sentences featured on language CDs, stilted sentences that leave one stranded mid-social interaction, the CD having failed to anticipate which way the conversation will swerve.

A chill wind rattled the windows of my house and I turned over the pages of Tamura's edition of *Wuthering Heights*, examining the illustrations. Ichihara Junko's seal-engraving technique made the pictures look like woodblock prints. In one of Ichihara's most arresting images, Catherine's ghost staggers across the page in a flurry of snow, her hair streaming back as if she is rushing into a headwind (fig. 9). Circlets of snow appear white against the black background that surrounds her figure; black circlets pass across Catherine's white dress. Ichihara reversed foreground and background as she engraved the *inkoku* block so as to have snow swirl against both black and white backdrops. "It's twenty years," moans Catherine's ghost voice. "Twenty years, I've been a waif for twenty years." In Tamura's accompanying translation, Catherine mourns the passage of time in Japanese.

In her edition of *Wuthering Heights*, Tamura juxtaposed passages from Brontë's original English with Japanese translations, and linked the se-

「さまよえるキャサリン」

Fig. 9. Ichihara Junko, *Samayoeru Kyasarin* [Wandering Catherine].
Tamura Taeko, trans. *E to genbun de tanoshimu Wuthering Heights* [Enjoy-
ing *Wuthering Heights* with illustrations and original text], p. 7. Courtesy of
Ichihara Junko, © Ichihara Junko.

lected scenes with brief plot summaries. I found the kitchen scene, which Tamura provided in English, followed by a glossary of words Japanese students might stumble over. She explained the word "degrade" for her students by likening it to *hin'i o sageru* in Japanese, which means Catherine's dignity or elegance would be lowered. In Tamura's translation of the passage, she wrote the phrase *hin'i ga sagatte shimau*, the final *shimau* a Japanese grammar construction used to suggest one is doing something that one shouldn't do, or to express regret for one's action. In Tamura's Japanese version, Catherine not only says she will be degraded by an alliance with Heathcliff, she anticipates with her grammar the regret she will experience if she participates in such an alliance. Tamura guided her Japanese readers through the difficult English; Brontë's line "he staid to hear no farther" led Tamura to elaborate on "farther," explaining how it usually connotes distance or degree, but how in this line it connotes what one usually indicates with the word "further."[9] I was impressed by Tamura's parsing of the word—I could not explain confidently in English the difference between farther and further—but I was also struck by how much effort she'd expended on a word that a native English reader would pass over like a bird flitting over a fence post.

I glanced around my office, at the scattering of *Wuthering Heights*–related manga, light novels, essay collections—only some of which I'd read in fits and starts. Why, I hadn't even read all of the English-language scholarship on the "I *am* Heathcliff" line, I realized, pulling a battered file folder from where it was wedged (how come? was there no method to my archive?) between folders dedicated to *Wuthering Heights* film versions and Brontë-influenced fashion references. The folder contained a sheaf of scholarly articles and chapters in which critics discuss Catherine's claim to be one with Heathcliff: Terry Eagleton calling "[t]he loving equality between Catherine and Heathcliff . . . a paradigm of human possibilities";[10] Graeme Tytler warning that identification with others is often a form of domination;[11] Daniel Cottom noting that "when Catherine is proclaiming her identification with Heathcliff . . . he is stealing away";[12] John Allen Stevenson suggesting that Heathcliff is "uniquely available to everyone else's power of projection."[13]

When Catherine claims she's Heathcliff, she aspires to being foreign to herself, to escaping the constricting bounds of her own subjectivity. It is not easy being Catherine—why *wouldn't* she want to be Heathcliff, who has the option of setting out on his own? He takes off from home as clouds appear inclined to thunder, and as his absence gets marked, a storm comes "rattling over the Heights in full fury" (85). No one knows where Heathcliff spends his three-year absence from the Heights, but the possibilities are enticing; Lockwood conjectures that he may have finished his education on the Continent or escaped to America, or embarked on a career as a highwayman (92). Catherine sets out in search of Heathcliff, but, of course, she has to return to the Heights, where she gets rebuked by Nelly for "standing bonnetless and shawlless to catch as much water as she could with her hair and clothes," and where she lapses into delirium (85). Heathcliff takes his strong feelings on the road; Catherine's passions collapse inward, manifesting themselves in a disease toxic enough to kill Edgar's mother when she invites Catherine to convalesce at Thrushcross Grange.

The window rattled; a lady bug husk blew across my desk. I could see Tamura's edition of *Wuthering Heights* slumped on my bookcase, its cheerful orange dust jacket stamped with the paisley-shaped flower and Catherine's line. Over my desk, three sumo wrestlers gazed down from the curling pages of a Japanese wall calendar. I thought of how Muraoka Hanako, the Japanese translator of *Anne of Green Gables*, rescued her precious manuscript from the firebombing of Tokyo. If my house were under siege, I would maybe rescue the dog. My book manuscript existed in so many forms, in e-mail attachments and on thumb drives and in spiral bound print-outs, it could never be destroyed.

All the years I had been working on my study of Japanese versions of *Wuthering Heights* I'd insisted that I wasn't writing about translation— mine was a study of *adaptations*, not translations, I stoutly maintained when people asked a translation question, inquiring, for example, how the servant Joseph's Yorkshire dialect gets translated into Japanese. One difficulty of translating *Wuthering Heights*, or so I'd been told, lay in the many Christian references that don't have equivalents in Japanese—wait! that was another topic I'd bracketed; I wasn't writing about *translation*. But now I imagined the ghost of Tamura-sensei looking down on me from heaven, or from whatever spiritual realm Japanese ghosts inhabit, and questioning my resolve. She had applied herself seriously to understanding Brontë novels and to making them more comprehensible to others. She had striven to master English, and she had worked to make sense of Brontë's difficult sentences.

By contrast, I had still not attended with sufficient care to what was arguably the *yōten* or gist of the novel, and the repeating refrain of my research. Catherine's "I *am* Heathcliff" line was the most important line for my study of Japanese versions of *Wuthering Heights,* since embedded in that line is a longing to be someone else, to transcend the boundaries of subjectivity and communicate fully with someone unlike oneself— which is what foreign language-learners try to do.[14] I wanted to believe that there was some continuity between my original project (to master *Wuthering Heights*) and my ultimate project (to master Japanese versions of *Wuthering Heights*), that no matter how Japanese writers and artists altered *Wuthering Heights,* that Catherine's line would serve as a signpost, kind of like the lime-daubed stones that Lockwood hopes will guide him when he returns to Thrushcross Grange after dark (31). But when Lockwood actually sets out, he realizes that a wet fall has confounded the deep swamps with the firmer path, and he has to rely on Heathcliff to find his way.

I, too, needed a guide, I thought, remembering a book I'd brought back from Japan, isolating it from Japanese gummy candy in my carry-on bag: Kobashi Sumio's *Arashi ga oka no nihongo hyōgen* (*Wuthering Heights* in Japanese expression).[15] I retrieved the Kobashi volume from a bookcase where it had gotten hidden behind two *meishi* wallets, portfolios holding the business cards of every Japanese person I'd ever met. In the same bookcase, I came across the Japanese *Little House in the Big Woods*: overdue!

Why Kobashi Sumio had taken such an interest in *Wuthering Heights* was not immediately apparent from his book, which was bound in navy with stiff brown end papers imprinted with a bamboo weave. It commences with an introduction, followed by a "reference catalog," containing a guide to Brontë's novel (publication data, plot summary, character listing, chronological list of events, variant Japanese spellings of Brontë's characters, list of Japanese translations, list of Kobashi-designated translator abbreviations). The reference catalog makes clear that Kobashi set about his book-writing task in a methodical and comprehensive manner. Kobashi was just the kind of single-minded scholar I thought I wanted to become when I set out to master *Wuthering Heights.* I would leave no sentence unexamined, I thought, when I carried *Wuthering Heights* with me to Japan. But when I started hauling *Wuthering Heights* all over Tokyo, and when I started hunting down Japanese versions in bookstores, and especially when I started trying to learn Japanese, my mind kept wandering. Kobashi, by contrast, maintained a clear sense of what he set out to do; he used *Wuthering Heights* as a means of studying grammatical structures and comparing translations. I imagined him pleasurably lining up his library of *Wuthering Heights* translations, and applying himself carefully to the same sentence in multiple versions.

I pondered the pages of Kobashi Sumio's book, which I'd discovered at the Waseda University library, but had been unable to find by means of online book purveyors. My copy had come from the author, whom I had queried by letter. "I wrote it in memory of my long life as an English teacher," Kobashi wrote in reply.[16] "The book is not an academic one and could not find a formal publishing company in my district. So, I published it privately, and . . . sent some to the University Library." Kobashi went on to say, "I shall be happy if this little book can be any help to you, a professor from a foreign country."

Kobashi had first read *Wuthering Heights* as a university student in an English version with notes in Japanese. "Having read it through, I bought the Japanese version. And with it at hand, I read it again and again."[17] Kobashi went on to recall, "I presented a short report on WH as an assignment. You know 'What one likes, one will do well.'" Kobashi went on to speak more generally about the status of *Wuthering Heights* in Japan, noting that it had been translated by more than 10 scholars, and some versions had been published again and again, and that many Japanese people are familiar with the Japanese title, "an easy and catchy Japanese name." Kobashi explained that he had written his book "to let the teachers and the students as well as the readers know that there are many Japanese expressions against one English word or sentence," before revealing that he would soon be 83 years old. "Please forgive me for my poor English," he wrote at the close of his well-written letter.

I began to translate the titles of the twenty-one sub-headings that make up Kobashi's third section, entitled "Translation Comparison." The headings and sub-headings were categorized according to sorting criteria I did not entirely understand. There were categories for sentences containing adverbial clauses, for exclamatory expressions, and for a mysterious something that I translated as "semi-verb." There was a category for long sentences and another for short sentences, as well as a category for sentences containing dialect and another for sentences containing inanimate subjects, including this one: "On that bleak hill top the earth was hard with a black frost and the air made me shiver through every limb." Kobashi had underlined "the air," the inanimate subject, I supposed, that was the subject of his interest.

Peeking ahead, I noticed that category number 20 was reserved for "mistranslation," but I stopped myself from jumping ahead to this more exciting-sounding heading, and settled down to deciphering the array of translations arranged beneath Kobashi's first selection, a sentence chosen because it included relative pronouns. Kobashi's first sentence selection was drawn from the second, more sluggish half of Brontë's novel, the half that many Japanese versions dispense with entirely in a manner of which I did not entirely disapprove. The sentence was one in which the younger Catherine discovers that someone has absconded with the stash of letters she's received from Linton Heathcliff. Kobashi transcribed,

> Never did any bird flying back to a plundered nest <u>which</u> it had left brim-ful of chirping young ones, express more complete despair in its anguished cries and fluttering, than she by her single "Oh!" and the change <u>that</u> transfigured her late happy countenance. (12)

After printing Brontë's sentence about the aggrieved second Catherine, Kobashi features four translations of the chirping bird sentence, translations ranging from Tanaka Seijirō's 1953 translation to Kōnosu Yukiko's 2003 translation.[18] I sat up a little straighter when I noted the inclusion of Kōnosu, with whom I'd had a brief encounter. I had asked Kōnosu to comment on her translation of Catherine's "I *am* Heathcliff" line. "Every previous translator before me," Kōnosu said, "translated it as 'I am Heathcliff.' That is the right way and precise way in English and Japanese."[19] "In a way, my translation is very risky," she laughed. "It easily can be exposed to criticism, but I decided to do it. . . . 'I am Heathcliff' is a curious expression, and its strangeness is important." I'd spent a memorable evening at a wine restaurant with Kōnosu, along with her editor and a Japanese novelist. At one point Kōnosu's editor, referencing the many Japanese versions of *Wuthering Heights*, said, "There is a version for children, for teenagers, for adults." Kōnosu added, "It's an advantage for us, because we can translate and remake it, but in the English language countries, it can't be done. You have only the original."[20] "We have only the original," I muttered to myself, repeating the sentence over and over like a Zen koan.

I closed my copy of Kobashi's book, with its array of Brontë sentences, each with its varied translations. Focus! I said to myself. I knew what I had to do, and Kobashi couldn't do it for me. I might not ever be able to read all the *Wuthering Heights* translations, but I could at least apply myself to the key sentence in Catherine's kitchen speech. I could try to understand how one Brontë line has gotten remade in Japan.

No sentence in *Wuthering Heights* dramatizes the difficulty of translation better than "I *am* Heathcliff," which vexes Japanese translators because of several key features of the Japanese language. In the English language, pronouns are commonplace—English speakers sprinkle "I" and "you" into conversations like salt on popcorn. But Japanese people often use honorifics or family position names to bypass the use of pronouns. When a woman checking out of a hotel accidentally leaves her wallet at the reception desk, it doesn't seem strange (or at least not to Japanese people) that the desk clerk, as he runs after her, calls, *Onē-sama, onē-sama*, or "Older sister, older sister." It's more polite to call someone older sister who is not your older sister than it is to call her "you." And when talking about one's self in Japanese, one avoids using the Japanese equivalent of "I" (*watashi*) whenever possible. Beginning students of Japanese use *watashi* indiscriminately in their stilted conversations ("I am a student," "I like sushi," "I study Japanese"), but when they do so, they draw too much attention to their "I-ness." They are actually saying something like: "As for me, I am a student," "As for me, I like sushi," "As for me, I study Japanese."

In most speaking situations, what or whom one is talking about is easily apparent. Occasionally, however, the Japanese eschewal of pronouns leads to confusion. For example, I once inquired after the children of a Japanese acquaintance, carefully not using *anata*, or "your," and so saying, "Children, how are they?" My interlocutor put her forefinger on her nose, in the Japanese version of pointing at oneself, so that she could clarify whether I was asking about her children or about children in general. In that pronoun-avoidant circumstance, I should have said, *Kurosawa-san no oko-san wa dōdesuka?* ("Ms. Kurosawa's children, how are they?").

Because of these pronoun complexities, it's difficult for Catherine to say that she is Heathcliff in Japanese. If she goes without a pronoun, she's merely saying "Heathcliff is," and it will not be clear she is talking about herself. But if she uses a pronoun, she says, "As for *me*, I am Heathcliff," shifting emphasis to herself from the verb. And that's only part of the problem. No single word in Japanese is equivalent to the English "I." Japanese people choose from a variety of pronominal options when talking about themselves. Of the many Japanese "I" variants, the novelist Mizumura Minae writes, "Each connotes a varying degree of culture (or its lack), urbanity and rusticity, femininity and masculinity, or even pompousness and humbleness. . . . And this floating 'I' renders impossible the notion of universal subjectivity implied in the 'I' of the European languages."[21] The nuances of the Japanese "I" spark debates among Japanese readers. I once listened as two scholars discussed how their reading of Heathcliff hinged on whether a translator makes him refer to himself as *boku* (a pronoun men use to refer to themselves) or *watashi* (a more formal and gender-neutral pronoun). "If he uses *boku*, he's not my Heathcliff," one of the women insisted. The other agreed, "He is pretending to be a gentleman; when he grows up he will say *watashi*."

Catherine might refer to herself as *atashi*, a feminization of the gender-neutral *watashi*. A translator who is trying to convey Catherine's famous line could write, *Atashi wa Hīsukurifu desu*, but the combination of the feminine "I" with the masculine name seems odd in Japanese. And if Catherine uses the male pronoun (*Boku wa Hīsukurifu desu*), that seems equally strange. You sometimes hear a Japanese girl use *boku*, but usually in a deliberately provocative way; she is probably the kind of boundary challenger who refuses to switch her phone to "manner mode" on the train.

I began by looking at Tamura's translation of Catherine's line: *Nerī, Watashi wa, Hīsukurifu sonomono nano yo*, or, in my translation, "Nelly, I am Heathcliff, the very thing."[22] Then I lined up the manga versions on my desk and opened them one after another to the kitchen scene. Many of the manga artists, I was happy to note, underscored the importance of the "I *am* Heathcliff" line by devoting large frames, or even two-page spreads, to close-up depictions of Catherine's face. The Japanese version of Catherine's line in Saitō Ikumi's manga becomes something like "Heathcliff, my life" or "He *is* my life" when translated back into English.[23] In Saitō's drawing, Catherine looks straight at the reader in extreme close-up, her words written vertically in large print on either side of her face; "Heathcliff" runs over her left ear, and "my life" runs along the right side of her neck. In Iwashita Hiromi's *Arashi ga oka*, Catherine's exclamation (*Hīsukurifu wa watashi nano!!*) is conveyed in a three-quarter frame, as if the reader is looking down on her from above (fig. 10).[24] Catherine, who is surrounded by radiating lines as if she is emitting beams of light, holds her fist over her heart as she speaks the line "Heathcliff is me," the Japanese line emphasized by two exclamation points, and the assertion perhaps softened a little by *nano*, which is often used by female speakers. In Morizono Miruku's manga version of *Wuthering Heights*, Catherine says, *Watashi wa Hīsukurifu nano yo!*, or "I am Heathcliff!" (The Japanese particle *yo* conveys the communication of new information.)[25] Morizono pulls out all the stops, devoting two full pages to a close-up of Catherine, set against white crazing and giant kanji sound effects. Catherine's line is written on a white jagged square in the midst of this stormy backdrop.

Fig. 10. Iwashita Hiromi, *Arashi ga oka* [Wuthering Heights], p. 39. Courtesy of Iwashita Hiromi, © Iwashita Hiromi.

There is also the variant of Hanabusa Yōko, in whose version of the kitchen scene, Catherine says, "No matter who I marry, we can't be separated," and "Heathcliff will always be by my side."[26] Hanabusa is the creator of a popular *shōjo* manga called *Lady!!*, the story of an Anglo-Japanese girl who goes to England to meet her father, the Viscount Marble. When I spoke to Hanabusa about the popularity of *Wuthering Heights* in Japan, she said, "A foreign country is something that we have longings for; it's something very far away that gives the feeling of yearning."[27]

Several of the manga versions owed a debt to William Wyler's 1939 film; Tamura's DVD copy had been sitting, unwatched, on my bookshelf now for several years. I turned it over in my hands, noting the all-region format that would allow me to watch it on an American DVD player. I could watch it in my living room without venturing out into the cold. As the film's soupy music rose and fell, I was struck by how little talking it contained. For vast stretches, Catherine and Heathcliff smolder in each other's presence, no subtitles necessary. In the film's version of the kitchen scene, Catherine, enacted by Merle Oberon, says, "He's more myself than I am," but the Japanese subtitles say, "I have a telepathic understanding of him," or, perhaps, "I have a communion of mind [with him]." A few frames later, when Merle Oberon speaks the line, "I *am* Heathcliff," the subtitled Merle says, "We are one in body and soul."[28]

I wandered back upstairs and pulled from a shelf full of Japanese *Wuthering Heights* editions, the translations of Abe Tomoji and Kōnosu Yukiko. Abe's was one of the earlier translations; Kōnosu's was one of the most recent. Abe dealt with the pronoun issue by having Catherine call herself *atashi*, the feminine version of the "I" pronoun. His Catherine says, "I am Heathcliff, Nelly! He is always, always in my mind."[29] Kōnosu's version, as she'd intimated when I met her, was longer. Her Catherine says something like, "Nelly, with Heathcliff I am one. That boy, no matter the time, forever, is in my mind."[30] I couldn't really tell how and why Kōnosu's Japanese phrasing would seem strange, as she'd suggested, to Japanese readers. I suspected that a good translator would not come up with the same English version that I did. I also suspected that even a superior translation might not convey the strangeness of the Japanese version. But I could see that Kōnosu was trying to avoid the awkwardness of linking a feminine pronoun to Heathcliff's name. Her wayward translation conveys the painful, impossible longing of Catherine's hopeful sentence. And here as I paused for a moment in the cold room, my desk covered with variants of Brontë's novel, a familiar mental boundary arose: I'm not here to analyze translations, I thought.

But what had I been doing if not translating for the last eight years? I'd spent my time turning manga Japanese into (bad) English, turning moderately polite English e-mail queries into theatrically polite Japanese ones, turning shopkeepers' quizzical gazes into an awareness that I was paying for a rice ball incorrectly. I'd been translating, translating, translating, I thought, the space heater humming next to my desk. Maybe I *was* writing a book about translation after all, even if, on a sentence-by-sentence basis,

I would never be a skilled translator of Japanese. Maybe, too, like Catherine, when she says, "I *am* Heathcliff," I was trying to translate myself into another person. All the time I had spent trying to understand Japanese versions of *Wuthering Heights* was time I had gotten to be someone other than myself, the person who took the same route to work every day, and whose colleagues could anticipate what she would say in department meetings.

And in that moment every language I had failed to learn came back to me as a language that had immeasurably enriched my life. I remembered the fruit stall in Lyon where a vendor had tolerated the verb tense problems in my melon request. I recalled an awkward conversation in an Italian hotel, the concierge abandoning hope and turning away. I remembered the fourth-grade classroom in which Mrs. Loughlin taught Spanish for a futile forty-five minutes a week. I remembered the time my friend Yoichi wrote out detailed train directions, and I stepped onto the wrong train anyway, Yoichi semaphoring his alarm on the opposite platform as the doors heaved shut. I had been translating nonstop for the past eight years, and lots of other people had been translating for me too, and I had been as single-minded as was possible given my life circumstances. But even if you are focused on understanding another culture's understanding of a single book, a ridiculously narrow project, you have to take some detours, and some of your routes will be confusing and you won't know where to disembark.

"SQUAWKKKKKK." A screech went up from the backyard, and the dog started running circles around the room and barking. Racing downstairs and out to the back porch, I grabbed a wooden pole my husband and I kept for scaring off hawks, who, now and again, glided down into the backyard and set the chickens flap-running for cover in an ungainly and vulnerable manner.

Perched on a fence post, a small red-tailed hawk, his head cocked, eyed the chickens, who were cowering under a frozen forsythia bush. I brandished my pole at the hawk, who seemed not the slightest bit alarmed by my action. Then, bellowing, I charged the hawk's fence post, the pole raised over my head like a sword. The hawk waited until I was close enough to see the yellow of his eyes, and then, with one flap of his wings, he lazily ascended, going only so far as the neighbor's denuded maple tree, from which aerie he looked down over my yard as the chickens scurried under my feet.

I stood guard for a while, my pole raised, as the chickens ventured back out over the ice rafts in the backyard. Two underdressed college students, clutching each other's arms, navigated down the alley behind my house. I lowered my pole as they walked by. Over my head, crows gathered in the upper boughs of a black walnut tree. Wind rattled the desiccated seed pods of a trumpet vine; the chickens darted in a panic. I stood alone in my backyard, pole at the ready. I had been working on my Brontë study for a long time. I thought about *Wuthering Heights* as a tiny pinhole into Japanese literature and culture, and about all the Japanese literature and culture I still wanted to absorb. The chickens edged toward their coop, brushing their beaks across the ground like minesweepers, and I locked them up for the night.

On Learning Japanese to Read *Wuthering Heights*

> It was quite regrettable that, given my innate stupidity and lack of
> scholarly ability, I had not attained any mastery of foreign literature,
> my supposed specialty.
> —Natsume Sōseki, preface to *Theory of Literature*
> (trans. Michael K. Bourdaghs)

Mastering a foreign language plays a large role in the fantasy life of educated Americans, the kind of people who dream of quitting their jobs and
starting a new life in an exotic setting. If they had extra time, they imagine,
they would use it to dust off the French they last used during a junior year
abroad, or to take up an entirely new language so that they could read a
Portuguese newspaper in São Paolo. These hopeful aspirants harbor these
dreams in blithe disregard of linguistic research on the ideal "window"
of language acquisition, a window that opens when one emerges from
the womb and which closes when one emerges from junior high. When
I started studying Japanese, my window of language acquisition had not
only closed, its sashes had been sealed with many coats of paint.

I wanted to learn Japanese for the most counterintuitive of reasons:
in order to be able to read Japanese adaptations of an English novel. I
also wanted to be able to order a melon soda at a Moss Burger restaurant
without having the counter clerk push a laminated English menu my way,
and to be able to converse in Japanese with my Japanese friends. But, most
pressingly, I wanted to be able to investigate Japanese versions of *Wuthering Heights* in much the same way that I was able to study Brontë's original
novel, a novel that I set out to read as an exercise in single-mindedness.
What had been deliberately designed to be a small, obsessively focused
endeavor was replaced by an impossible octopoid project from which
larger tentacular questions sprang: Why are there so many Japanese translations of *Wuthering Heights*? What is the appeal of Catherine (*Kyasarin*)

and Heathcliff (*Hīsukurifu*) for Japanese people? What is the difference between adaptation and translation? What constitutes intellectual mastery? And, more pressingly: would I ever master the Japanese indirect passive verb form?

The indirect passive verb form, also known as the adversative passive, is a linguistic version of passive aggression that does not exist in English. In English, the passive voice can be used to avoid agency, and so it is a favorite construct of government bureaucrats ("Mistakes were made") and academics ("The abundance of translations can be understood as proof of the cultural globalization in progress in this era"). In Japanese, too, one can use the passive verb form in this way, but you can also use a passive verb to convey annoyance. For example, you can say, "The baby cried" in a way that expresses something more like, "I was cried at by the baby," and, in so doing, communicate your displeasure at the baby's racket. By using the indirect passive verb form you can say that your husband ate the last piece of cake, and also convey how aggrieved you are by his greediness.[1]

My foreign language facility paled in comparison to that of the Brontë sisters, citizens of a world in which foreign language aptitude was the badge of a well-educated person. Emily Brontë, along with her sister Charlotte, enrolled in Constantin Héger's school in Brussels so that she could learn French and German. "Lessons were taught exclusively in French and no concessions were expected or sought for the fact that the Brontës were as yet not fluent in the language," writes Juliet Barker of the Pensionnat Héger, which catered expressly to Belgians.[2] For the Brontë sisters, French and German skill was vital to their career plans; in order to open a school for girls, they had to convince the parents of potential students that they were accomplished enough in foreign languages to ensure that their future students would be able to read a *plat de jour* in Paris or discuss *die blume* with a florist in Bonn.

But even nineteenth-century writers with greater financial independence applied themselves to foreign languages with alacrity. Byron not only learned Italian, he learned the Venetian dialect he needed in order to be able to carry on an affair with the wife of his landlord. Shelley so fully internalized Italian vocabulary that it came to affect his English usage, or so argues the Shelley scholar Stuart Curran. When Shelley writes in "Ode to the West Wind" that "the sea-blooms and the oozy woods," hearing the wind's voice, "tremble and despoil themselves," he draws on the Italian word *spogliarsi* (to undress, strip, to divest oneself). Shelley absorbed Italian literature and language, immersing himself in its particularities, maintains Curran.[3] Mary Shelley read the Italian translation of *Clarissa*, the longest novel in the English language; Byron devoured a thirty-volume collection of Italian history.

Byron and the Shelleys had pressing reasons for wanting to reinvent themselves in foreign exile. Byron was fleeing scandalous rumors of an affair with his half-sister; Percy Shelley had abandoned a wife and two children to take up with the daughter of his intellectual heroes Mary Wollstonecraft and William Godwin. But poets who had not become persona non grata in Romantic-era polite society also read several languages—Samuel Taylor Coleridge translated a raft of German poems into English, and also his own poems into German. And even idiosyncratically educated people who lived on moors with erratic fathers soldiered their way through Rousseau or Goethe, or tackled some Latin. Among the few Emily Brontë manuscripts that survive are fragments of her translation of Virgil's *Aeneid*. When Brontë's character Nelly Dean wants to assert her intellectual ambitions, she does so by claiming she's looked into every book in the Linton family library "unless it be that range of Greek and Latin, and that of French." She goes on to say, "Those I know one from another: it is as much as you can expect of a poor man's daughter."[4] William Crimsworth, the protagonist of Charlotte Brontë's novel *The Professor*, auditions for a job by translating English business letters into French and German under the watchful eye of a company operative. Crimsworth writes, "I showed him my countenance with the confidence that one would show an unlearned man a letter written in Greek."[5] Her editor notes that Brontë wrote the title "The Professor" on a slip of paper and stuck it over her first title, "The Master," the original title underscoring the character's pride in his linguistic accomplishment, as well as Brontë's preoccupation with mastery.[6]

Mary Shelley, too, showcased the foreign language skills of her fictional characters. The creature in *Frankenstein* is a language savant. Cast off by his creator and left to wander on his own through Germany, he learns French by eavesdropping on the expatriate De Lacey family. He sets up a classroom for himself in a lean-to connected to their cottage, and teaches himself by nonstop listening, much in the way my friend Maiko, upon landing in Des Moines, learned English by binge-watching *South Park* episodes. At first Shelley's creature is "baffled in every attempt."[7] "Their pronunciation was quick," he recalls of the De Lacey family members, "and the words they uttered, not having any apparent connexion with visible objects, I was unable to discover any clue by which I could unravel the mystery of their reference." But within several revolutions of the moon, he learns the words "fire," "milk," "bread," and "wood." "My days were spent in close attention," the creature recalls, "that I might more speedily master the language."[8] His efforts pay off when, upon the arrival of the non-French-speaking Safie, he is able to boast that he improved "more rapidly than the Arabian, who understood very little, and conversed in broken accents, whilst [he] comprehended and could imitate almost every word that was spoken."

Mary Shelley conceived of the idea for *Frankenstein* while summering in Switzerland. Byron came up with the premise of *Childe Harold's Pilgrimage* while traveling through Portugal. Even the homebody Wordsworth took as source material for *The Prelude* his travels in France. Where the Romantic poets did not go was Japan. One may occasionally come across mentions of Japan in Romantic-era writing, but mostly these are mentions of a wood varnish and not a country. When Jane Austen's heroine Catherine Morland encounters a mysterious cabinet in her sleeping quarters at Northanger Abbey, it is described as "black and yellow Japan of the handsomest kind."[9]

Emily Brontë, who lived several decades after Austen, had no practical use for Japanese. But then, even today, very few people who do not live in Japan have a practical use for learning the Japanese language. And Japanese is among the most difficult languages for a native English speaker to master, or so says the U.S. Foreign Service Institute, which divides their intensive language classes into three categories corresponding to level of difficulty: twenty-four-week classes for "world" languages (for example, Spanish, French, Portuguese, and Dutch); forty-four-week classes for "hard" languages (such as Hindi, Russian, and Thai), and eighty-eight-week classes for "super-hard" languages (Arabic, Chinese, Japanese, and Korean). One of the several reasons that Japanese is super-hard for English speakers (and vice versa) is that the basic Japanese sentence construction is the reverse of the English pattern of noun-verb-direct object. So, whereas in English I say, "I drink coffee," in Japanese, instead, I say, "As for me, coffee drink." The direct object (coffee) comes before the verb (drink), and in most cases the agent of the sentence disappears. (In conversation, one would not say "As for me" (*watashi*) because it would be clear to the listener that one was talking about one's self.)

I arrived in Japan with a plan to master *Wuthering Heights*, and I departed from Japan with a plan to master the Japanese language. I hoped to document my mastery by means of the Japanese Language Proficiency

Test (JLPT), which assesses Japanese mastery at five different levels ranging from level 5 (easy-peasy) to level 1 (impossibly difficult). Many people take the exam in order to prove to a potential employer that they can speak Japanese well enough to work in Japan. For that reason, they don't bother to take the level 5 or 4 exams; a minimum of level 2 proficiency is typically required by Japanese employers, and, since the test is given only once a year in the United States, for most people it makes sense to skip over the easiest exams. I, however, decided to work my way through all the levels in a systematic fashion, and so took the level 5 a year after I came home from Japan, around the time my older daughter started college. I went on to pass the level 4 test as she embarked on her sophomore year. But the level 5 and level 4 tests were mere throat-clearing for the more meaningful level 3 test, which I would take in her junior year, the year before my younger daughter departed for college. Passing the JLPT3 would certify that I was making real progress in my attempt to master Japanese, and would also distract me from the fact that my husband and I would soon be alone with our children's pets.

As part of my resolve to pass the JLPT3, I divorced myself from the Internet, and this left me with too much time to feel feelings as I sat in my study drilling Japanese grammar. Downstairs, my younger daughter was slowly and pleasurably reading *Les Misérables* in translation, the dog's muzzle resting on her knee. Soon she would be doing her reading in a far-off dormitory! Up until recently the dog had padded into her room to settle down for the night, leaving the imprint of his drool on her sheets, but recently the dog had started wandering into other people's rooms and flopping over on his side. "Do you think he knows she'll soon be leaving for college?" I asked my husband when the dog sprawled uncomfortably on the hardwood floor next to our bed.

Second-language specialists talk about active versus passive language learning, or, language skills you can quick-draw like a Wild West shooter versus language skills for which you have to fumble as you would for misplaced keys. In Japanese, whenever you count something, you have to indicate the total number of items with a counter word that's specific to the items being counted; there are different counters for cats (*hiki*) and birds (*wa*). (Japanese children learn a tongue twister—*niwa ni wa ni wa niwatori ga iru*, or, "In the garden there are two chickens"—which plays on the similarity between the word for garden [*niwa*] and the counter for two chickens [*ni wa*] and the word for chicken [*niwatori*].) Passive language skills are of no use when someone inquires whether you have any pets and you can only recall the counter for apples (*tsu*: small round objects) instead of the counter for dogs (*hiki*: four-legged animals).

Some years ago, a linguist measured the English acquisition rate of a three-year-old boy named Mikihide, the son of Japanese parents who had enrolled him in an American preschool.[10] Mikihide, an active and inquisitive child who probably knew how to count both apples and dogs in Japanese, had acquired at the end of seven months an impressive passive vocabulary. He could understand what was required of him if asked to "sit down," "take one," or "please push me"; he could also follow the plotline of *Speed Racer*, his favorite cartoon. But Mikihide's active vocabulary, the words he confidently spoke, comprised only 260 words (or 300 by his mother's more generous estimate). My passive knowledge of Japanese might fill an Olympic-size swimming pool, whereas my active knowledge wouldn't overflow an inflatable kiddie pool.

In Japan, too, there are many people possessed of a vast repository of English vocabulary and grammar who, nonetheless, do not feel capable of speaking in English. Because Japanese people do not necessarily come in contact with many native English speakers, and because English classes in Japan are often taught by Japanese teachers who, although they have a tighter grip on English grammar than most Americans do, may not regularly converse with native speakers, Japan is a country full of hesitant English speakers.[11] Almost everyone I spoke to in Japan could speak English better than I could speak Japanese, and all of them perceived their English-speaking skills as embarrassingly limited. This included a Japanese acquaintance who was able to discourse in English on the literary oeuvre of Akutagawa Ryūnosuke, the father of the Japanese short story, whereas I frequently confused the Japanese verbs for "to read" (*yomu*) and "to drink" (*nomu*).

Cognizant that I had barely passed the listening sections in my previous JLPT tests, and wanting to improve my conversational skills, I registered at The Mixxer, "a free educational website for language exchanges via Skype."[12] The Mixxer participants introduce themselves by writing brief introductory profiles and by uploading images to represent themselves. In my profile, I strove to sound business-like but modest. I explained that I had been studying Japanese for four years but that my spoken Japanese was poor. I wrote that I taught English at an American university and that I would be happy to speak to English learners of all levels of proficiency. Because I wrote my profile in both English and Japanese, because I advertised my teacher status, because I understood my target audience better than the man who used the screen name "delinquent habits" and uploaded a photo of his pit bull, I received many contact requests. Not long after registering on The Mixxer, I received invitations to chat from a student in Nagoya who was trying to raise his TOEFL score, from a travel agent living in Orlando who couldn't understand his American clients, from a film buff in Saitama who had a fondness for Rose Byrne, and from a retiree in Morioka whose Mixxer photo was a Tomcat fighter plane.

There is a fourteen- or fifteen-hour time difference between Iowa City and Tokyo (there is no daylight saving time in Japan); for that reason, it's not possible to have a Skype conversation with a Japanese person during business hours unless one of you is an insomniac. Weekdays, I would stumble out of bed so that I could talk to someone in Japan before she went to bed; Saturday evenings I would talk to Japanese people for whom it was Sunday a.m. Together, we all cast out to sea in our Skype skiffs, the light fading in Japan as the sun rose in Iowa, or the dawn brightening over Tokyo as the sun set in Davenport.

I spoke to my Mixxer partners in the most unforgiving of foreign language-speaking circumstances—with my laptop camera turned off, and so without the assistance of visual cues. I had no idea whether the Morioka man was hirsute or bald, nor did I know whether he was speaking from a *manshon* (a high-rise multi-unit building) or an *apāhto* (a low-rise rental unit building). Anyone who has ever tried to answer the telephone in a foreign country will acknowledge the high degree of language facility a blind speaking situation requires. Since the person on the other end of the line cannot see you struggling to find words, you are reduced to using only those words you can easily recall, words which may or may not be sufficient for the conversation at hand.

As the December test date drew near, the days clattered by like the leaf-vacuuming trucks that hove through my neighborhood. Morning, noon, and night I reviewed Japanese flash cards—surreptitiously during department meetings, overtly in the interval between the ministrations of a dental hygienist and the conclusive review of the dentist herself, distractedly while walking the dog. Even though I was diverted from my study of *Wuthering Heights*, I felt as though the weather of *Wuthering Heights* was blowing around me. Brontë conveys the bleakness of the period just after Catherine's death and burial by having Isabella read late into the night, saying, "It seemed so dismal to go upstairs, with the wild snow blowing outside" (175). Characters in Brontë's novel are constantly mentioning that their tea has grown cold or that their dinner is no longer warm. They angle to get closer to the fire, just as, in my house, everyone sprawled in front of the gas fireplace, the sole warm spot in a house penuriously heated, everyone shivering when wind blew down the vestigial chimney and blew out the flames.

With the Japanese Language Proficiency Test test day almost in sight, I turned flash cards at a frantic pace, attempting to master the approximately 750 words on the JLPT3 vocabulary list that a former test taker had compiled. The dog and I circled the block, with me mumbling Japanese words, and with him foraging for pizza crusts near apartment dumpsters. In the weeks before I took the JLPT3, my conversation partners all said, *Ganbatte kudasai*, which is the Japanese equivalent of "Good luck," but which literally means "Persevere please," and to which I replied, *Ganbarimashō* ("I will do my best"). Once, while in a train station in Japan, my daughter and I watched a Japanese mother, toddler gripped in one hand, a baby strapped to her chest, drag a suitcase up a flight of stairs. The toddler was cross and uncooperative. As my daughter and I moved closer to see if we could help, we heard the reluctant child, say either *Ganbaranai* (I do not persevere) or *Ganbarenai* (I cannot persevere). "That's so sad!" said my daughter just before we startled the mother by swooping in and carrying her bag upstairs. Up until then, we hadn't known it was *possible* to use the negative form (I do not persevere), let alone the negative potential form (I cannot persevere) of the verb *ganbaru*, so cheerfully and frequently do Japanese people deploy the positive form of this verb. But as I trudged around my neighborhood with the dog rooting for garbage, I felt the weight of negative potentiality.

I showed up at the Chicago test site, carrying a battery of sharpened pencils and no cell phone since the test registration materials declared that if one's cell phone went off in the middle of the test, one's test would be immediately invalidated. I didn't trust my cell phone to stay silenced even if I turned it off, so I left it in the car when my husband dropped me in front of the test site. Every other person of my age was either administering the exam or waiting, like a pit-stop crew member, to hand over sandwiches when the test takers emerged during breaks. When I'd taken the JLPT5 and JLPT4 in years past, the parents of test takers had leaped up when the test room doors opened, and then settled back to playing Candy Crush or reading magazines when the test takers retreated back inside. In previous years, I'd allowed myself to feel smugly superior to the waiting parents, but now I watched with envy as a *chūnen josei* (middle-aged woman) pulled out a *People* magazine and a Snickers bar.

As I waited in a lounge area outside the testing rooms, eyeing my fellow test takers, one of whom, a green-haired boy in a Pokémon T-shirt, was *only now* sharpening his pencils, my other life flashed before me. A few months before, I had given a talk on my *Wuthering Heights* project at a Canadian university where the audience was assembled around a table large enough to accommodate the board of the New York Stock Exchange. I talked to the gathered Canadian academics from the head of the boardroom table as if I were a business tycoon, telling them about the meaning of the Japanese title of *Wuthering Heights*, describing the important role played by Edmund Blunden in the Japanese popularization of *Wuthering Heights*, and showing them clips from the 1939 film *Wuthering Heights*. Just before I was introduced, a friend warned me to watch out for a cluster of old men during the Q and A, and, sure enough, as soon as I stopped speaking, a hand shot up from the ancients. The questioner was keen-eyed and ruddy-faced; he wanted to know if I had seen the Spanish film version of *Wuthering Heights* (I had not), and whether I knew the Japanese estimation of Emily Brontë's poetry (I did not), and if I knew whether there were Japanese translations of Emily Brontë's poetry (I did not), and at that point the moderator gestured toward a graduate student at the foot of the board room table, who suggested, helpfully, that maybe I should look at the critical scholarship on fanfiction, and I agreed that I should, but secretly resisted.

Now I was surrounded by Japanophile teenagers who almost certainly had a greater knowledge of fanfiction than I did. Near the JLPT registration table, the green-haired boy was talking smack to a girl clutching a Hello Kitty wallet. "My *sensei* told me I could probably pass the level 2 exam, but I decided to take it easy and start with the level 3," the boy said to the girl. We all edged closer to the sign-up table. "I've heard the level 3 is pretty hard," the girl said, stabbing at her cell phone. "I did a homestay in Sendai, and my host family told me my Japanese was very good," the boy persisted, but the girl had stopped listening.

At the head of the registration line an official-looking woman was checking off names on a list. In Japanese, she asked the green-haired boy his name, and in Japanese he responded, throwing in a comment about the weather, the show-off. I practiced in my head how to introduce myself in the third-year Japanese manner, rather than in the less-polite first-year manner, but when I got to the head of the line, the registration woman glanced up at me and switched into English.

The chapter of *Wuthering Heights* that begins directly after Catherine's funeral begins with an account of the weather, a glimpse of winter tramp-ling the first vestiges of spring. "That Friday made the last of our fine days, for a month," Nelly recalls. "In the evening, the weather broke; the wind shifted from south to north-east, and brought rain, first, and then sleet, and snow" (171). When I got settled in my assigned test room, it was smooth going at first; I lined up my entrance ticket and pencils at the edge of my desktop, and followed along as the proctor, whom I recognized from the year before—hello, old friend!—handed out test booklets and answer sheets. I wrote my name and my birthdate and carefully darkened the lozenges underneath each letter and number. I sat expectantly in my seat and watched a digital clock count down to the official test-starting second, and even if I did not work my way through the vocabulary sec-tion of the test with total confidence, I blackened to the end of the sec-tion with five seconds to spare. Of the weather change after Catherine's death, Brontë writes, "One could hardly imagine that there had been three weeks of summer: the primroses and crocuses were hidden under wintry drifts: the larks were silent, the young leaves of the early trees smitten and blackened" (171). Just so did the testing room darken during the gram-mar section, which consisted of hollowed-out sentences, series of blank spaces with one space starred, followed by Japanese phrases one had to arrange correctly in order to determine which phrase should be placed in the starred space.

Japanese sentence structure is notable for its flexibility; the phrases on my test booklet spun around like ribbon gymnasts. And when, after a ten-minute break—the parents bountiful as vending machines; the test takers ravenous as wolves—we returned to the testing room, and the reading section commenced, oh, how dreary, and chill, and dismal that section did creep over! Nothing in the level 5 and level 4 tests prepared me for the level 3 reading section, in which one was asked to figure out whether the child's crèche at a local library was open on the third Thursday of the month when the third Thursday of the month fell on a holiday, or, pos-sibly, whether it was open on all the days other than Thursday, except on holiday occasions. All around me pencils scratched and pages turned; the other test takers were answering questions about driving directions and borrowing guidelines as I stalled over childcare availability.

"I'm pretty sure I failed it," I gloomed to my husband and daughters, who were waiting to pick me up after the exam. "That's what you said after you took the level 5 and the level 4," said my husband encouragingly, as he waited for an SUV to back out of a parking space. "Look, that's what's his name," I yelled as I saw one of my former classmates standing by the curb. "He must have been taking the test too." "Hey, Summercorn," I called, waving frantically. "How'd you do?" I was not really sure what my classmate's name was, having only heard the Japanized version of it we spoke in class, where Smith-san became *Sumisu-san*, but Summercorn waved and drew closer. "I don't know. I think I did OK, but the level 2 listening section was kind of hard for me. How about you?" Level 2! Summercorn had taken the second-hardest JLPT level!

Before we headed back to Iowa City, we dropped my older daughter off at O'Hare airport; she was headed back to college. In Japanese, one uses the kanji 上 (*ue*, or above) to distinguish an older daughter from a younger (下 *shita*, or below) one. Trailing behind both daughters, I carried my giant collection of index cards into the airport terminal, and threw away a rubberbanded pack each time we passed a trash receptacle. My index card collection had been as tall as a wedding cake, but fat lot of good it had done me, I thought, as I waved goodbye to my above daughter at the departure gate. A thousand index cards lighter, I rode back to Iowa City, seething quietly. My below daughter sat in the back seat reading *Les Mis*.

In the months after the JLPT3 test, as I waited for my scores to come in the mail, I tried to carry on with my work on Japanese versions of *Wuthering Heights*, but I did so sullenly, the dog twitching at my feet. For months I'd intended to read a children's book edition of *Wuthering Heights*, part of what I liked to call my *archive*, a surfeit of books and manga that kept migrating around the house. I climbed up to the attic, the dog traipsing after me up two flights of steps. The dog had a fear of going downstairs; he would follow me up into the higher reaches of the house and then get stranded there. "You can do it!" I'd call from the kitchen, but he'd whimper until I'd climb back up the stairs and talk him down. Sometimes when he heard kibble hitting his food bowl he'd stand at the top of the stairs, pawing the top step.

The attic contained a toy Noah's ark and some block puzzles and a stack of board games and a spindly-legged doll chair that presented a safety hazard to toddlers, who tried to climb into it. The attic walls were lined with bookcases holding the remains of my daughters' childhood books, or at least the ones that I liked—I'd winnowed out the annoying Clifford series and the lesser Curious George books. I suddenly remembered the scene in *Wuthering Heights* in which Linton Heathcliff and Cathy Linton find a cupboard containing "a heap of old toys; tops, and hoops, and battledoors, and shuttlecocks." "One was marked C.," Cathy recalls, "and the other H.; I wished to have the C., because that stood for Catherine, and the H. might be for Heathcliff, his name; but the bran came out of H., and Linton didn't like it" (248). Suddenly that inconsequential scene—the children squabble with each other and then sing songs—seemed terribly sad. I passed my eyes over the bookshelves quickly, found the children's book version of *Arashi ga oka* and ran downstairs. And then I ran back up in order to rescue the marooned dog.

The children's *Arashi ga oka*, written by Mori Michiyo,[13] featured Catherine and Heathcliff on the cover looking as if they were characters in *Hans Brinker and the Silver Skates* (fig. 11). They had the pink cheeks and vaguely Mitteleuropean children's mountain wear that I associate with children's literature I read as a child. Heathcliff wore a pullover sweater and had a red ribbon tied in a bow at his neck; Catherine's dress had a triangular bib bodice edged in lace. Heathcliff stood behind Catherine with his hands on her shoulders in a brotherly manner as they both looked off into the distance, perhaps anticipating a ski trip to the mountains that loom behind their heads.

Mori Michiyo's edition of *Wuthering Heights* provided *furigana* next to all the kanji, even the kanji for *Arashi ga oka*. *Furigana* are small-font *hiragana* or *katakana* that are placed next to kanji to assist readers who may not be familiar with difficult kanji characters. Even in texts aimed at adults, such as newspaper articles or novels, rarely-used kanji are sometimes supplemented by *furigana* that tell the reader how to read these kanji. The children's edition of *Wuthering Heights* was pitched at a grade schooler's reading level, but I still found myself flipping through the pictures, feeling vaguely humiliated by how dependent I was on the *furigana*. "I thought I'd be fluent by now," I said to the dog, who cocked his head, listening for the words "cheese" and "treat."

When the JLPT3 results finally arrived, they came in a business-sized envelope. My husband had left the letter on top of the foyer radiator next to some college solicitations for my younger daughter. After taking the JLPT5 and the JLPT4 exams, I had received large cardboard envelopes containing certificates of successful completion, but this envelope was an unimpressive dispatch, no bigger than the utility bill. When I picked up the JLPT letter, it was as warm as a piece of toast, but more deadly. At first the news did not seem so bad; I'd received a respectable "B" grade for both vocabulary and grammar, but my total score was only 72/180. And written in the left bottom quadrant of the score report sheet was the word *gōkaku* (合格), meaning "success" or "passing," preceded by the dreaded kanji *fu* (不) which

Fig. 11. Mori Michiyo, *Arashi ga oka* [Wuthering Heights] book jacket,
© Kaisei-sha, 1954. Courtesy of Kaisei-sha Publishing Company, Limited.

negates what comes after it, and which I knew from the word *fuan* (不安), which means "anxiety" or "unrest," spelled nothing but trouble. *Fuan* level high, I turned my attention to the "Understanding JLPT Score Reports and Certificates of Proficiency," which, on the Japanese side, provided *furigana*, as if acknowledging that the weaker test-takers might have a need for this reading crutch. I turned directly to the English-language translation the test organizers also provided, and quickly figured out that, although I'd made it through the vocabulary and grammar sections and even the listening section with points to spare, I had drastically underperformed on the reading section, commanding only sixteen out of the total sixty points, three points short of the minimal score I needed to pass.

"That's too bad, Mom," my younger daughter called from the couch as I sloped upstairs. "I am never going to master Japanese," I thought, looking out my study window and pondering the implacable advance of mental decline. Across the street, a little boy revved the wheels of a metal truck until his mother called him inside. I sat for a few minutes thinking about my reading test score, and wondering if it was time to call the whole thing off. "I don't love *Wuthering Heights*," I admitted, as under my desk chair, the dog whistled in his sleep.

If I were to list books I love, *Wuthering Heights* wouldn't even be in the top ten, I thought, doodling in my project notebook.

Best-Loved Books

1. Flannery O'Connor, *A Good Man Is Hard to Find*
2. Wallace Stevens, *The Palm at the End of the Mind*
3. Tanizaki Junichirō, *The Makioka Sisters* (the Edward Seidensticker translation)
4. L. Rust Hills, *How to Do Things Right*
5. Barbara Pym, *Excellent Women*
6. Jean Webster, *Daddy-Long-Legs*
7. Samuel Richardson, *Clarissa*
8. Julie Hecht, *Do the Windows Open?*
9. Henry James, *The Aspern Papers*
10. Adrienne Rich, *Diving into the Wreck*
11. Ann Rule, *The Stranger Beside Me*
12. Emily Brontë, *Wuthering Heights*

The list-making was pleasurable because I was writing with a yellow Pilot Kakuno fountain pen that had a smiley face imprinted on the nib. I recalled *The Pillow Book*, in which Sei Shōnagon makes lists of times of year and mountain peaks and dispiriting things.

Dispiriting Things

1. Failing the JLPT3 exam
2. Being illiterate in Japanese
3. Not being able to finish my *Wuthering Heights* project because I am never going to be able to read Japanese
4. No longer being a person who can count on passing tests if she studies hard enough
5. Possibly being a person who can't read Japanese because her brain is deteriorating and her learning/forgetting balance has tipped into the negative
6. Facing a bleak future in which I call my above daughter by my below daughter's name, or call both of them by the dog's name

In Jean Webster's *Daddy-Long-Legs* (number 6), which I could remember because I read it before senescence set in, the orphan Judy Abbott describes *Wuthering Heights* (number 12, *maybe*) as her favorite book, but worries that she herself is no Emily Brontë. "Sometimes a dreadful fear comes over me that I'm not a genius," she writes.[14] My dreadful fear was that I would never have the basic competence I needed to finish writing my book. Judy Abbott worries that there is a ceiling on her ambition; I worried that under my ambition there was no floor. I had just that morning mixed up the Japanese words for light and dark, confidently telling my conversation partner that *Persuasion* is Jane Austen's most light and upbeat novel. If I couldn't learn to read as well as a Japanese junior high school student, I would never be able to complete my study of Japanese versions of *Wuthering Heights*. I'd just keep beavering away until the day when my family sadly (I hoped) emptied my office files and trundled my *Arashi ga oka* notes to the recycling bins that were part of a new sustainability initiative. Maybe my project ought to be recycled now, I thought.

I trudged back up to my study with the dog, and sat down in my desk chair. Just visible at the far end of the desk's surface was the Mori Michiyo edition of *Wuthering Heights*; I pulled the pink-cheeked Catherine and Heathcliff out from under a pile of Manila folders. The book's pages were brittle; the Japanese girls who had once read it were by now *otoshiyori*, a polite term for old people. I thought of Mori Michiyo, who had died in 1977 at age seventy-six, and whose version of *Wuthering Heights* was listed in Japanese Wikipedia as a "retelling" rather than a translation, this in keeping with her biographer's claim that Mori's translations, "extremely free and original in interpretation of the texts," might best be characterized as "Mori Michiyo's own creative works."[15] I recalled going to Jinbōchō, a Tokyo neighborhood full of antiquarian bookstores, with my conversation partner Miharu, who put in a request for Mori's volume, and I recalled finding my way back to the neighborhood on my own when the volume arrived.

The dog's wheezing interrupted my reverie. I remembered that I hadn't passed the JLPT3 exam, and that there were still forty-eight thousand kanji I couldn't recognize. I thought of the moment in *Wuthering Heights* when Heathcliff ceases his pursuit of revenge. "I get levers and mattocks to demolish the two houses, and train myself to be capable of working like Hercules," he says, "and when everything is ready, and in my power, I find the will to lift a slate off either roof has vanished!" (323) I'd never come close to lifting the slate off anything, I thought. I felt like lying down on the floor of my study, in the same position in which Nelly finds the dead Heathcliff, his face lashed with rain from an open casement. I should quit before I become a wild-haired Casaubon bent over a kanji dictionary.

I remembered the language savants whom I'd encountered in my attempt to learn Japanese. There was Nakahama Manjirō, a fourteen-year-old fisherman who, in 1842, five years before Emily Brontë published *Wuthering Heights*, washed up on an island from which he was rescued by American whalers, and who, within a few weeks began to speak English, or so it was claimed.[16] There was Edward Seidensticker, whose landmark translation of Kawabata Yasunari led to Kawabata winning the Nobel Prize in Literature, and whose wonderful translation of Tanizaki's *The Makioka Sisters* led me to love that novel. Seidensticker reportedly memorized a Japanese dictionary on a slow boat ride to Japan, an approach to vocabulary-building he recommended to his students.[17] The take-home message seemed to be that it took a transpacific boat journey to provide the study conditions necessary for passing successfully from English to Japanese.

I am older than Manjiro and Seidensticker, I thought sadly, my eye passing over the books on my desk as the dog mooched at my knee. "When's the last time anyone walked you?" I asked. Noting my accusatory tone, the dog shot me the sidelong glance to which he resorts when he's been caught rolling in something dead, and skulked away. Just then my eye snagged on my kanji bible, James W. Heisig's *Remembering the Kanji*. Heisig, a professor of religion who devised an ingenious technique for teaching himself how to remember kanji, prefaces his book with a warning, next to which I'd drawn three penciled stars. I opened my secondhand Heisig and turned to the relevant passage. "It seems worthwhile to give some brief thought to any ambitions one might have about 'mastering' the Japanese writing system," Heisig writes.[18]

I thought about my plan to master *Wuthering Heights*, and of my revised plan to master the Japanese language so that I could read Japanese versions of *Wuthering Heights*. I thought of the time I had spent reading *Wuthering Heights* without mastering Brontë's novel, and of the time I had spent studying for the JLPT without mastering Japanese. I thought of my trip to the specialized book area in Jinbōchō, and of the moment when I'd managed to purchase Mori Michiyo's book, and I took comfort in having small pockets of temporary knowledge.

Heisig insists that his method for learning kanji is intended only as an aid to get one "close enough to the characters to befriend them." "Let them surprise you, inspire you, enlighten you, resist you, and seduce you," Heisig writes. "They cannot be mastered without a full understanding of their long and complex history and an insight into the secret of their unpredictable vitality—all of which is far too much for a single mind to bring to the tip of a single pen."

Yes, exactly, I thought, drawing a favorite kanji with my yellow fountain pen on Heisig's title page. There the book's prior owner had penciled phrases in Vietnamese alongside helpful English translations: "You look pretty!" "You need to eat more," "How are *you*?" Under the last phrase was written "Literally means (are you healthy?)." I wondered how far my predecessor had gotten in her kanji study. I thought about letting the kanji surprise me, enlighten me, resist me, seduce me. But first there was the dog to walk. So eager was he to get outside that when I rose from my desk, he forgot his fears and hurtled down the stairs.

Notes

For works published in Japanese, citations are given in the order of family name followed by given name. For works published in English, citations are given in the order of given name followed by family name.

Introduction

1. Erika Ingham, the assistant curator at the National Portrait Gallery (London), confirmed that Branwell Brontë's portrait (NPG 1725) was the centerpiece of an exhibition devoted to the Brontës organized by Seiyu Ltd. and Seibu Department Stores, Ltd. The portrait was exhibited first at Ikebukuro Seibu Museum, Tokyo (2–11 October 1987) and then at Seibu Takarazuka, near Osaka (15–26 October 1987).

2. John Elliott Cairnes, quoted in Mark R.D. Seaward's introduction to *Sixty Treasures,* written and compiled by Juliet R. V. Barker (Haworth, West Yorkshire: Brontë Society, 1988).

3. Patsy Stoneman's "Exhibitions of Brontëana" entry in *The Oxford Companion to the Brontës* notes that the Brontë Society loaned first editions and Brontë personal possessions to this exhibition, and Stoneman provides a better translation of the title: "The Breath of the Wilderness of Haworth: The Brontë Sisters and *Wuthering Heights*." Christine Alexander and Margaret Smith, *The Oxford Companion to the Brontës* (Oxford: Oxford University Press, 2011). Online.

4. From 2009 to 2010 I taught American literature and culture at Japan Women's University and Tsuda College. I am grateful for the encouragement and support I received from the faculty and students at both of those institutions.

5. The novel's furious energies are highlighted in Anne Carson's "The Glass Essay," in which the narrator notes approvingly, "She knows how to hang puppies, / that Emily." Carson, *Glass, Irony and God* (New York: New Directions, 1995), 4.

6. Louis A. Renza, *"A White Heron" and the Question of Minor Literature* (Madison: University of Wisconsin Press, 1984); T. J. Clark, *The Sight of Death: An Experiment in Art Writing* (New Haven: Yale University Press, 2006); Geoff Dyer, *Zona* (New York: Pantheon, 2012).

7. *Derrida*, dir. Kirby Dick and Amy Ziering Kofman (Jane Doe Films, 2002).

8. E. M. Forster, *Aspects of the Novel* (London: Edward Arnold, 1927), 19.

9. Ingrid Geerken describes *Wuthering Heights* as "a literary treatise on wild grief," situating the novel in the context of the Brontë family history of loss and nineteenth-century mourning culture. Ingrid Geerken, "'The Dead Are Not Annihilated': Mortal Regret in *Wuthering Heights*," *Journal of Narrative Theory* 34.3 (Fall 2004): 377.

10. Henry James qtd. by Lucasta Miller, *The Brontë Myth* (London: Jonathan Cape, 2001), x.

11. Elizabeth Gaskell, *The Life of Charlotte Brontë* (London: Oxford University Press, 1966), 109; hereafter cited in text.

12. Miller, *The Brontë Myth*, 170.

13. Qtd. in Juliet Barker, *The Brontës* (New York: Pegasus, 2010), 182. The Gondals are the inhabitants of an imaginary island invented by the Brontë children; Sally Mosley was a family retainer. As Barker notes, Emily yokes the fantastic and the quotidian in the diary fragment.

14. Juliet Barker, Emily Brontë, *Oxford Dictionary of National Biography*, online.

15. Charlotte Brontë, "Editor's Preface to the New [1850] Edition of *Wuthering Heights*," in Emily Brontë, *Wuthering Heights*, ed. Pauline Nestor (London: Penguin Classics, 2008), liii.

16. Charlotte Brontë, qtd. in "A Note on the Text," in Brontë, *Wuthering Heights*, ed. Nestor, xl.

17. Haun Saussy has described literary competency as "the supercompetency you need to deal with the superdiscourse that is literature." Saussy, "Language and Literature—a Pedagogical Continuum?" *Profession 2005*, ed. Rosemary G. Feal (New York: Modern Language Association, 2005), 117.

18. Japanese speaking and writing skills came slightly more easily. I sought out Japanese conversation partners on the language exchange website The Mixxer (language-exchanges.org). I also made extensive use of lang-8.com, a website where native speakers volunteer to correct written texts in their languages of origin in exchange for the opportunity to have their foreign-language writing attempts corrected by speakers of their target languages.

19. Ōgi Yuzuha, *Arashi ga oka* [Wuthering Heights, English translation published as *Rising Storm*] (Tokyo: Kaiōsha Comics, 2003).

20. *Hanako to Anne*, NHK [Japanese Broadcasting Corporation], 31 March 2014 to 27 September 2014. Calvin Trillin has written about Prince Edward Island as a hotspot for Japanese tourists. Calvin Trillin, "Anne of Red Hair," *New Yorker*, 5 August 1996, 56–61. Terry Dawes is making a documentary about the Japanese affection for Lucy Maud Montgomery's novel.

21. The shogunate forbade the import of Christian books beginning in the 1640s, but books on more practical subjects (such as navigation) were permitted. As Andrew Gordon writes, a small flow of Western books and Chinese translations were allowed in the following decades. "A modest tradition of Dutch-language scholarship of the West took root, primarily in Nagasaki. Its practitioners looked into Western natural science, medicine, and botany in particular and compiled a dictionary and maps" (45). By the 1840s, these Dutch scholars had turned to the study of military technology. Andrew Gordon, *A Modern History of Japan: From Tokugawa Times to the Present*, 3rd ed. (New York: Oxford University Press, 2014). See also Rebekah Clements's *A Cultural History of Translation in Early Modern Japan* (Cambridge: Cambridge University Press, 2015).

22. John Ruskin, *Modern Painters, The Complete Works of John Ruskin*, 26 vols. (Philadelphia: Reuwee, Wattley & Walsh, 1891), 22:368.

23. Wolfgang Schivelbusch, *The Railway Journey: The Industrialization of Time and Space in the Nineteenth Century* (Berkeley: University of California Press, 1986), 69. Schivelbusch is also my source of information about the compression of travel times.

24. George Henry Lewes, *The Leader*, 28 December 1850, reprinted in Emily Brontë, *Wuthering Heights*, ed. Beth Newman (Peterborough, Ontario: Broadview Editions, 2007), 371.

25. Tom Toro cartoon, *New Yorker*, 23 April 2012, 47.

26. Gaskell, *Life of Charlotte Brontë*, 340.

27. Iwakami Haruko counted 17 translations of *Wuthering Heights* when she published in 2002 her excellent Brontë reception history and analysis of one of the first translations of *Jane Eyre*; at least three more have been published since that time. See Iwakami's "The Brontës in Japan: How *Jane Eyre* Was Received in the Meiji Period (1868–1912)," *Brontë Studies* 27 (July 2002): 91–99. In a separate article, written in Japanese, Iwakami details the early reception of *Wuthering Heights,* documenting critics' mentions of Emily Brontë and her novel in advance of its earliest translation. Iwakami, "*Arashi ga oka no juyō— Meiji ki kara Taishō Shōwa shoki* [The Brontës in Japan: How *Wuthering Heights* was received in Japan between the late 19th and the early 20th centuries], *Shiga daigaku kyōiku gakubu kyō* [Shiga University Education Department Bulletin] 58 (2008): 15-23. Professor Iwakami's work on Brontë reception history served as a crucial foundation for my research.

28. Walter Benjamin, "The Task of the Translator," in *Walter Benjamin: Selected Writings*, vol. 1 (1913–1926), ed. Marcus Bullock and Michael W. Jennings, trans. Harry Zohn (Cambridge, Mass.: Belknap Press of Harvard University Press, 1996), 256.

29. Brontë, *Wuthering Heights*, ed. Nestor, 19.

30. Okada Ryōichi includes *Wuthering Heights* in *Kaikaburareta meisaku* [Overestimated masterpieces], a book which challenges readers to judge independently five vaunted Western literary works. Okada, *Kaikaburareta meisaku* [Overestimated masterpieces] (Tokyo: Sairyusha, 2007).

31. Even now, having studied Japanese for eight years, I read Japanese at a snail's pace, leaving a penciled trail of definitions in the margins.

32. A. Lloyd, "Introduction," Kōyō Ozaki, *The Gold Demon*, trans. A. Lloyd and M. Lloyd (Tokyo: Seibundo, 1917), xii.

33. A. Lloyd, "Introduction," Kōyō Ozaki, *The Gold Demon*, xii–xiii.

34. The rich culture of translation in Japan resonated for me as evidence of intellectual curiosity and cosmopolitanism. However, Harasawa Masayoshi takes a more skeptical view, linking it to what he describes as a categorical imperative or driving force of the Japanese nation: "to Japanize everything that is at all foreign to us." Harasawa goes on to write: "It is only when in contact with its translation that they are really at ease with an English novel, essay, poem or whatever. In the subconscious of the whole nation, to read Shakespeare, for example, is to read him in translation." Masayoshi Harasawa, "Japanese Culture: The Ultimate Destiny of English Language Teaching in Japan," in *The Teaching of English in Japan*, ed. Ikuo Koike, Masao Matsuyama, Yasuo Igarashi, and Koji Suzuki (Tokyo: Eichosha, 1978), 550, 554. I am grateful to Myles Chilton's *English Studies Beyond the 'Center': Teaching Literature and the Future of Global English* (New York: Routledge, 2016) for drawing my attention to Harasawa's article.

35. Japan is not the only country in which the Brontës' novels have been remediated and adapted. See Patsy Stoneman's comprehensive and absorbing *Brontë Transformations: The Cultural Dissemination of "Jane Eyre" and "Wuthering Heights"* (London: Prentice Hall, 1996). Vladimir Nabokov describes how Don Quixote gradually lost contact with the book that bore him, "leaving his creator's desk and roaming space after roaming Spain." Just so has Heathcliff come to range beyond the novel he inhabits. Vladimir Nabokov, *Lectures on "Don Quixote,"* ed. Fredson Bowers (New York: Harcourt Brace Jovanovich, 1983), 112.

36. Of course, as I came to realize, the processes of adaptation and translation are intertwined. See the keen critical insights gathered in Laurence Raw's *Translation, Adaptation and Transformation* (New York: Continuum, 2012). Raw views translation and adaptation studies as "fundamentally different yet interrelated processes" (3).

37. For a book that comprehensively addresses a Western novel's reception in Japan, please see Tsuyoshi Ishihara's excellent *Mark Twain in Japan*, in which Ishihara describes how Japanese readers and writers transformed, distorted, and rejected aspects of Twain and his works. Ishihara, *Mark Twain in Japan: The Cultural Reception of an American Icon* (Columbia: University of Missouri Press, 2005). For a rich coverage of the reception of William Blake in Japan, see the essays gathered by Steve Clark and Masashi Suzuki in *The Reception of Blake in the Orient* (London: Continuum, 2006). On the reception of Coleridge in the East, see *Coleridge, Romanticism and the Orient*, ed. David Vallins, Kaz Oishi, and Seamus Perry (New York: Bloomsbury Academic, 2013).

38. Kazuhito Matsumoto, "'Exophony' in the Midst of the Mother Tongue: Resources Between Languages," in *Doing English in Asia: Global Literature and Culture*, ed. Patricia Haseltine and Sheng-mei Ma (New York: Lexington, 2016), 17–18.

39. Matsumoto, "'Exophony,'" 26.

40. Tawada Yoko qtd. in Matsumoto's "'Exophony,'" 18.

Chapter One

1. *Examiner*, January 1848, 21–22, reprinted in *The Brontës: The Critical Heritage*, ed. Miriam Allott (London: Routledge & Kegan Paul, 1974), 220.

2. *Britannia*, 15 January 1848, 42–43, reprinted in Allott, *The Brontës*, 223.

3. *Douglas Jerrold's Weekly Newspaper*, 15 January 1848, 77, reprinted in Allott, *The Brontës*, 228.

4. Unsigned notice in the *New Monthly Magazine*, January 1848, lxxxii, reprinted in Allott, *The Brontës*, 228.

5. Emily Brontë, *Wuthering Heights*, ed. Pauline Nestor (New York: Penguin Classics, 2008), [3]. Page citations hereafter provided in main body of text.

6. Borges qtd. in Stephen Bayley, "Books We Hate to Love," *Los Angeles Times*, 3 March 2006, online. Brontë may use this uncommon word, Janet Gezari suggests, to connote a secret place that is difficult to penetrate. Gezari writes, "His [Lockwood's] naive belief that the Heights is open to his inspection is repeatedly undermined, even as he enters more and more deeply into its innermost recesses and hidden places." Emily Brontë, *The Annotated "Wuthering Heights,"* ed. Janet Gezari (Cambridge, Mass.: Belknap Press of Harvard University Press, 2014), 44–45n13.

7. The title page is reprinted in Brontë, *Wuthering Heights*, ed. Nestor, unpaginated front matter.

8. Charlotte Brontë to Thomas DeQuincey, 16 June 1847, in *The Letters of Charlotte Brontë*, ed. Margaret Smith, 3 vols. (Oxford: Clarendon Press, 1995–2004), 1:530. Juliet Barker notes that a year after its publication, only two copies of *Poems* had been sold. Barker, *The Brontës* (New York: Pegasus, 2010), 589.

9. "Nothing creditable can be accomplished without application and diligence," Smiles writes in a typical passage. Samuel Smiles, *Self-Help; with Illustrations of Character, Conduct, and Perseverance*, Author's Revised and Enlarged Edition (New York: Wm. L. Allison, [1884]), vii. "The books were congenial to the spirit of the period," the scholar Okada Akiko writes, going on to note, more surprisingly, that Smiles introduced the Romantic poets to Japanese readers as models of self-help. "For example, Shelley became a great poet after toil and hardship, Byron became famous in spite of the adversity he faced because of lameness, and Keats was a genius of humble origin." Okada, *Keats and English Romanticism in Japan* (Bern, Switzerland: Peter Lang, 2006), 27. See also Sukehiro Hirakawa's *Japan's Love-Hate Relationship with the West* on Nakamura Masanao's translation of *Self-Help*, and on early translations of Western literature more generally. Hirakawa, *Japan's Love-Hate Relationship with the West* (Folkstone, Kent: Global Oriental, 2005).

10. Mizutani Futo explained his translation of Charlotte Brontë's title (as *Riso kajin*, or "An ideal lady") by talking about how the protagonist's taste and temper perfectly suited Rochester. "He had been looking for an ideal lady throughout Europe," Mizutani wrote. "After ten years of vain quest, he finally found one back home." The title and Mizutani's explanation suggest how, as Iwakami Haruko points out, the viewpoint was shifted from that of Jane to that of Rochester, confusing the point that *Jane Eyre* "is a story of a woman who achieved a loving marriage by her own will." Iwakami, "The Brontës in Japan: How *Jane Eyre* Was Received in the Meiji Period (1868–1912)," *Brontë Studies* 27 (July 2002): 96. The passages I quote from Mizutani are Iwakami's translations.

11. Iwakami, "The Brontës in Japan," 96. *Little Lord Fauntleroy*, too, was published serially, beginning in July 1890 with the first six installments coming out in book form in 1892. The complete translation in book form, released in 1897, became one of the best sellers of the period, going through one hundred printings by 1926. Iwakami contrasts the runaway success of *Fauntleroy* with the canceled *Jane Eyre* serialization, speculating that the *Fauntleroy* translator, Wakamatsu Shizuko, introduced an idealized image of a Western home, one in which (according to Iwakami's translation of Wakamatsu's statement), children were angels who could "detain their fathers who go astray and remind their mothers of integrity." Wakamatsu's plain colloquial translation style may also have contributed to the *Fauntleroy* translation's success. "She was so adept in translating dialogue that each character was very natural and lively," Iwakami writes, comparing Wakamatsu's dialogue to the new colloquial style of Futabatei Shimei in his novel *Ukigumo* [*The Drifting Clouds* (1887–1889)], which was published around the same time. At a moment when Japanese translators of Western works felt free to abridge according to their own whims, giving priority to story over literary style or voice, Futabatei was the first to argue for a sensitivity to a writer's style when translating works. Iwakami, 95.

12. Elizabeth Napier, "The Problem of Boundaries in *Wuthering Heights*," *Philological Quarterly* 63.1 (1984): 96. See also Susan Stewart, "The Ballad in *Wuthering Heights*," *Rep-*

resentations 86.1 (Spring 2004), especially 183. See too Dorothy Van Ghent's excursus on the windowpane as "the medium, treacherously transparent, separating the 'inside' from the 'outside,' the 'human' from the alien and terrible 'other.'" Van Ghent, *The English Novel: Form and Function* (New York: Holt, Rinehart and Winston, 1953), 161.

13. Quoted by Kato Yuji in "Herman Melville and Modern Japan: A Speculative Re-Interpretation of the Critical History," *Leviathan: A Journal of Melville Studies* 8.3 (2006): 11. Kato's source is Abe Tomoji's *Meruviru* [Melville] (Tokyo: Kenkyusha, 1934).

14. Takeshi Saitō, "Edmund Blunden, Poet," *Today's Japan* 5.3 (1960): 37. The decade of the 1920s was a period of Keats ascendance in Japan, with Saitō playing a decisive role in the dissemination of Keats knowledge. See Yoshikazu Suzuki, "'A candle that must melt away': Early Keats Scholarship in Japan," *English Romanticism in East Asia*, ed. Suh-Reen Han. Praxis Series. *Romantic Circles*. December 2016. Online. See also Okada's *Keats and English Romanticism in Japan* for an engaging, comprehensive account of Japanese Keats reception.

15. Dr. Toyoda qtd. by Yamato Yasuo, "Three Notes," in *English Studies in Japan: Essays and Studies Presented to Dr Yasuo Yamato in Honour of His Sixtieth Birthday* (Tokyo: English Literary Society of the Nihon University, 1958), 371.

16. Edmund Blunden to Richard Cobden-Sanders, 15 August 1925, Edmund Blunden Papers, Special Collections, The University of Iowa Libraries.

17. Edmund Blunden to Richard Cobden-Sanders, 31 March 1927, Edmund Blunden Papers, Special Collections, The University of Iowa Libraries.

18. Tamotsu Sone, "Edmund Blunden, Teacher," *Today's Japan* 5.3 (1960): 54.

19. Sone, "Edmund Blunden, Teacher," 54.

20. Sōseki Natsume, preface to *"Theory of Literature" and Other Critical Writings*, trans. Michael K. Bourdaghs, *Theory of Literature and Other Critical Writings*, ed. Michael K. Bourdaghs, Atsuko Ueda, and Joseph A. Murphy (New York: Columbia University Press, 2009), 48. See also Sōseki's *Spring Miscellany and London Essays*, trans. Sammy I. Tsunematsu (Boston: Tuttle, 2002), 7, and Damian Flanagan's insightful introductory account of Sōseki's two-year course of study in London in Sōseki Natsume, *The Tower of London: Tales of Victorian London*, trans. Damian Flanagan (London: Peter Owen, 2005).

21. Sōseki, preface to *Theory of Literature*, 44–45.

22. Sōseki, "Professor Craig," *The Tower of London*, 158.

23. Jay Rubin, "Translator's note," Sōseki Natsume's *Sanshirō: A Novel*, trans. Jay Rubin (London: Penguin Books, 2009), xlv.

24. Minae Mizumura, *The Fall of Language in the Age of English*, trans. Mari Yoshihara and Juliet Winters Carpenter (New York: Columbia University Press, 2015), 139.

25. Mizumura, *Fall of Language*, 154.

26. Mizumura, *Fall of Language*, 136.

27. Edmund Blunden to Richard Cobden-Sanders, 18 June 1824, Edmund Blunden Papers, Special Collections, The University of Iowa Libraries.

28. Qtd. in Barry Webb, *Edmund Blunden: A Biography* (New Haven: Yale University Press, 1990), 145.

29. Qtd. in Webb, *Edmund Blunden*, 163.

30. Qtd. in Webb, *Edmund Blunden*, 164.

31. Qtd. in Webb, *Edmund Blunden*, 202–203.

32. Webb, *Edmund Blunden*, 151.

33. Particles, for students of Japanese, like the determiners "the" and "a" for Japanese students of English, are little surrender flags that the non-native speaker waves every time she speaks or writes. At one point I speculated that when Wim Wenders gave the name *Tokyo-Ga* to his documentary homage to the auteur Ozu Yasujirō, he did so to mark his inability to understand the Japanese language—I assumed that the title "ga" evokes the Japanese particle *ga*. I couldn't have been more wrong, as a reader of this book in manuscript pointed out—Wenders' "ga" evokes the Japanese word *ga*, which means "image" or "picture." As I rewatched the film, I belatedly registered Wenders' many direct references to image-making, and to the differences between the images of Tokyo he was preserving and the ones he admired in Ozu's films. Still, Wenders' evocative film has much to say about linguistic bafflement. The most poignant moment in *Tokyo-Ga* comes when Ozu's cameraman hands Wenders one of Ozu's scripts. Wenders conveys the magical quality of the moment—he has before him an artifact actually used by the master, a sheaf of pages that passed from Ozu's hand to the cameraman's hand to Wenders—before admitting, sadly, in voice-over, "I couldn't decipher a single word, not even the title."

34. The manga artist Iwashita Hiromi and his editor Fujī Junya said that it would be impossible to come up with a better title than *Arashi ga oka*, which has an ominous quality that gives people the notion that something is going to happen. Iwashita observed that all Japanese people know this title, even though few have read the novel. Iwashita Hiromi and Fujī Junya, conversation with the author, Minami Machida, Tokyo, Japan, 18 August 2012. Kurosawa Ayako served as interpreter.

35. Professor Iki Kazuko, conversation with author, North American Society for the Study of Romanticism Supernumerary Conference, Tokyo, Japan, 13 June 2014.

36. In *Brontë Transformations*, Patsy Stoneman describes her interview with "Twinkles" Hunter, the actress who played the child Catherine in A. V. Bramble's 1920 film. Patsy Stoneman, *Brontë Transformations: The Cultural Dissemination of "Jane Eyre" and "Wuthering Heights"* (London: Prentice Hall, 1996), 115.

37. Kyoko Hirano, in *Mr. Smith Goes to Tokyo*, points out that under the Occupation, government films showing revenge as a legitimate motive, or depicting brutality as triumphant, were prohibited. *Wuthering Heights*, although more subdued in Wyler's film version than in Brontë's original, skated close to these prohibitions. *Mr. Smith Goes to Tokyo: Japanese Cinema Under the American Occupation, 1945–1952* (Washington, D.C.: Smithsonian Institution Press, 1992), 44. Hila Shachar, in her treatment of the filmic afterlives of *Wuthering Heights*, suggests that Wyler's 1939 film version turns Catherine and Heathcliff into "models of the eternal and transcendent nature of Western values," and goes on to assert that almost every subsequent screen adaptation of *Wuthering Heights* is indebted to Wyler's imagery and continues to repeat it. Hila Shachar, *Cultural Afterlives and Screen Adaptations of Classic Literature: "Wuthering Heights" and Company* (New York: Palgrave Macmillan, 2012), 48–49.

38. Hiroshi Kitamura, email message to author, 25 October 2016.

39. Hiroshi Kitamura, *Screening Enlightenment: Hollywood and the Cultural Reconstruction of Defeated Japan* (Ithaca, N.Y.: Cornell University Press, 2010), 102.

40. Kitamura, *Screening Enlightenment*, 100.

41. Abé Mark Nornes, "For an Abusive Subtitling," *Film Quarterly* 52.3 (1999): 20.

42. Ota Tatsuo qtd. in Nornes, "For an Abusive Subtitling," 27.

43. Donald Richie, *A Hundred Years of Japanese Film* (New York: Kodansha International, 2001), 21.

44. Hiroshi Komatsu and Frances Loden, "Mastering the Mute Image: The Role of the *Benshi* in Japanese Cinema," *Iris: A Journal of Theory on Image and Sound* 22 (Autumn 1996): 34.

45. The scene has assumed an unusually large place in the cultural imagination, serving, for example, as the inspiration for Kate Bush's 1978 hit pop song "Wuthering Heights."

46. "The cruelty of the dream is the gratuitousness of the violence wrought on a child by an emotionally unmotivated vacationer from the city, dreaming in a strange bed," writes Van Ghent. *The English Novel*, 160.

47. John Collick, "Dismembering Devils: The Demonology of *Arashi ga oka* (1988) and *Wuthering Heights* (1939)," in *Novel Images: Literature in Performance*, ed. Peter Reynolds (New York: Routledge, 1993), 40. Collick attributes this comment to Yoshida, whom he interviewed in 1991. Yoshida's film is available on DVD. *Arashi ga oka* [Wuthering Heights], directed by Yoshida Yoshishige (1988; Tokyo: Geneon Entertainment, 2005), DVD.

48. Maki Okumura, "Intrusion of the Stranger: Yoshishige Yoshida's Version of *Wuthering Heights*," *Brontë Studies* 29 (July 2004): 126. Okumura also discusses the influence on Yoshida's film of George Bataille's writings on the relationship between the sacred and the profane.

49. Okumura quotes an interview in which the director Yoshida describes this scene as conveying that Kinu feels that she has the same *oni* (demon) inside herself as Onimaru does. Okumura, "Intrusion of the Stranger," 129.

50. Collick, "Dismembering Devils," 38–39.

51. Hirokane Kenshi, *Atogaki* [afterword], in Saitō Ikumi, *Arashi ga oka* (1939) [Wuthering Heights (1939)], story by Kanno Hiroshi, *Sekai meisaku mūbī* [World masterwork movie] (Tokyo: Mangabank, 2007), 146–47.

52. I wasn't the first person to compare readers of *Wuthering Heights* to Lockwood. Stevie Davies writes, "Like the callow narrator of *Wuthering Heights*, Lockwood, we resolve with each reading, 'I don't care—I will get in!'" Davies, *Emily Brontë: Heretic* (London: The Women's Press, 1994), xi. Vivienne Rundle, in her dissertation "Framing the Reader: Interpretation and Design in Victorian and Early Modern Narrative," writes in detail about Lockwood as "reader-surrogate." PhD diss., University of Pennsylvania, 1992, 122.

53. Hirokane, *Atogaki* [afterword], in Saitō Ikumi, *Arashi ga oka (1939)* [Wuthering Heights (1939)], 156.

54. Stevie Davies suggests that Emily Brontë's works "uniquely compel and arouse us *because* they forbid our full comprehension; again and again the door is shut, leaving us stranded, at best half-in and half-out." Davies, *Emily Brontë*, xi.

Chapter Two

1. Jennifer Robertson chronicles Takarazuka Revue history and provides a fascinating analysis of the complicated gender dynamics of the all-female troupe. Her ground-

breaking study informs my work in this chapter. See Robertson, *Takarazuka: Sexual Politics and Popular Culture in Modern Japan* (Berkeley: University of California Press, 1998). More recent studies of the Takarazuka Revue include Leonie R. Stickland's *Gender Gymnastics: Performing and Consuming Japan's Takarazuka Revue* (Melbourne: Trans Pacific Press, 2008) and Makiko Yamanashi's *A History of the Takarazuka Revue Since 1914: Modernity, Girls' Culture, Japan Pop* (Boston: Global Oriental, 2012).

2. Emily Brontë, *Wuthering Heights*, ed. Pauline Nestor (New York: Penguin Classics, 2008), 323–24. Hereafter page citations provided in text of chapter.

3. In Beth Newman's view, "Isabella's rude awakening from her romantic fantasies . . . provide[s] a sustained critique of the romance novel." Newman, introduction to Brontë, *Wuthering Heights*, ed. Beth Newman (Peterborough, Ontario: Broadview Editions, 2007), 24. Joyce Carol Oates calls *Wuthering Heights* "a romance that brilliantly challenges the basic presumptions of the 'romantic.'" Oates, "The Magnanimity of *Wuthering Heights*," *Critical Inquiry* 9.2 (1982): 436.

4. *Dream Girls*, dir. Kim Longinotto and Jano Williams (Twentieth Century Vixen, 1994).

5. Sue Wise writing about the critical consensus on Elvis in "Sexing Elvis," *On Record: Rock, Pop, and the Written Word*, ed. Simon Frith and Andrew Goodwin (New York: Pantheon, 1990), 396.

6. Judith Butler, *Gender Trouble: Feminism and the Subversion of Identity* (New York: Routledge, 1990), 123. Jennifer Robertson suggests that the company has managed both "to uphold the dominant ideal of heterosexuality and to inform a lesbian subcultural style" (73). The Western literary works adopted by the Takarazuka producers, she goes on to write, became "a site of transvestism in Japanese popular culture." Robertson, *Takarazuka*, 76.

7. Koshiro Miyako, conversation with author, Yokohama, Japan, 18 August 2012. Kurosawa Ayako served as interpreter.

8. Nishiyama Sen, one of the diplomatic interpreters Kumiko Torikai writes about in *Voices of the Invisible Presence: Diplomatic Interpreters in Post–World War II Japan*, intentionally looked away from the speaker whose words he was interpreting in order to make him look at the listener. The speakers, he said, should be interacting with each other rather than with the interpreter. Torikai, *Voices of the Invisible Presence: Diplomatic Interpreters in Post–World War II Japan* (Philadelphia: John Benjamins, 2009), 118–19.

9. Roland Barthes, *Empire of Signs*, trans. Richard Howard (New York: Hill and Wang, 1982), 4. See also D. A. Miller's account of using *Empire of Signs* as his point of departure as he prepared for a trip to Japan. Miller, *Bringing Out Roland Barthes* (Berkeley: University of California Press, 1992).

10. More recently, Wao Yōka performed the role of Velma Kelly in a Takarazuka production of *Chicago* staged at Lincoln Center, New York City, in July 2016.

11. *Arashiga ga oka* [Wuthering Heights], Takarazuka Snow Troupe, directed by Ōta Tetsunori (1997; Takarazuka Creative, 2006), DVD.

12. Mizumura Minae, conversation with author, Oiwake, Japan, 13 August 2012.

13. Utsumi Shigenori, *Fain romansu Utsumi Shigenori Takarazuka kageki sakuhinshū* [Fine romance Utsumi Shigenori Takarazuka opera anthology] (Takarazuka City, Japan: Takarazuka Creative, 2000). Compact Disk.

14. Ōta Tetsunori, [Wuthering Heights], Bow Hall Stage, May 31-June 15, Takarazuka Opera Company (Takarazuka City, Japan: Takarazuka kagekidan, 1997). I am grateful to Ōta Tetsunori for giving me a bound copy of this script.

15. Utsumi Shigenori, *Arashi ga oka* [Wuthering Heights], *Takarazuka kageki kyaku hon to haiyaku* [Takarazuka Opera Company script and cast list], Shinjuku Coma Stadium, May 3-28, 1969; *Takarazuka Arashi ga oka*, May 3-28, 1969. English synopsis. Takarazuka *Wuthering Heights* fan magazine, 1969.

16. In this category of slightly defamiliarized English expressions I place an empathic imperative that I saw posted in the stall of a woman's bathroom: "Let's handle the public things with great care for everyone's comfortable use."

17. Virginia Woolf, "Haworth, November, 1904," *The Essays of Virginia Woolf*, ed. Andrew McNeillie, 3 vols. (New York: Harcourt Brace Jovanovich, 1986–1988), 1:8.

18. For a fascinating treatment of this topic, see Ivan Kreilkamp, "Petted Things: *Wuthering Heights* and the Animal," *Yale Journal of Criticism* 18 (Spring 2005): 87–110.

19. Nishiyama Sen qtd. in Torikai's *Voices of the Invisible Presence*, 118–19.

20. Ōta Tetsunori, conversation with the author, Takarazuka City, Japan, 20 August 2012. Kurosawa Ayako served as interpreter.

21. Monzaemon Chikamatsu, *The Love Suicides at Sonezaki*, in *Four Major Plays of Chikamatsu*, trans. Donald Keene (New York: Columbia University Press, 1961), 49.

22. Monzaemon Chikamatsu, *The Love Suicides at Amijima*, in *Four Major Plays*, 207.

23. Chikamatsu, *Love Suicides at Amijima*, 207.

24. Utsumi Shigenori, *Arashi ga oka* [Wuthering Heights].

Chapter Three

1. Iwashita Hiromi, *Arashi ga oka* [Wuthering Heights] (Tokyo: Nihonbungeisha, 2009).

2. Hanabusa Yōko, *Arashi ga oka* [Wuthering Heights], Grimm Fairy Tale Comics (Tokyo: Bunkasha, 2007).

3. Sakurai Mineko, *Arashi ga oka* [Wuthering Heights], Grimm Fairy Tale Comics (Tokyo: Bunkasha, 2012).

4. Suzuka Reni, *Arashi ga oka* [Wuthering Heights], Famous Love Comics 2, explanation by Edo Daisuke (Tokyo: Telehouse, 1989), 10.

5. Koyama Kariko and Yamagata Hirō, *Manga dewakaru piketi no nijūichi seiki no shihon* [Understanding by means of manga Thomas Piketty's *Capital in the Twenty-First Century*] (Tokyo: Takarajimasha, 2015).

6. Emily Brontë, *Wuthering Heights*, ed. Pauline Nestor (London: Penguin Classics, 2008), 82; page citations hereafter provided in text of chapter.

7. Morizono Miruku, *Arashi ga oka* [Wuthering Heights], Manga sekai no bungaku 8 [Manga world literature 8] (Tokyo: Sekai bunkasha, 1996).

8. Morizono, afterword, *Arashi ga oka* [Wuthering Heights], 268. (My translation.)

9. Jay Rubin, *Making Sense of Japanese: What the Textbooks Don't Tell You* (New York: Kodansha International, 1998), 110.

10. Hiromi Tsuchiya Dollase, "Early Twentieth-Century Japanese Girls' Magazine

Stories: Examining Shōjo Voice in *Hanamonogatari* (Flower tales)," *Journal of Popular Culture* 36.4 (2003): 725–26.

11. Kyōtei Ōson, preface to *Little Women*, qtd. in Dollase, "Japanese Girls' Magazine Stories," 726. See also Kazuko Watanabe's account of teaching *Little Women* in Japan. Watanabe, "Reading *Little Women*, Reading Motherhood in Japan," *Feminist Studies* 25.3 (Fall 1999): 698–709.

12. Dollase, "Japanese Girls' Magazine Stories," 727.

13. Rebecca Suter writes, "Like the 'glass mask' of the title, female identity is presented as something that needs to be learned, and even once acquired, is constantly in danger of shattering." Suter, "From Jusuheru to Jannu: Girl Knights and Christian Witches in the Work of Miuchi Suzue," *Mechademia* 4 (2009): 246.

14. I found helpful and delightful the pop culture wiki tvtropes.org, which details iconic and recurring themes and images found in the *Glass Mask* anime series.

15. Miuchi Suzue, *Garasu no kamen* [Glass mask] (Tokyo: Hakusensha, 1978), 7:17. (My translation.)

16. Miuchi Suzue, conversation with the author, Kichijōji, Musashino, Tokyo, 17 August 2012. Kurosawa Ayako served as interpreter.

17. A Noh drama version of *Kurenai tennyo* [Crimson goddess] was performed in 2006 to sellout crowds in Tokyo and Osaka. For a brief discussion of this production as part of an appeal to younger audiences, see Mariko Anno and Judy Halebsky, "Innovation in Nō: Matsui Akira Continues a Tradition of Change," *Asian Theatre Journal* 31.1 (2014): 134–35. For an illustrated account of the making of the new *Kurenai tennyo* production, see Miuchi Suzue and Hikawa Mariko's *Shinsaku nō Kurenai tennyo no sekai—Garasu no kamen yori* [New Noh crimson goddess world—based on Glass Mask] (Tokyo: Hakusensha, 2006).

18. Emily Brontë, *Arashi ga oka* [*Wuthering Heights*], trans. Abe Tomoji, 2 vols. (1961; repr., Tokyo: Iwanami shoten, 1991–92).

19. Miuchi Suzue, *Garasu no kamen* [Glass mask], 7:124–25.

20. Shimura Takako, *Aoi hana* [Sweet Blue Flowers], 8 vols. (Tokyo: Ōtashuppan, 2005–2013), 2:47 (My translation.)

21. Miuchi Suzue, *Garasu no kamen* [Glass mask], 7:104.

22. Miuchi Suzue, *Garasu no kamen*, [Glass mask], 8:15 and 8:20.

23. Beth Newman, introduction, Emily Brontë, *Wuthering Heights*, ed. Beth Newman (Peterborough, Ontario: Broadview Press, 2007), 27.

24. Juliet Barker, "Emily Brontë," *Oxford Dictionary of National Biography*, online.

25. Pauline Nestor, introduction to Emily Brontë, *Wuthering Heights*, ed. Pauline Nestor, xviii. Nestor's source is Elizabeth Gaskell's *The Life of Charlotte Brontë*.

26. Charlotte Brontë, "Editor's Preface to the New [1850] Edition of Wuthering Heights," reprinted in Brontë, *Wuthering Heights*, ed. Nestor, l and lii.

Chapter Four

1. Mizumura Minae, *Honkaku shōsetsu* [*A True Novel*] (Tokyo: Shinchōsha, 2002).

2. Minae Mizumura, "Renunciation," *Yale French Studies* 69 (1985): 81–97.

3. Leopoldo Brizuela and Oliverio Cohelo, "Interview with Minae Mizumura," *La Nacion* (Buenos Aires), 1 March 2008, 3.

4. Kōno Taeko and Tomioka Taeko, *Arashi ga oka futari tabi* [Duo journey in *Wuthering Heights*] (Tokyo: Bungeishunjū, 1986); Kōno Taeko, *Gikyoku Arashi ga oka* [Wuthering Heights: A play] (Tokyo: Kawade shobō shinsha, 1970); Taeko Kōno, *Toddler, Hunting & Other Stories*, trans. Lucy North (New York: New Directions, 1996). Kōno has also written critical essays that address Brontë's work. See *Kōno Taeko zenshū* [Taeko Kōno complete works] (Tokyo: Shinchōsha, 1994–95). Kōno was the first president of the Brontë Society of Japan. See the Brontë Society entry in Christine Alexander and Margaret Smith's *The Oxford Companion to the Brontës* (Oxford: Oxford University Press, 2003), 105–6.

5. Emily Brontë, *Wuthering Heights*, ed. Pauline Nestor (London: Penguin Books, 2008), 324; page citations hereafter provided in text of chapter. Ayako Miura, *Freezing Point*, trans. Hiromu Shimuzu and John Terry (Wilmington, Del.: Dawn Press, 1986), 348 and 426. Miura's contemporary, the novelist Tsushima Yūko (1947–2016), too, has expressed her interest in *Wuthering Heights*, writing an essay about Catherine in *Hon no naka shōjotachi* [Girls in books] (Tokyo: Chūōkōronsha, 1989).

6. Sachiko Schierbeck, "Miura Ayako," in *Japanese Women Novelists in the 20th Century: 100 Biographies, 1990–1993* (Copenhagen, Denmark: Museum Tusculanum Press, 1994), 207. More recently, the novelist Aoyama Nanae, too, evokes *Wuthering Heights* when she tracks the relationship of two young lovers from childhood to old age in her novel *Meguri ito* [Circulating threads], in which her heroine echoes Catherine's "I *am* Heathcliff" by saying, "Tetsuharu is me." Aoyama Nanae, *Meguri ito* (Tokyo: Shueisha, 2013). I am indebted to Kawasaki Akiko's account of this novel, and also to her account of Kōno Taeko's work. See Kawasaki, "Japanese Adaptations of *Wuthering Heights*: Taeko Kono, *Gikyoku Arashi-ga-oka*, Minae Mizumura, *A True Novel*, and Nanae Aoyama, *Meguri-ito*," in *Buronte to 19 seiki Igirisu* [The Brontës and Nineteenth-Century Great Britain] (Osaka, Japan: Osaka Kyoiku Tosho, 2015), 315–29. My thanks to Mizumura Minae for drawing my attention to Kawasaki's excellent article. I also received assistance in understanding the influence of Brontë on Aoyama's work from Tanizaki Yui and Hakui Ryoko, and from Aoyama Nanae herself.

7. Minae Mizumura, *A True Novel*, trans. Juliet Winters Carpenter (New York: Other Press, 2013), 159. Hereafter page citations provided in text of chapter.

8. "About IWP," International Writing Program (University of Iowa), https://iwp.uiowa.edu/about-iwp.

9. Minae Mizumura, *The Fall of Language in the Age of English*, trans. Mari Yoshihara and Juliet Winters Carpenter (New York: Columbia University Press, 2015), 19.

10. Mizumura, *The Fall of Language*, 21.

11. Mizumura, *The Fall of Language*, 12.

12. Mizumura, *The Fall of Language*, 15.

13. This is the translation of the song's Japanese lyrics that was contributed by "Sedgwick" to the web site www.jpopasia.com.

14. Hisaaki Yamanouchi, *The Search for Authenticity in Modern Japanese Literature* (Cambridge: Cambridge University Press, 1978), 36.

15. Yamanouchi, *The Search for Authenticity*, 36.

16. Judith Thurman, "The Kimono Painter," in *Cleopatra's Nose: 39 Varieties of Desire* (New York: Farrar, Straus and Giroux, 2007), 261.

17. Junichirō Tanizaki, *The Makioka Sisters*, trans. Edward G. Seidensticker (New York: Vintage Books, 1995), 30.

18. Thurman, "The Kimono Painter," 261. In my experience, Japanese people graciously share their kimono culture with foreigners. When my daughters attended a Japanese high school, the school mothers lassoed them into borrowed *yukata* so that they could join their classmates in a traditional dance. When Katy Perry decked herself out in kimono, *tabi* socks, and geisha makeup at the 2013 American Music Awards, a costume criticized by some American commentators for its cultural appropriation, my Japanese conversation partner shrugged.

19. Isaac Titsingh, *Illustrations of Japan* (London: R. Ackermann, 1822), 99.

20. See the literary offerings compiled in *Shōjo sekai bungaku zenshū* [Girls' library of world literature], 30 vols. (Tokyo: Kaisei-sha, 1960–64), and in *Sekai meisaku bunko* [World masterpiece library], 140 vols. (Tokyo: Kaisei-sha, 1954–61).

21. Mizumura Minae, conversation with author, Oiwake, Nagano, Japan, 13 August 2012.

22. Minae Mizumura, "The Japanese Language: An Endangered Heritage," interview by Kōno Michikazu, *Japan Echo* 36.2 (2009). Online.

23. Aiko Ito and Graeme Wilson, introduction to *I Am a Cat* by Natsume Sōseki, trans. Aiko Ito and Graeme Wilson (Boston: Tuttle, 2002), xvi. *Wagahai* means "I" but with a nuance of arrogance.

24. Mizumura, "The Japanese Language: An Endangered Heritage."

25. Iwakami Haruko and Okumura Maki, conversation with the author, Kusatsu, Shiga Prefecture, 20 June 2014.

26. Iwakami, conversation with author. See also Iwakami Haruko, review (in Japanese) of *A True Novel*, by Minae Mizumura, trans. Juliet Winters Carpenter, *Brontë Studies* 5.6 (2014): 39–42.

27. Juliet Winters Carpenter, conversation with author, Kyoto, Japan, 19 June 2014.

28. Vladimir Nabokov, *Lectures on "Don Quixote,"* ed. Fredson Bowers (New York: Harcourt Brace Jovanovich, 1983), 29.

29. Nabokov, *Lectures on "Don Quixote,"* 75.

30. Jorge Luis Borges, qtd. in Alberto Manguel, *With Borges* (London: Telegram, 2006), 43.

31. Jorge Luis Borges, *The Total Library: Nonfiction 1922–1986*, ed. Eliot Weinberger, trans. Esther Allen, Suzanne Jill Levine, and Eliot Weinberger (New York: Penguin, 2001), 93. Contemporary theorists of translation take the Borgesian view to a further extreme, linking translation failure to genre innovation. See Emily Apter's *Against World Literature: On the Politics of Untranslatability* (New York: Verso, 2013). Apter takes up Franco Moretti's suggestion that, when transplanted from their native soil, literary forms undergo morphological innovation, leading Apter to ask, "Are new genres made by virtue of translation failure?" (50). See also Laurence Raw, *Translation, Adaptation and Transformation* (New York: Continuum, 2012).

32. In a blog post for the Society of Children's Book Writers & Illustrators Japan Translation Group, Carpenter has written about her work with students on translating passages from Mizumura's novel. See "One Passage, Seven Translations—Minae Mizumura." https://ihatov.wordpress.com/tag/juliet-winters-carpenter/.

33. Richard Blakeborough, *Wit, Character, Folklore and Customs of the North Riding of Yorkshire* (London: Henry Frowde, 1898), 120.

34. Carpenter's translation of Mizumura's *A True Novel* won the 2014–2015 Japan-

U.S. Friendship Commission Prize for the Translation of Japanese Literature, as well as the 2014 Lewis Galantiere Award. Mizumura's *Honkaku shōsetsu* won the 2002 Yomiuri Prize for Literature.

35. Miuchi Suzue, conversation with the author, Kichijōji, Musashino, Tokyo, 17 August 2012.

36. Lafcadio Hearn, "Furosodé," *In Ghostly Japan* (Boston: Little, Brown, and Company, 1899), 12.

37. Takeo Arishima, *A Certain Woman*, trans. Kenneth Strong (Tokyo: University of Tokyo Press, 1978), 135.

38. Mizumura Minae, conversation with author, Tokyo, 10 June 2014.

39. Mizumura's *Haha no isan* has been published in Juliet Winters Carpenter's translation *Inheritance from Mother* (New York: Other Press, 2017).

40. Mizumura, *The Fall of Language*, 153. This observation by Mizumura helped me to understand a charge that has been leveled against the novelist Ōe Kenzaburō, who has been accused of writing Japanese "that reads like a translation from a Western language." Translator's note to Kenzaburō Ōe, *The Silent Cry*, trans. John Bester (New York: Kodansha International, 1974), 1. Another translator of Ōe's work, John Nathan, writes, "Ōe consciously interferes with the tendency to vagueness which is considered inherent in the Japanese language." Nathan notes critics' accusation that Ōe's prose "reeks of butter," a way of saying "he has alloyed the purity of Japanese with constructions from Western languages." Kenzaburō Ōe, *A Personal Matter*, trans. John Nathan (New York: Grove Press, 1969), ix.

41. In his manga version of Brontë's novel, Iwashita Hiromi provides a clarifying schematic drawing of this scene. Iwashita Hiromi, *Arashi ga oka* [Wuthering Heights] (Tokyo: Nihonbungeisha, 2009), 143.

Chapter Five

1. Tamura Taeko, trans. *E to genbun de tanoshimu Wuthering Heights* [Enjoying *Wuthering Heights* with illustrations and original text], *Inkoku* [seal illustrations] by Ichihara Junko. Osaka: Osaka Kyōiku Tosho, 2007).

2. Emily Brontë, *Wuthering Heights*, ed. Pauline Nestor (London: Penguin Classics, 2008), 82. Hereafter page citations provided in text of chapter.

3. Laura Ingalls Wilder, *Ōki na mori no chiisa na ie* [*Little House in the Big Woods*], trans. Onchi Mihoko, illustrations by Garth Montgomery Williams (Tokyo: Fukuinkanshoten, 1973). Takayama Hiromi helped with translation.

4. Ichihara Junko, letter to author, 23 November 2013.

5. Emily Brontë, *Wuthering Heights*, abridged and simplified by E.M. Attwood, annotated by Katsuji Takamura and Miyuki Kino (Tokyo: Eichosha, 1974); Emily Brontë, *Arashi ga oka* [*Wuthering Heights*], E. M. Attwood abridged version, translated by students in Tamura Taeko's Yomiuri Bunka Center class, 2008.

6. Tamura Taeko, conversation with author, Kadoma, Osaka, Japan, 23 August 2012.

7. *Ai no arashi* [Storm of love], midday drama directed by Yamamoto Takanori, Matsuoi Hideji, Fukuda Shinji, Ono Toshikazu, and Hanadō Junji (Nagoya, Japan: Tōkai Television, 1986); *Shin ai no arashi* [New storm of love], midday drama directed by

Kaneko Yoshiichi, Koike Tadakazu, and Shimazaki Toshiki (Nagoya, Japan: Tōkai Television, 2002).

8. Emily Brontë, *Arashi ga oka* [*Wuthering Heights*]. Translation and notes by Nakaoka Hiroshi. English Treasury (Tokyo: Gogaku Shunjusha, 2002).

9. Tamura Taeko, trans. *E to genbun de tanoshimu Wuthering Heights*, 23.

10. Terry Eagleton, *Myths of Power: A Marxist Study of the Brontës* (New York: Macmillan, 1975), 103.

11. Graeme Tytler, "'Nelly, I *am* Heathcliff!': The Problem of 'Identification' in *Wuthering Heights*," *Midwest Quarterly* 47.2 (2006): 178.

12. Daniel Cottom, "I Think; Therefore, I Am Heathcliff," *ELH* 70.4 (2003): 1083.

13. John Allen Stevenson, "'Heathcliff Is Me!': *Wuthering Heights* and the Question of Likeness," *Nineteenth-Century Literature* 43.1 (1988): 71.

14. Claire Kramsch writes, "In language learning, desire is first of all escape—the urge to escape from a state of tedious conformity with one's present environment to a state of plenitude and enhanced power." Kramsch, *The Multilingual Subject: What Foreign Language Learners Say about their Experience and Why It Matters* (Oxford: Oxford University Press, 2009), 14.

15. Kobashi Sumio, *Arashi ga oka no nihongo hyōgen* [*Wuthering Heights* in Japanese expression] (Okayama: Sanmon insatsujo, 2012).

16. Kobashi Sumio, letter to author, 20 June 2014.

17. Kobashi Sumio, letter to author, 2 July 2014.

18. Emily Brontë, *Arashi ga oka* [*Wuthering Heights*], trans. Kōnosu Yukiko (Tokyo: Shinchōsha, 2003). Emily Brontë, *Arashi ga oka* [*Wuthering Heights*], trans. Tanaka Seijirō, 2 vols. (Tokyo: Shinchōsha, 1953).

19. Kōnosu Yukiko, conversation with author, Nishi Ogikubo, Tokyo, 17 June 2014. I later discovered Kōnosu's essay "*Arashi ga oka o yomu* [Reading *Wuthering Heights*] in *Shōjo wa hon o yonde otona ni naru* [Girls, grow up with books!] (Tokyo: Gendai kikakushitsu, 2015), pp. 81–106. In this essay, Kōnosu describes how she came to *Wuthering Heights* by way of Jean Webster's *Daddy-Long-Legs*, and reread Brontë's novel in college. She also says that she finds the second half of the novel, which is often excised in Japanese versions, the most interesting, and she argues for the central importance of Nelly Dean, calling her the agent of the story, and comparing her to a lone ferryman steering a barge on a river.

20. Hakui Ryoko and Kōnosu Yukiko, conversation with author, Nishi Ogikubo, Tokyo, 17 June 2014. The novelist Tanizaki Yui also contributed to this lively conversation.

21. Minae Mizumura, "On Translation," *91st Meridian*, International Writing Program, University of Iowa. https://iwp.uiowa.edu/sites/iwp/files/Minae_translation.pdf.

22. Tamura Taeko, trans. *E to genbun de tanoshimu Wuthering Heights*, 26.

23. In Saitō's manga, the line reads: *Hīsukurifu koso watashi no inochi*. Saitō Ikumi, *Arashi ga oka* [Wuthering Heights], story by Kanno Hiroshi (Tokyo: Mangabank, 2007), unpaginated.

24. Iwashita Hiromi, *Arashi ga oka* [Wuthering Heights] (Tokyo: Nihonbungeisha, 2009), 39.

25. Morizono Miriku. *Arashi ga oka* [Wuthering Heights], *Manga sekai no bungaku* 8 [Manga world literature 8] (Tokyo: Sekai bunkasha, 1996), 94–95.

26. In Hanabusa's manga, Catherine says: *Atashitachi wa hanarenai!! Atashi ga dare to*

kekkon shitemo kawarani. Atashi wa Hīsukurifu o zutto soba ni oite okumono!! Hanabusa Yōko, *Arashi ga oka* [Wuthering Heights], Grimm Fairy Tale Comics (Tokyo: Bunkasha, 2007), unpaginated.

27. Hanabusa Yōko and Sanazaki Harumo, conversation with author, Roppongi, Minato City, Tokyo, 16 August 2012.

28. The subtitle reads: *Watashitachi wa isshin doutai. Arashi ga oka* [*Wuthering Heights*], dir. William Wyler, *Mizuno Haruo no DVD de miru sekai meisaku eiga* [Haruo Mizuno's world masterwork movie] (Tokyo: Keep Co., Ltd., 2005). DVD.

29. In Abe's Japanese translation, Catherine says, *Atashi wa Hīsukurifu nano yo, Neri! Kare wa, itsudemo, istudemo, atashi no kokoro no naka ni iru.* Emily Brontë, *Arashi ga oka* [*Wuthering Heights*], trans. Abe Tomoji, 2 vols. (Tokyo: Iwanami shoten, 1991–92), 1:139.

30. In Kōnosu's translation, Catherine says, *Nerī, watashi wa Hīsukurifu to hitotsu na no yo—ano ko wa donna toki demo, itsumademo, watashi no kokoro no naka ni iru.* Emily Brontë, *Arashi ga oka* [*Wuthering Heights*], trans. Kōnosu Yukiko, 172.

Coda

1. A Japanologist who read this book in manuscript countered my association of this point of grammar with passive aggression, and sent me running back to my Japanese textbook, where, it is true, there was no mention of aggression, but where I found the indirect passive example sentence I had recalled. The textbook writer translated *Watashi wa akachan ni nakareta* as "The baby cried on me. (literally: I was cried by the baby)." Yukiko Abe Hatasa, Kazumi Hatasa, and Seiichi Makino, *Nakama 2: Japanese Communication, Culture, Context* (New York: Houghton Mifflin, 2000), 442. Unable to let go of my misinterpretation of this grammar construction, I thought fondly of a line from William Maxwell's *The Chateau.* Maxwell writes of an American couple sojourning in France: "They stood in line under a sign—*Personnes Isolées*—that had for them a poignancy it didn't have for those who were more at home in the French language." William Maxwell, *The Chateau* (New York: Alfred A. Knopf, 1961), 108.

2. Juliet Barker, *The Brontës* (New York: Pegasus Books, 2010), 448.

3. Stuart Curran, "Byron and Shelley: Becoming Italian" (paper presented at the North American Society for the Study of Romanticism Supernumerary Conference, Tokyo, Japan, June 2014).

4. Emily Brontë, *Wuthering Heights*, ed. Pauline Nestor (New York: Penguin Classics, 2008), 63. Hereafter page citations provided in text of chapter.

5. Charlotte Brontë, *The Professor*, ed. Margaret Smith and Herbert Rosengarten (Oxford: Clarendon Press, 1987), 13.

6. Margaret Smith, introduction to Charlotte Brontë, *The Professor*, xxx.

7. Mary Shelley, *Frankenstein; or, The Modern Prometheus*, ed. D. L. Macdonald and Kathleen Scherf (Peterborough, Ontario: Broadview Press, 1994), 140.

8. Mary Shelley, *Frankenstein*, 146.

9. Jane Austen, *Northanger Abbey*, ed. Claire Grogan (Peterborough, Ontario: Broadview Press, 2002), 170.

10. Midori Yoshida, "The Acquisition of English Vocabulary by a Japanese-Speaking Child," in *Second Language Acquisition: A Book of Readings*, ed. Evelyn Marcussen Hatch (Rowley, Mass.: Newbury House, 1978), 91–100.

11. For a rich array of essays discussing the common practice of, and polemical issues related to, English language teaching in Japan, see the giant anthology *The Teaching of English in Japan*, ed. Ikuo Koike, Masao Matsuyama, Yasuo Igarashi, and Koji Suzuki (Tokyo: Eichosha, 1978). This collection includes Masayoshi Harasawa's essay "Japanese Culture: The Ultimate Destiny of English Language Teaching in Japan," in which Harasawa historicizes and criticizes the focus on translation in English language teaching, writing, "English is a language that requires us first and foremost to speak it or hear it spoken in order to meet the needs of the moment. This communication aspect of English has nothing at all to do with translation or rather translation will only work as a vicious interference in the process." Harasawa, "Japanese Culture," 554. More recently, Myles Chilton has noted the way in which foreign language education, as a result of globalization, has become instrumentalized as a tool for communication rather than as "a medium of expression or representation." Myles Chilton, *English Studies Beyond the 'Center': Teaching Literature and the Future of Global English* (New York: Routledge, 2016), 4.

12. The Mixxer, Dickinson College, http://www.language-exchanges.org/.

13. Mori Michiyo, *Arashi ga oka* [Wuthering Heights], vol. 99 in *Sekai meisaku bunko* [World masterpiece library] (Tokyo: Kaisei-sha, 1954).

14. Jean Webster, *Daddy-Long-Legs* (New York: Puffin Books, 2010), 45.

15. James Morita, "Mori Michiyo," *Japanese Women Writers: A Bio-Critical Sourcebook*, ed. Chieko I. Mulhern (Westport, Conn.: Greenwood Press, 1994), 235.

16. Manjirō wrote the first Japanese guide to English conversation. See Takashi Inui, *Jon Manjirō no eikaiwa* [John Manjiro's English conversation manual] (Tokyo: Jieirisāchishuppan, 2010).

17. Juliet Winters Carpenter, conversation with the author, Kyoto, Japan, 19 June 2014.

18. James W. Heisig, introduction to *Remembering the Kanji: A Complete Course on How Not to Forget the Meaning and Writing of Japanese Characters*. vol. 1, 6th ed. (Honolulu: University of Hawai'i Press, 2011), 7.

Works Consulted

"About IWP." International Writing Program (University of Iowa). https://iwp.uiowa. edu/about-iwp.

Ai no arashi [Storm of love]. Midday drama. Dir. Yamamoto Takanori, Matsuoi Hideji, Fukuda Shinji, Ono Toshikazu, and Hanadō Junji. Nagoya, Japan: Tōkai Television, 1986.

Alexander, Christine and Margaret Smith. *The Oxford Companion to the Brontës*. Oxford: Oxford University Press, 2011. Online.

Allott, Miriam, ed. *The Brontës: The Critical Heritage*. London: Routledge & Kegan Paul, 1974.

Anno, Mariko, and Judy Halebsky. "Innovation in Nō: Matsui Akira Continues a Tradition of Change." *Asian Theatre Journal* 31.1 (2014): 126–52.

Aoyama Nanae. *Meguri ito* [Circulating threads]. Tokyo: Shūeisha, 2013.

Apter, Emily. *Against World Literature: On the Politics of Untranslatability*. London and New York: Verso, 2013.

Arashi ga oka [Wuthering Heights]. Takarazuka Snow Troupe. Dir. Ōta Tetsunori. Starring Wao Yōka. Takarazuka City: Takarazuka Creative, 2006. DVD.

Arashi ga oka [Wuthering Heights]. Dir. William Wyler. *Mizuno Haruo no DVD de miru sekai meisaku eiga* [Haruo Mizuno's world masterwork movie]. Tokyo: Keep Co., Ltd., 2005. DVD.

Arashi ga oka [Wuthering Heights]. Dir. Yoshida Yoshishige. Tokyo: Geneon Entertainment, 2005. DVD.

Arishima, Takeo. *A Certain Woman*. Trans. Kenneth Strong. Tokyo: University of Tokyo Press, 1978.

Austen, Jane. *Northanger Abbey*. Ed. Claire Grogan. Peterborough, Ontario: Broadview Press, 2002.

Avakian, Monique. *The Meiji Restoration and the Rise of Modern Japan*. Englewood Cliffs, New Jersey: Silver Burdett Press, Inc., 1991.

Azuma, Hiroki. *Otaku: Japan's Database Animals*. Trans. Jonathan E. Abel and Shion Kono. Minneapolis: University of Minnesota Press, 2009.

Azuma Ryūmei. *Konna ai o shitemitai arashi ga oka yori arashi ga oka* [Wanting to see a love like this: Wuthering Heights]. Tokyo: Tenkeidō, 1987.

Barker, Juliet. *The Brontës*. New York: Pegasus, 2010.

Barker, Juliet. "Emily Brontë." *Oxford Dictionary of National Biography*. Online.

Barthes, Roland. *Empire of Signs*. Trans. Richard Howard. New York: Hill and Wang, 1982.

Bayley, Stephen. "Books We Hate to Love." *Los Angeles Times*, 3 March 2006. http://articles.latimes.com/2006/mar/03/opinion/oe-bayley3.

Beilenson, Peter and Harry Behn, trans. *Haiku Harvest*. Japanese Haiku Series IV. Mount Vernon, NY: The Peter Pauper Press, 1962.

Benfey, Christopher. *The Great Wave: Gilded Age Misfits, Japanese Eccentrics, and the Opening of Old Japan*. New York: Random House, 2003.

Benjamin, Walter. "The Task of the Translator." In *Walter Benjamin: Selected Writings*. Vol. 1. *1913-1926*. Ed. Marcus Bullock and Michael W. Jennings. Trans. Harry Zohn. Cambridge: Belknap Press of Harvard University Press, 1996. 253-63.

Bernard, Donald R. *The Life and Times of John Manjiro*. New York: McGraw-Hill, 1992.

Blakeborough, Richard. *Wit, Character, Folklore and Customs of the North Riding of Yorkshire*. London: Henry Frowde, 1898.

Blumberg, Rhoda. *Shipwrecked!: The True Adventures of a Japanese Boy*. New York: Harper Collins, 2001.

Blunden, Edmund. *Lectures in English Literature*. Tokyo: Kodokwan & Co., Ltd., 1952.

Blunden, Edmund. Edmund Blunden Papers. Special Collections. The University of Iowa Libraries.

Borges, Jorge Luis. *The Total Library: Nonfiction, 1922-1986*. Ed. Eliot Weinberger. Trans. Esther Allen, Suzanne Jill Levine, and Eliot Weinberger. New York: Penguin, 2001.

Brizuela, Leopoldo, and Oliverio Cohelo. "Interview with Minae Mizumura." *La Nacion* (Buenos Aires), 1 March 2008, 1-14. http://mizumuraminae.com/pdf/MinaeMizumuraInterviewLaNacionRevised20140411.pdf.

Brontë, Charlotte. *The Letters of Charlotte Brontë*. Ed. Margaret Smith. 3 vols. Oxford: Clarendon Press, 1995-2004.

Brontë, Charlotte. *The Professor*. Ed. Margaret Smith and Herbert Rosengarten. Oxford: Clarendon Press, 1987.

Brontë, Emily. *The Annotated "Wuthering Heights."* Ed. Janet Gezari. Cambridge, Mass.: Belknap Press of Harvard University Press, 2014.

Brontë, Emily. *Arashi ga oka* [*Wuthering Heights*]. E.M. Attwood abridged version. Translated by the students in Tamura Taeko's Yomiuri Bunka Center class, 2008.

Brontë, Emily. *Arashi ga oka* [*Wuthering Heights*]. Translation and notes by Nakaoka Hiroshi. English Treasury. Tokyo: Gogaku Shunjusha, 2002.

Brontë, Emily. *Arashi ga oka* [*Wuthering Heights*]. Novel Theater Series. Ed. Nakaoka Hiromi. Tokyo: Gogaku Shunjusha, 1972.

Brontë, Emily. *Arashi ga oka* [*Wuthering Heights*]. Trans. Abe Tomoji. 2 vols. Tokyo: Iwanami shoten, 1991-92. Abe's translation first published 1960-61.

Brontë, Emily. *Arashi ga oka* [*Wuthering Heights*]. Trans. Funayama Kaoru. Vol. 10. *Shōjo sekai bungaku zenshū* [Girls' library of world literature]. Tokyo: Kaisei-sha, 1961.

Brontë, Emily. *Arashi ga oka* [*Wuthering Heights*]. Trans. Kawashima Hiromi. 2 vols. Tokyo: Iwanami shoten, 2004.

Brontë, Emily. *Arashi ga oka* [*Wuthering Heights*]. Trans. Kono Ichirō. Tokyo: Chūōkōronsha, 1993.

Brontë, Emily. *Arashi ga oka* [*Wuthering Heights*]. Trans. Kōnosu Yukiko. Tokyo: Shinchōsha, 2003.

Brontë, Emily. *Arashi ga oka* [*Wuthering Heights*]. Trans. Onodera Takeshi. 2 vols. Tokyo: Kōbunsha, 2010.

Brontë, Emily. *Arashi ga oka* [*Wuthering Heights*]. Trans. Tanaka Seijirō. 2 vols. Tokyo: Shinchōsha, 1953.

Brontë, Emily. *Arashi ga oka* [*Wuthering Heights*]. Trans. Tanaka Yasuo. 2 vols. Kyoto: Miyaobi Shuppansha, 2001–2002.

Brontë, Emily. *Arashi ga oka* [*Wuthering Heights*]. Trans. Yamato Yasuo. Tokyo: Kadokawa shoten, 1998. Yamato's translation first published 1932.

Brontë, Emily. *E to genbun de tanoshimu "Wuthering Heights"* [Enjoying *Wuthering Heights* with illustrations and original text]. Trans. Tamura Taeko. *Inkoku* [seal illustrations] by Ichihara Junko. Osaka: Osaka Kyōiku Tosho, 2007.

Brontë, Emily. *Wuthering Heights*. Abridged and simplified by E. M. Attwood. Annotated by Katsuji Takamura and Miyuki Kino. Tokyo: Eichosha, 1974.

Brontë, Emily. *Wuthering Heights*. Ed. Pauline Nestor. New York: Penguin Classics, 2008.

Brontë, Emily. *Wuthering Heights*. Ed. Beth Newman. Peterborough, Ontario: Broadview Editions, 2007.

Butler, Judith. *Gender Trouble: Feminism and the Subversion of Identity*. New York: Routledge, 1990.

Carpenter, Juliet Winters. "One Passage, Seven Translations—Minae Mizumura." SCBWI Japan Translation Group (Society of Children's Book Writers & Illustrators). https://ihatov.wordpress.com/tag/juliet-winters-carpenter/.

Carson, Anne. *Glass, Irony and God*. New York: New Directions, 1995.

Chikamatsu, Monzaemon. *Four Major Plays of Chikamatsu*. Trans. Donald Keene. New York: Columbia University Press, 1961.

Chilton, Myles. *English Studies Beyond the 'Center': Teaching Literature and the Future of Global English*. New York: Routledge, 2016.

Chitham, Edward. *The Birth of "Wuthering Heights": Emily Brontë at Work*. New York: St. Martin's Press, 1998.

Cho, Heekyoung. *Translation's Forgotten History: Russian Literature, Japanese Mediation, and the Formation of Modern Korean Literature*. Cambridge: Harvard University Asia Center, 2016.

Clark, Steve, and Masashi Suzuki, eds. *The Reception of Blake in the Orient*. New York: Continuum, 2006.

Clark, T. J. *The Sight of Death: An Experiment in Art Writing*. New Haven: Yale University Press, 2006.

Clements, Rebekah. *A Cultural History of Translation in Early Modern Japan*. Cambridge: Cambridge University Press, 2015.

Collick, John. "Dismembering Devils: The Demonology of *Arashi ga oka* (1988) and *Wuthering Heights* (1939)." In *Novel Images: Literature in Performance*. Ed. Peter Reynolds. New York: Routledge, 1993. 34–48.

Complete Japanese Verb Guide. Compiled by The Hiroo Japanese Center. Rutledge, Vermont: Tuttle Publishing, 1989.

Cottom, Daniel. "I Think: Therefore, I Am Heathcliff." *ELH* 70.4 (2003): 1067–88.

Curran, Stuart. "Byron and Shelley: Becoming Italian." Paper presented at the North American Society for the Study of Romanticism Supernumerary Conference, Tokyo, Japan, June 2014.

Davies, Stevie. *Emily Brontë: Heretic*. London: The Women's Press, 1994.

Derrida. Dir. Kirby Dick and Amy Ziering Kofman. Jane Doe Films, 2002.

Dollase, Hiromi Tsuchiya. "Early Twentieth Century Japanese Girls' Magazine Stories: Examining Shojo Voice in Hanamonogatari (Flower tales)." *Journal of Popular Culture* 36.4 (Spring 2003): 724–55.

Dream Girls. Dir. Kim Longinotto and Jano Williams. Twentieth Century Vixen, 1994.

Dyer, Geoff. *Zona*. New York: Pantheon, 2012.

Eagleton, Terry. *Myths of Power: A Marxist Study of the Brontës*. New York: Macmillan, 1975.

Foer, Joshua. *Moonwalking with Einstein: The Art and Science of Remembering Everything*. New York: Penguin, 2011.

Forster, E. M. *Aspects of the Novel*. London: Edward Arnold, 1927.

Frank, Katherine. *A Chainless Soul: A Life of Emily Brontë*. Boston: Houghton Mifflin, 1990.

Fraser, Rebecca. *The Brontës: Charlotte Brontë and Her Family*. New York: Crown Publishers, Inc., 1988.

Fujimoto, Yoko. "Contexts and 'Con-textuality' of Minae Mizumura's *Honkaku-Shosetsu*." *Bulletin of the Graduate Division of Letters, Arts and Sciences of Waseda University* 52.2 (2007): 19–37.

Fujimoto, Yukari. "Takahashi Macoto: The Origin of Shōjo Manga Style." Trans. Matt Thorn. *Mechademia* 7 (2012): 24–55.

Gaskell, Elizabeth. *The Life of Charlotte Brontë*. London: Oxford University Press, 1966.

Geerken, Ingrid. "'The Dead Are Not Annihilated': Mortal Regret in *Wuthering Heights*." *Journal of Narrative Theory* 34.3 (2004): 373–406.

Gomi Tarō. *Nihongo gitaigo jiten* [Dictionary of Japanese mimetic words]. Tokyo: Kodansha, 2004.

Gordon, Andrew. *A Modern History of Japan: From Tokugawa Times to the Present*. 3rd ed. New York: Oxford University Press, 2014.

Haiku Harvest: Japanese Haiku Series IV. Trans. Peter Beilenson and Harry Behn. Mount Vernon, New York: Peter Pauper, 1962.

Hanabusa Yōko. *Arashi ga oka* [Wuthering Heights]. Grimm Fairy Tale Comics. Tokyo: Bunkasha, 2007.

Hanako to Anne. NHK [Japanese Broadcasting Corporation], 31 March 2014—27 September 2014. Television.

Hara Chieko. *Arashi ga oka satsujin jiken* [Wuthering Heights murder case]. Tokyo: Bunkasha, 2009.

Harasawa, Masayoshi. "Japanese Culture: The Ultimate Destiny of English Language Teaching in Japan." In *The Teaching of English in Japan*. Ed. Ikuo Koike, Masao Matsuyama, Yasuo Igarashi, and Koji Suzuki. Tokyo: Eichosha, 1978. 547–57.

Hardwick, Elizabeth. *Sleepless Nights*. New York: New York Review Books, 2001.

Hardy, Alec M. *Edmund Blunden*. London: Longmans, Green & Co., 1958.

Hass, Robert, ed. and trans. *The Essential Haiku: Versions of Bashō, Buson, and Issa*. Hopewell, New Jersey: The Ecco Press, 1994.

Hatasa, Yukiko Abe, Kazumi Hatasa, and Seiichi Makino. *Nakama 2: Japanese Communication, Culture, Context*. New York: Houghton Mifflin, 2000.

Hearn, Lafcadio. *In Ghostly Japan*. Boston: Little, Brown, 1899.

Heisig, James W. *Remembering the Kanji: A Complete Course on How Not to Forget the Meaning and Writing of Japanese Characters*. Vol. 1. 6th ed. Honolulu: University of Hawai'i Press, 2011.

Hirakawa, Sukehiro. *Japan's Love-Hate Relationship with the West*. Folkstone, Kent: Global Oriental, 2005.

Hirano, Kyoko. *Mr. Smith Goes to Tokyo: Japanese Cinema Under the American Occupation, 1945–1952*. Washington, D.C.: Smithsonian Institution Press, 1992.

Hirokane Kenshi. *Atogaki* [Afterword]. Saitō Ikumi. *Arashi ga oka (1939)*. [Wuthering Heights (1939)]. Story by Kanno Hiroshi. *Sekai meisaku mūbī* [World masterwork movie]. Tokyo: Mangabank, 2007. 156–57.

Hirono Yumiko. *Nazotoki "Arashi ga oka"* [The anatomy of Wuthering Heights]. Kyoto: Shōraisha, 2015.

Hutcheon, Linda with Siobhan O'Flynn. *A Theory of Adaptation*. New York: Routledge, 2012.

Ishihara, Tsuyoshi. *Mark Twain in Japan: The Cultural Reception of an American Icon* Columbia: University of Missouri Press, 2005.

Ito, Aiko, and Graeme Wilson. Introduction to *I Am a Cat* by Sōseki Natsume. Trans. Aiko Ito and Graeme Wilson. Boston: Tuttle, 2002. vii–xvi.

Ito, Ken K. *An Age of Melodrama: Family, Gender, and Social Hierarchy in the Turn-of-the-Century Japanese Novel*. Stanford: Stanford University Press, 2008.

Iwakami Haruko. *"Arashi ga oka dai 9 kyū o eibun kaishaku suru—I am Heathcliff o chūshin ni"* [An explanation of *Wuthering Heights* chapter 9, focusing on "I am Heathcliff"]. *Brontë Studies* 5.3 (2011): 85–96.

Iwakami Haruko. "The Brontës in Japan: How *Jane Eyre* Was Received in the Meiji Period (1868–1912)." *Brontë Studies* 27 (July 2002): 91–99.

Iwakami Haruko. *"Arashi ga oka no juyō—Meiji ki kara Taishō Shōwa shoki"* [The Brontës in Japan: How *Wuthering Heights* was received in Japan between the late 19th and the early 20th centuries]. *Shiga daigaku kyōiku gakubu kiyō* [Shiga University Education Department Bulletin] 58 (2008): 15–23.

Iwakami Haruko (Japanese). Review of *A True Novel*, by Minae Mizumura. Trans. Juliet Winters Carpenter. *Brontë Studies* 5.6 (2014): 39–42.

Iwashita Hiromi. *Arashi ga oka* [Wuthering Heights]. Tokyo: Nihonbungeisha, 2009.

James, William. *The Varieties of Religious Experience: A Study in Human Nature*. New York: Longmans, Green, and Co. 1903.

Jisho. A Japanese-English dictionary. Created by Kim Ahlström, Miwa Ahlström, and Andrew Plummer. www.jisho.org.

Kaneko, Hisakazu. *Manjiro, The Man Who Discovered America*. Boston: Houghton Mifflin Company, 1956.

Kantor, Jodi. "The Literary Critic's Shelf of Shame." *Slate*, 6 March 2001. http://www.slate.com/articles/arts/culturebox/2001/03/the_literary_critics_shelf_of_shame.html.

Kato, Yuji. "Herman Melville and Modern Japan: A Speculative Re-Interpretation of the Critical History." *Leviathan: A Journal of Melville Studies* 8.3 (2006): 11–18.

Kawasaki, Akiko. "Japanese Adaptations of *Wuthering Heights*: Taeko Kono, *Gikyoku Arashi-ga-oka*, Minae Mizumura, *A True Novel*, and Nanae Aoyama, *Meguri-ito*." In *Buronte to 19 seiki Igirisu* [The Brontës and Nineteenth-Century Great Britain]. Osaka, Japan: Osaka Kyoiku Tosho, 2015. 315–29.

Keene, Donald. *Japanese Literature: An Introduction for Western Readers*. New York: Grove Press, Inc., 1955.

Keene, Donald. *Modern Japanese Literature*. New York: Grove Press, 1956.

Kenkō. *Essays in Idleness*. Trans. Donald Keene. New York: Columbia University Press, 1967.

Kitamura, Hiroshi. *Screening Enlightenment: Hollywood and the Cultural Reconstruction of Defeated Japan*. Ithaca, N.Y.: Cornell University Press, 2010.

Kobashi Sumio. *Arashi ga oka no nihongo hyōgen* [*Wuthering Heights* in Japanese expression]. Okayama: Sanmon insatsujo, 2012.

Koike, Ikuo, Masao Matsuyama, Yasuo Igarashi, and Koji Suzuki, eds. *The Teaching of English in Japan*. Tokyo: Eichosha, 1978.

Komatsu, Hiroshi, and Frances Loden. "Mastering the Mute Image: The Role of the *Benshi* in Japanese Cinema." *Iris: A Journal of Theory on Image and Sound* 22 (Autumn 1996): 33–52.

Kōno, Taeko. *Gikyoku Arashi ga oka* [Wuthering Heights: A play]. Tokyo: Kawade shobō shinsha, 1970.

Kōno Taeko. *Kōno Taeko zenshū* [Kōno Taeko complete works]. Tokyo: Shinchōsha, 1994–95.

Kōno, Taeko. *Toddler-Hunting and Other Stories*. Trans. Lucy North. New York: New Directions, 1996.

Kōno Taeko and Tomioka Taeko. *Arashi ga oka futari tabi* [Duo journey in Wuthering Heights]. Tokyo: Bungeishunjū, 1986.

Kōnosu Yukiko. *Arashi ga oka o yomu* [Reading *Wuthering Heights*]." In *Shōjo wa hon o yonde otona ni naru* [Girls, grow up with books!]. Tokyo: Gendai kikakushitsu, 2015). 81–106.

Koyama Kariko and Yamagata Hirō. *Manga dewakaru piketi no nijūichi seiki no shihon* [Understanding by means of manga Thomas Piketty's "Capital in the 21st Century"]. Tokyo: Takarajimasha, 2015.

Kramsch, Claire. *The Multilingual Subject: What Foreign Language Learners Say about their Experience and Why It Matters*. Oxford: Oxford University Press, 2009.

Kreilkamp, Ivan. "Petted Things: *Wuthering Heights* and the Animal." *Yale Journal of Criticism* 18.1 (Spring 2005): 87–110.

Langenscheidt Pocket Japanese Dictionary. New York: Langenscheidt, 2006.

Lewes, George Henry. Review of *Wuthering Heights* and *Agnes Grey*. *The Leader*, 28 December 1850. Reprinted in Emily Brontë, *Wuthering Heights*. Ed. Beth Newman. Peterborough, Ontario: Broadview Editions, 2007. 369–71.

Lutz, Deborah. *The Brontë Cabinet: Three Lives in Nine Objects*. New York: W.W. Norton & Company, 2015.

Lynch, Deidre. "On Going Steady with Novels." *The Eighteenth Century* 50.2 (2009): 207–19.

Manguel, Alberto. *With Borges*. London: Telegram, 2006.

Matsumoto, Kazuhito. "'Exophony' in the Midst of the Mother Tongue: Resources between Languages." In *Doing English in Asia: Global Literature and Culture*. Ed. Patricia Haseltine and Sheng-mei Ma. New York: Lexington, 2016. 17–18.

Maxwell, William. *The Chateau*. New York: Alfred A. Knopf, 1961.

Miller, D.A. *Bringing Out Roland Barthes*. Berkeley: University of California Press, 1992.

Miller, J. Hillis. *The Disappearance of God: Five Nineteenth-Century Writers*. Cambridge: Belknap Press of Harvard University Press, 1963.

Miller, Lucasta. *The Brontë Myth*. London: Jonathan Cape, 2001.

Miuchi Suzue. *Garasu no kamen* [Glass mask]. Vols. 7 and 8. Tokyo: Hakusensha, 1978.

Miuchi Suzue and Hikawa Mariko. *Shinsaku nō Kurenai tennyo no sekai—Garasu no kamen yori* [New Noh crimson goddess world—based on Glass Mask]. Tokyo: Hakusensha, 2006.

Miura, Ayako. *Freezing Point*. Trans. Hiromu Shimuzu and John Terry. Wilmington, Del.: Dawn Press, 1986.

Miyabe Miyuki. *Osoroshi: Mishimaya henchō hyaku monogatari kotohajime* [Frightening: The beginning of 100 unusual stories at the Mishima store]. Tokyo: Kadokawa shoten, 2008.

Miyoshi, Masao. "The Invention of English Literature in Japan." In *Trespasses: Selected Writings*. Ed. Eric Cazdyn. Durham: Duke University Press, 2010. 111–26.

Mizumura, Minae. *The Fall of Language in the Age of English*. Trans. Mari Yoshihara and Juliet Winters Carpenter. New York: Columbia University Press, 2015.

Mizumura, Minae. "Finishing the Unfinished Soseki. A talk presented at Cornell University, Ithaca, New York, 9 November 1989. http://mizumuraminae.com/pdf/FinishingtheUnifinished20080303Website.pdf.

Mizumura Minae. *Honkaku shōsetsu* [*A True Novel*]. 2 vols. Tokyo: Shinchōsha, 2002.

Mizumura, Minae. *Inheritance from Mother*. Trans. Juliet Winters Carpenter. New York: Other Press, 2017.

Mizumura, Minae. "The Japanese Language: An Endangered Heritage." Interview by Kōno Michikazu. *Japan Echo* 36.2 (2009). Online.

Mizumura, Minae. "On Translation." *91st Meridian*. International Writing Program, University of Iowa. https://iwp.uiowa.edu/sites/iwp/files/Minae_translation.pdf.

Mizumura, Minae. "Renunciation." *Yale French Studies* 69 (1985): 81–97.

Mizumura, Minae. *A True Novel*. Trans. Juliet Winters Carpenter. 2 vols. New York: Other Press, 2013.

Mori, Maryellen T. "The Liminal Male as Liberatory Figure in Japanese Women's Fiction." *Harvard Journal of Asiatic Studies* 60.2 (2000): 537–94.

Mori Michiyo. *Arashi ga oka* [Wuthering Heights]. Vol. 99. *Sekai meisaku bunko* [World masterpiece library]. Tokyo: Kaisei-sha, 1954.

Morizono Miruku. *Arashi ga oka* [Wuthering Heights]. *Manga sekai no bungaku 8* [Manga world literature 8]. Tokyo: Sekai bunkasha, 1996.

Mulhern, Chieko I., ed. *Japanese Women Writers*. Westport, Conn.: Greenwood Press, 1994.

Nabokov, Vladimir. *Lectures on "Don Quixote."* Ed. Fredson Bowers. New York: Harcourt Brace Jovanovich, 1983.

Nagaike, Kazumi. *Fantasies of Cross-dressing: Japanese Women Write Male-Male Erotica*. Boston: Brill, 2012. E-book.

Napier, Elizabeth. "The Problem of Boundaries in *Wuthering Heights*." *Philological Quarterly* 63.1 (1984): 95–107.

Natsume, Sōseki. *I Am a Cat*. Trans. Aiko Ito and Graeme Wilson. Boston: Tuttle Publishing, 2002.

Natsume, Sōseki. *Sanshirō: A Novel*. Trans. Jay Rubin. London: Penguin, 2009.

Natsume, Sōseki. *Spring Miscellany and London Essays*. Trans. Sammy I. Tsunematsu. Boston: Tuttle, 2002.

Natsume, Sōseki. *"Theory of Literature" and Other Critical Writings*. Ed. Michael K. Bourdaghs, Atsuko Ueda, and Joseph A. Murphy. New York: Columbia University Press, 2009.

Natsume, Sōseki. *The Tower of London: Tales of Victorian London.* Trans. Damian Flanagan. London: Peter Owen, 2005.

Nomura, Mizuki. *Book Girl and the Famished Spirit.* Trans. Karen McGillicuddy. New York: Yen On, 2011.

Nomura Mizuki. *Bungaku shōjo to uekawaku gōsuto* [Book girl and the famished spirit]. Tokyo: Enterbrain, 2006.

Nornes, Abé Mark. "For an Abusive Subtitling." *Film Quarterly* 52.3 (1999): 17–34.

Oates, Joyce Carol. "The Magnanimity of *Wuthering Heights.*" *Critical Inquiry* 9.2 (1982): 435–49.

Ōe, Kenzaburō. *A Personal Matter.* Trans. John Nathan. New York: Grove Press, 1969.

Ōe, Kenzaburō. *The Silent Cry.* Trans. John Bester. New York: Kodansha International, 1974.

Ogi, Fusami. "Female Subjectivity and Shoujo (girls) Manga (Japanese comics): Shoujo in Ladies' Comics and Young Ladies' Comics." *Journal of Popular Culture* 36.4 (2003): 780–803.

Ōgi Yuzuha. *Arashi ga oka* [Wuthering Heights]. Tokyo: Kaiōsha, 2003.

Ōgi, Yuzuha. *Rising Storm* [English translation of *Arashi ga oka*]. Trans. C. Pellikka. Houston, Texas: DramaQueen, 2005.

Okada, Akiko. *Keats and English Romanticism in Japan.* Bern, Switzerland: Peter Lang, 2006.

Okada Ryōichi. *Kaikaburareta meisaku* [Overestimated masterpieces]. Tokyo: Sairyusha, 2007.

Okumura, Maki. "Intrusion of the Stranger: Yoshishige Yoshida's Version of *Wuthering Heights.*" *Brontë Studies* 29 (July 2004): 125–34.

Ōta Tetsunori. Script and Direction. *Arashi ga oka* [Wuthering Heights]. Bow Musical. Takarazuka Opera Company. Takarazuka City, Japan: Takarazuka kagekidan, 1997.

Ozaki, Kōyō. *The Gold Demon.* Trans. A. Lloyd and M. Lloyd. Tokyo: Seibundo, 1917.

Preus, Margi. *Heart of a Samurai: Based on the True Story of Nakahama Manjiro.* New York: Amulet Books, 2010.

Raw, Laurence. *Translation, Adaptation and Transformation.* New York: Continuum, 2012.

Renza, Louis A. *"A White Heron" and the Question of Minor Literature.* Madison: University of Wisconsin Press, 1984.

Richie, Donald. *A Hundred Years of Japanese Film.* New York: Kodansha International, 2001.

Robertson, Jennifer. *Takarazuka: Sexual Politics and Popular Culture in Modern Japan.* Berkeley: University of California Press, 1998.

Rubin, Jay. *Making Sense of Japanese: What the Textbooks Don't Tell You.* New York: Kodansha International, 1998.

Rundle, Vivienne. "Framing the Reader: Interpretation and Design in Victorian and Early Modern Narrative." PhD diss., University of Pennsylvania, 1992.

Ruskin, John. *Modern Painters.* In *The Complete Works of John Ruskin.* 26 vols. Philadelphia: Reuwee, Wattley & Walsh, 1891.

Saitō Ikumi. *Arashi ga oka (1939)* [*Wuthering Heights* (1939)]. Story by Kanno Hiroshi. Sekai meisaku mūbī [World masterwork movie]. Tokyo: Mangabank, 2007.

Saitō, Takeshi. "Edmund Blunden, Poet." *Today's Japan* 5.3 (1960): 33–37.

Saitō, Takeshi. "English Literature in Japan: A Brief Sketch." *Studies in English Literature* 8.3 (1928): 344–57.

Saitō, Takeshi. *Keats' View of Poetry*. London: Cobden-Sanderson, 1929.

Sakurai Mineko. *Arashi ga oka* [Wuthering Heights]. Tokyo: Bunkasha, 2012.

Sanger, Charles Percy. "The Structure of *Wuthering Heights*." *Hogarth Essays* XIX. London: Hogarth Press, 1926.

Saussy, Haun. "Language and Literature—a Pedagogical Continuum?" *Profession 2005*. Ed. Rosemary G. Feal. New York: Modern Language Association, 2005. 113–21.

Schierbeck, Sachiko. *Japanese Women Novelists in the 20th Century: 104 Biographies, 1900–1993*. University of Copenhagen, Denmark: Museum Tusculanum Press, 1994.

Schivelbusch, Wolfgang. *The Railway Journey: The Industrialization of Time and Space in the Nineteenth Century*. Berkeley: University of California Press, 1986.

Seaward, Mark R.D. "Introduction." In *Sixty Treasures: The Brontë Parsonage Museum*. Haworth, West Yorkshire: Brontë Society, 1988.

Sei Shōnagon. *The Pillow Book*. Trans. Meredith McKinney. London: Penguin Books, 2006.

Seiichi, Makino, and Michio Tsutsui. *A Dictionary of Basic Japanese Grammar*. Tokyo: Japan Times, 1989.

Sekai meisaku bunko [World masterpiece library]. 140 vols. Tokyo: Kaisei-sha, 1954–61.

Shachar, Hila. *Cultural Afterlives and Screen Adaptations of Classic Literature: "Wuthering Heights" and Company*. New York: Palgrave Macmillan, 2012.

Shelley, Mary. *Frankenstein; or, The Modern Prometheus*. Ed. D. L. Macdonald and Kathleen Scherf. Peterborough, Ontario: Broadview Press, 1994.

Shimura Takako. *Aoi hana* [*Sweet Blue Flowers*]. Vols. 1 and 2. Tokyo: Ōtashuppan, 2006.

Shin ai no arashi [New storm of love]. Midday drama. Dir. Kaneko Yoshiichi, Koike Tadakazu, and Shimazaki Toshiki. Nagoya, Japan: Tōkai Television, 2002.

Shōjo sekai bungaku zenshū [Girls' library of world literature]. 30 vols. Tokyo: Kaisei-sha, 1960–64.

Sischy, Ingrid. "Selling Dreams." *New Yorker*, 28 Sept. 1992. 84–103.

Smiles, Samuel. *Self-Help; with Illustrations of Character, Conduct, and Perseverance*. Author's Revised and Enlarged Edition. New York: Wm. L. Allison, [1884].

Smith, Janet S. Shibamoto. "Translating True Love: Japanese Romance Fiction, Harlequin-Style." In *Gender, Sex and Translation*. Ed. José Santaemilia. Northampton, MA: St. Jerome Publishing, 2005. 97–116.

Sone, Tamotsu. "Edmund Blunden, Teacher." *Today's Japan* 5.3 (1960): 53–58.

Stevenson, John Allen. "'Heathcliff Is Me!': *Wuthering Heights* and the Question of Likeness." *Nineteenth-Century Literature* 43.1 (1988): 60–81.

Stewart, Susan. "The Ballad in *Wuthering Heights*." *Representations* 86.1 (Spring 2004): 175–97.

Stickland, Leonie R. *Gender Gymnastics: Performing and Consuming Japan's Takarazuka Revue*. Melbourne: Trans Pacific Press, 2008.

Stoneman, Patsy. *Brontë Transformations: The Cultural Dissemination of "Jane Eyre" and "Wuthering Heights."* London: Prentice Hall, 1996.

Suter, Rebecca. "From Jusuheru to Jannu: Girl Knights and Christian Witches in the Work of Miuchi Suzue." *Mechademia* 4 (2009): 241–56.

Suzuka Reni. *Arashi ga oka* [Wuthering Heights]. Famous Love Comics 2. Explanation by Edo Daisuke. Tokyo: Telehouse, 1989.

Suzuki, Yoshikazu. "'A candle that must melt away': Early Keats Scholarship in Japan." *English Romanticism in East Asia*. Ed. Suh-Reen Han. Praxis Series. *Romantic Circles*. December 2016. www.rc.umd.edu/prasix/eastasia/prasix.2016.eastasia.suzuki.html.

Takarazuka, Arashi ga oka. May 3–May 28, 1969. English Synopsis. Takarazuka *Wuthering Heights* fan magazine, 1969.

Takashi Inui. *Jon Manjirō no eikaiwa* [John Manjiro's English conversation manual]. Tokyo: Jieirisāchishuppan, 2010.

Tamura Taeko, trans. *E to genbun de tanoshimu Wuthering Heights* [Enjoying *Wuthering Heights* with illustrations and original text]. *Inkoku* [seal illustrations] by Ichihara Junko. Osaka: Osaka Kyōiku Tosho, 2007.

Tanizaki, Junichirō. *The Makioka Sisters*. Trans. Edward G. Seidensticker. New York: Vintage Books, 1995.

Thormählen, Marianne, ed. *The Brontës in Context*. Cambridge: Cambridge University Press, 2012.

Thurman, Judith. "The Kimono Painter." In *Cleopatra's Nose: 39 Varieties of Desire*. New York: Farrar, Straus and Giroux, 2007. 261–78.

Titsingh, Isaäc. *Illustrations of Japan*. London: R. Ackerman, 1822.

Toku, Masami. "Shojo Manga! Girls' Comics! A Mirror of Girls' Dreams." *Mechademia* 2 (2007): 19–32.

Torikai, Kumiko. *Voices of the Invisible Presence: Diplomatic Interpreters in Post–World War II Japan*. Philadelphia: John Benjamins, 2009.

Toro, Tom. "This moor got a great Yelp review." Cartoon. *New Yorker*, 23 April 2012.

Trillin, Calvin. "Anne of Red Hair." *New Yorker*, 5 August 1996, 56–61.

Trivedi, Harish. "Translating Culture vs. Cultural Translation." *91st Meridian*. International Writing Program. University of Iowa. https://iwp.uiowa.edu/91st/vol4-num1/translating-culture-vs-cultural-translation.

Tsushima Yūko. *Hon no naka no shōjotachi* [Girls in books]. Tokyo: Chūōkōronsha, 1989.

Tytler, Graeme. "'Nelly, I *am* Heathcliff!': The Problem of 'Identification' in *Wuthering Heights*." *Midwest Quarterly* 47.2 (2006): 167–81.

Ukai, Nobumitsu. "Catherine Earnshaw as the Spine of a Book—The Duplication of Self in *Wuthering Heights*." Kyushu University. Japanese Institutional Repository Online.

Utsumi Shigenori. *Arashi ga oka* [Wuthering Heights]. *Takarazuka kageki kyaku hon to haiyaku* [Takarazuka Opera Company script and cast list]. Shinjuku Coma Stadium. May 3-28, 1969.

Utsumi Shigenori. *Fain romansu Utsumi Shigenori Takarazuka kageki sakuhinshū* [Fine romance Utsumi Shigenori Takarazuka opera anthology]. Takarazuka City, Japan: Takarazuka Creative, 2000. Compact Disk.

Vallins, David, Kaz Oishi, and Seamus Perry, eds. *Coleridge, Romanticism and the Orient*. New York: Bloomsbury Academic, 2013.

Van Ghent, Dorothy. *The English Novel: Form and Function*. New York: Holt, Rinehart and Winston, 1953.

Vogler, Thomas A., ed. *Twentieth Century Interpretations of "Wuthering Heights."* Englewood Cliffs, N.J.: Prentice-Hall, Inc., 1968.

Watanabe, Kazuko. "Reading *Little Women*, Reading Motherhood in Japan." *Feminist Studies* 25.3 (Fall 1999): 698–709.

Watson, Melvin R. "*Wuthering Heights* and the Critics." *Trollopian*. 3.4 (1949): 243–63.

Watson, Richard A. *The Philosopher's Demise: Learning to Speak French*. Boston: David Godine, 2003.

Webb, Barry. *Edmund Blunden: A Biography*. New Haven: Yale University Press, 1990.

Webster, Jean. *Daddy-Long-Legs*. New York: Puffin, 2010.

Wenders, Wim, dir. *Tokyo-Ga*. In *Banshun* [Late spring]. Dir. Ozu Yasujirō. Wim Wenders Produktion. Criterion Collection: Janus Films, 2006. DVD.

Wilder, Laura Ingalls. *Ōki na mori no chiisa na ie* [*Little House in the Big Woods*]. Trans. Mihoko Onchi. Illustrations by Garth Montgomery Williams. Tokyo: Fukuinkan-shoten, 1973.

Wise, Sue. "Sexing Elvis." In *On Record: Rock, Pop, and the Written Word*. Ed. Simon Frith and Andrew Goodwin. New York: Pantheon, 1990. 390–98.

Woolf, Virginia. "Haworth, November, 1904." In *The Essays of Virginia Woolf*. Ed. Andrew McNeillie. 3 vols. New York: Harcourt Brace Jovanovich, 1986–1988. 1:5–9.

Wyler, William, dir. *Wuthering Heights*. Haruo Mizuno's World Masterwork Movies. Tokyo: Keep Co., Ltd., 2005. DVD.

Yamanashi, Makiko. *A History of the Takarazuka Revue Since 1914: Modernity, Girls' Culture, Japan Pop*. Boston: Global Oriental, 2012.

Yamanouchi, Hisaaki. *The Search for Authenticity in Modern Japanese Literature*. Cambridge: Cambridge University Press, 1978.

Yamato, Yasuo. "Three Notes." In *English Studies in Japan: Essays and Studies Presented to Dr Yasuo Yamato in Honour of His Sixtieth Birthday*. Tokyo: English Literary Society of the Nihon University, 1958. 349–382.

Yildiz, Yasemin. *Beyond the Mother Tongue: The Postmonolingual Condition*. New York: Fordham University Press, 2012.

Yoshida, Midori. "The Acquisition of English Vocabulary by a Japanese-Speaking Child." In *Second Language Acquisition: A Book of Readings*. Ed. Evelyn Marcussen Hatch. Rowley, Mass.: Newbury House, 1978. 91–100.

Yoshida Yoshishige, dir. *Arashi ga oka* [Wuthering Heights]. Tokyo: Geneon Entertainment, 2005. DVD.

Youdelman, Rachel. "An Interview with Japanese Brontë Scholar Seiko Aoyama." *Brontë Society Transactions* 25.2 (October 2000): 160–67.

Index

Note: Page numbers in *italics* refer to illustrative matter.